Swimming with Frogs

A Dream on a Shoestring

Robert Cooper

Best wishes Cyril
Robert
March 2014

Published in 2014 by FeedARead.com Publishing

A CIP catalogue record for this title is available from the British Library

For my wife who doubted this book would ever be, and for Eileen, whose valuable assistance and encouragement made sure it would.

For my Dad whose financial support helped make this book possible.

Special thanks to Howard Gardener who created my cover.

1

I felt sorry for Greg as he lay wrapped like a foetus around the roll-bags. Lulled by the continual drone of the engine, he'd eventually fallen into a restless sleep beside me and I could see again the small boy my adult son had once been. He'd given up asking how much longer hours ago and my backside had long since given up any sensation of feeling somewhere during the twenty-four-hour drive in an overloaded lorry travelling down through France.

Through the window on my left I could see the valley if not the house and as the last kilometres of the *route Nationale* disappeared under the front wheels of the truck, the early morning sun threw its first beams above the distant horizon.

I pictured my new wife Jenny at the house; sipping her precious morning tea and trying to recover from the same journey in our car - but I knew she would be worrying about our lengthened arrival time. I could visualise also the seemingly lifeless form of my daughter Emily as she lay sleeping on the couch.

I turned left into the lane and five minutes later a feeling of great relief washed over me as I cut the engine at the top of our drive. Greg didn't stir and I sat behind the steering wheel in blissful silence and realised at last that I had arrived at 'Prieu' with the first lorry load of all our worldly goods from England.

The relief of actually getting here safely was immense, and now the constant pain radiating down my left leg from my sciatic nerve paled into insignificance as I sat silently in the driver's seat reflecting on the events that had brought me here. But was coming here to a foreign country and a language I couldn't speak or understand the biggest mistake of my life?

During the preceding years I'd already been married and divorced twice and had a string of casual relationships while living on my own. I had a nice apartment and an enjoyable social life and yet I still seemed to be missing something.

I had developed an adult attitude and enjoyment of Naturism, the pursuance of which had led me to a reputable club for like-minded people to the north of London. The club's fifteen acres were originally bought as virgin woodland in the nineteen thirties by the father of the present owners. Disillusioned by his life in London as an engineer, he had seen an advertisement in a newspaper for the land and decided to buy it.

He arrived at the tiny local railway station with his wife, their suitcases and a box of tools, and they walked the near mile to their acquisition to start a new life. It seemed that even then some people wanted to opt out of the rat race.

Then during the Second World War, friends hoping to escape the wartime bombings came with their families and built wooden cabins within the grounds to live in; they pioneered a naturist community that remains almost unchanged to this day.

Over the passing years cabin ownership changed as people moved on or became too old and incapable, but some stayed until they died. Then the cabins were bought by younger families with enthusiasm to undertake renovation and modernisation; and for the twenty five residences still there, the same circle continues.

The minute population was diverse and came from many walks of life. There was a retired stunt man and TV producer while another was a funeral director. One lady was a personal assistant to a director within a multinational drug company and one was a bus driver. There were grave diggers and market traders, a retired army sergeant and a retired police Superintendent. Two ward sisters – both retired, and the list went on.

Today Spielplatz naturist club has a private membership of hundreds and some are fortunate and own a cabin or caravan plot where they are allowed to reside during the summer season from April to September.

The club bought an ex-war barrack hut during those early years to provide a warm place for all to meet; now it had become a comfortable bar and small bistro with facilities for regular dance functions, and there was also a sauna cabin. The original outdoor swimming pool which was a steel tank filled with green water and accessed by a ladder, had now become an inviting crystal clear modern heated pool with an enclosed sun terrace and seating.

Entry to the grounds can only be attained through the steel gates and a coded keypad, but inside the gates the same staunch preservation of the natural environment that was conceived all those years ago still exists today. There is peace and tranquillity there that is rare to find elsewhere.

The people I met there showed a real friendliness and warmth to me and I soon discovered that naturism bridged most social and class circles. I felt at home there and so when I discovered that Number 29 was for sale I just had to view this small wooden cabin that measured six metres square. It had a small kitchen, an even smaller bathroom, and one long living room.

Leslie the owner had a concerned family, who out of necessity for his own safety had moved him into residential care. He was a petite man with a long grey beard, and he was often seen in the grounds wearing a hooded orange track suit and half-length black wellies; it soon earned him a nickname and he became affectionately known as 'the Gnome'.

Then in his 80's, he was disorientated and forgetful and he had become a danger unto himself as I quickly discovered. Burn marks on the wooden floor from an aged heater, melted plastic plates solidified under the cooker grille and an electrical installation that was a catastrophe waiting to happen.

The cabin framework was constructed from five centimetre square timber with feather-edge planking outside and soft Tentex boarding inside, and no insulation. It had a sloping roof which comprised of many layers of very tired roofing felt which was covered in a thick layer of moss, but it didn't leak.

The living room had panelled walls with each panel showing different wallpaper, and there were thirty power sockets, some with timers and controls at Leslie's bedside to activate his various lights and appliances. The bathroom and kitchen extension were a later addition and constructed again with a timber frame but clad inside and out with asbestos sheets.

His tiny bathroom said it all; most of the walls were mirrored and the area that remained was papered with a pattern of naked ladies, and folk who remembered said it cost him a small fortune for the few rolls he used.

Residents who knew him said that during his earlier years at Number 29 he rode an old BSA motorcycle, and that he would often arrive with a new lady friend as pillion. These were the days before a boundary fence was added to the grounds, and one neighbour recalled a visit she made to Leslie telling how astonished she was to see the horse from the adjoining paddock poking its head through the window to join the squirrels for a hand-offered tit bit.

Fifty per cent of the garden was being lost to a Rhododendron, and there was a Russian vine overtaking the whole front wall of the cabin and doing its best to lift off the roof.

I met the clubs management and was accepted for residential suitability and gave notice on my rented flat. All I needed now was the money to pay for it.

Despite my best efforts it seemed that banking establishments did not have any criteria for lending money to buy a wooden dwelling in a naturist club, and nobody would advance me the required sixteen thousand five hundred pounds required, so I borrowed the lot from my Dad.

A keen naturist also, he retired from the fire service at fifty after he had spent thirty five years putting out fires; and then he joined the fire research establishment and worked into his seventies lighting them. I learned many of my practical skills from his endless source of advice and he would keenly come over for the day to assist me as I slowly built a new cabin over the top of the old one, and then as each new area was completed I removed the old cabin piece by piece from the inside.

The finished much bigger building was a modern well insulated contemporary home, with one bedroom, en suite and a superb fully-fitted kitchen which inspired my love of cooking.

But during the years that I spent rebuilding my cabin, my life was changing rapidly and after thirty five years I became disillusioned with my career in engineering, and I resigned my position as Works Manager. I made a career change into direct sales which was mostly evening work, but it gave me valuable daylight hours towards finishing my cabin.

I had been thinking how refreshing it would be to meet someone with similar interests, someone with a like-minded appreciation of the countryside and nature with whom I could share my life. I thought that this was very unlikely at my age and so I resigned myself to live alone, with the consolation that casual relationships could partly fill the gap; and then I met Jenny.

It was a quiet mid-week afternoon and the warm sunshine had enticed me into the pool. I dried and placing my towel down on the bench I sat to talk. She was warm and friendly and conversation flowed easily between us as we sat naked together facing the pool in near empty grounds.

She had beautiful eyes which sparkled in the sunshine reflecting from the pool and her dark hair was short and cut in a feminine style which curled gently forward under her ears and framed an attractive face with a warm smile. We chatted on no specific topics, and I confess I flirted openly, convinced that this confident lady was very much married. That was the last I saw of her for five months.

I thought it suited me fine to continue with the affair of nearly two years' duration that I was having with a married woman. For me it was uncomplicated seeing her for just a couple of occasions each week; sometimes we went out but mostly I cooked dinner. When I woke she would have gone.

I knew she had fallen in love with me and would have been thrilled to enter into something permanent, had I not been honest with her right from the start about my expectations. I never loved her but I was very fond of her and as the time between seeing each other grew longer and longer, her marriage failed - doomed as it was, and she eventually found someone who wanted to commit.

We parted as close friends in the knowledge that at that time we had been there for each other and I missed her.

Plunging again full tilt into finishing my home took a great effort of enthusiasm especially when the sun was out and the grounds at the weekends were full with many new friends. For company and nourishment it was all too easy to pop over to the bar and restaurant and stay there in the sun on the terrace.

So many members with identical Christian names always caused confusion. There was Busy Ann and Andy's Ann, Sailor John and Beastie John because he worked for a company called B. East; BT Allan a telephone engineer, and Brian had become Hairy Brian because he was.

Hairy Brian ran the restaurant and on quieter days I would sit with him and chat about food and cooking; he had once been a chef and I learned much from his experiences. If he became busy I sometimes pitched in and helped and then he asked me if I would cover him and cook the Sunday lunches; I was boosted by his confidence in my ability but I had never cooked lunch for thirty or more people.

Slowly summer drifted by in glorious days spent doing exactly as I pleased. Sales work was stimulating and the only distraction from the paradise where I lived, and although my earnings requirements were now greatly reduced, the peaks and troughs of commission caused some hiccoughs.

As Christmas approached Brian again asked me to help him, to prepare and serve all the food for the mid December club dinner Dance; a lovely evening when the whole inner area of the bar and restaurant is laid to bursting point with tables and chairs. Members not seen for many months and regulars all arrive dressed appropriately for the tradition which is always fully booked.

I was chatting with Brian one day when he raised the topic of my solitary life. I divulged that while I wasn't entirely content I was also reluctant to embark into another blind alley; but I did admit that there was a place in my life if I met right person.

"Well…" he said, "…You never know who will turn up for the dinner dance."

2

Ferrying the empty platters back into the kitchen we congratulated ourselves on the success of the buffet for the Dinner-Dance and I received grateful thanks for my assistance.

Happy members and guests dispersed to the bar or cloakroom while we seized the opportunity to rearrange the tables and reveal the dancing area ready for the waiting band.

An hour later the band were in full swing during which time the dishwasher in the kitchen hadn't stopped as we strived to achieve some sort of order in preparation for the following day's Sunday lunches and business as usual.

But one thing I hadn't failed to notice during our clearing of the tables, and one that I hoped would materialise was that Jenny was there. By then I had discovered that her circumstances were very similar to my own and finding we had parts of our lives in common, I plucked up the courage to ask her to dance. She agreed and as I held her close she felt so comfortable in my arms.

Inside the clubhouse the heat was intense and we joined the many like-minded revellers outside on the terrace for a breather. Engrossed in our new-found friendship we suddenly realised the extent of the December temperature outside, and that those not so engrossed as us had sensibly returned inside long ago.

We danced again, this time a little closer until at last we realised that almost everybody else had gone home and we retired back to my cabin for coffee. At six the following morning we were still talking and I had a dinner date for the next day. I cooked.

It must have been the stuffed fillet of pork with apricot sauce that did it, because we've been together ever since.

At first while awaiting the finalisation of things with her estranged husband, she always returned home for the sake of the family. They were unsettling times, and unsure exactly at that time as to where we were going she wanted to buy a cabin of her own. Eventually the right one came up and she bought it, so we became neighbours, enjoying a relationship together and totally immersed in the club activities and social life.

I soon learned that she was a very practical lady who took a keen interest in my conversion project and she often helped me. I reciprocated with practical help and advice as Jenny remodelled her kitchen.

Then during the winter months I was soon spending more time living with Jenny, as both myself and her aged Siamese cat called Sulin took advantage of her wood burning stove and the cosy warmth it provided.

Not actually living at Number 29 gave me more time to work towards its completion as I could just stop and close the door, then return the next day and pick up where I left off. Coming back to Jenny's cabin one day gave me an example of her capabilities. She had removed a built-in cupboard, and plumbed in her newly acquired washing machine in its place.

"Why didn't you ask me?" I complained and was quickly countered by, "Well you're too busy on your own place to help me, and I'm quite capable of doing it myself!"

She was, but together we had quickly discovered that it was going to be necessary to spend a lot of money on essential repairs to her cabin.

Jenny had spoken about a house that she owned in the south of France during our opening conversations; I had forgotten all about it until we discussed that we needed a break.

She said, "I need to go to France to check on the house, will you come with me and we can have the break we both need."

So it was arranged, a ferry from Dover to Calais and a very long drive.

I have been to France two or three times before, when my children were younger and I have always enjoyed being there, falling quickly into the lifestyle, albeit in holiday mode; now I was going again and looking forward to a proper holiday, one that was for me well overdue.

An early start from home at four in the morning landed us safely on French soil at eight o'clock on a chilly February morning, with five hundred and seventy miles in front of us. We shared the driving with Jenny taking the lions share because she knew the route so well and it avoids most of the boring motorways and their tolls, in favour of the almost empty scenic route.

France has a population very similar to England but it has five times the area, with very different architecture and cultures as you move from region to region. Travelling south you can see the gradual change.

We passed through customs and leaving Calais we joined the unavoidable motorway together with a snake of disembarking vehicles all going in the same southerly direction; all seemingly possessed by some implanted need to be where ever their journey terminates...Yesterday.

Slowly our snake dispersed - and apart from the odd car which appeared in our rear view mirror from nowhere and which was intent on overtaking a GB plate whatever the road conditions – we found that we had the road to ourselves for the best part of two hundred and fifteen kilometres towards Rouen.

Passing through the open countryside I saw sleepy farms where cows were grazing in fields as big as English villages and I swear I saw them smiling. We passed under bridges that exhibited metal statues which depicted sports scenes, and then I was amazed to see the stainless steel contemporary monument to the past Viking presence.

With the motorways eventually behind us we crossed the river *Seine* and the *Ile Lacroix*. The elevated road gives a brief glimpse of the city of Rouen which is famous for its many churches whose spires reach skywards displaying the mason's craft. This historic city was a home to Eleanor of Aquitaine, queen of England to Henry II, (1133-89), it is said that her blood line still flows in the English Monarchy today.

The southern side of Rouen exposed its industrial area, and the biggest railway marshalling yard I'd ever seen. There were railway lines as far as I could see in any direction, with many lines of motionless rolling stock, in some places over the whole length of visible track. The whole area was enveloped in an intricate web of overhead power cables; the effect was that of a huge spider's nest with all the wagons like stunned prey. It's a place with countless traffic lights and road signs pointing in every direction that we were glad to leave behind us, and it surprised us that we managed to negotiate through it unscathed and to our relief we entered open country once more.

We avoided the congestion of Paris and travelled to the west side of the nation's capital. En route we came across our first roundabout that testified to the modern thinking of French planners, but not until we were upon it did we realise that the four grazing cows were in fact made of concrete.

We passed Evreux and Dreux, and continued on and on along roads so long and straight that we wondered if they were left from Napoleonic times, then in the distance we saw the emerging silhouette of Chartres cathedral, but as the road we were on never allowed us to see more than that, we promised ourselves that one day we would visit this magnificent building.

Our plan was to stop for an overnight stay at Blois to break the journey, and then set off again early for the final push to Lot-et Garonne. Now as we approached Blois, we were glad that most of the day's driving was behind us and we looked forward to a shower, an aperitif, and our first French cuisine of the trip. At mid-evening we sat in the restaurant with drooping eyelids and decided to call it a day, we slid into bed and were asleep in seconds.

At six o'clock – fortunately because we wanted an early start - we were woken by the inimitable French cockerel in the yard outside. He was lucky that most hotel windows only open for ventilation and not for the launching of missiles.

As the light emerged from the fresh morning sky we passed through villages still rubbing the sleep from their eyes, and I saw an elderly lady wrapped up in her winter coat with an apron showing from below, and I watched as she ambled home with the day's *baguette* under one arm, warm and fresh from the *boulangerie*; and I could imagine that her table for *petit dejeuner* was probably already laid.

I was now excitedly awaiting our arrival at the house and I found this last lap the most interesting, but as the roads were now winding continually it was hard to maintain the same pace as yesterday, and I realised the difference in the countryside that I'd overlooked the day before when I was travel weary; it was like driving from the flatness of Norfolk straight into Devon and Cornwall.

The landscape had become dramatic with rolling hills and ancient *châteaux* overlooking estates that were once owned by Marquis and Comte who had made some of their fortunes by bleeding the peasants of tax. Some estates are still owned by their descendants whose farming techniques have changed with the times to become big business. But maintaining an historical building is an expense that is rarely covered by farm income and so they open their doors to the public, allowing us to delight in the grandeur of the past. The more practical of us might also wonder how these magnificent structures were achieved to such architectural accuracy without the aid of a JCB, site crane or laser level.

I awoke sleepily in the passenger seat after another little doze and noticed the descending road along a deep gorge that gave me the first sight of Nontron perched on a precipice of the far bank and accessible by turning left over the high arched stone bridge.

On a subsequent trip, we crossed the bridge and entered the town where we stopped for lunch in a very tradition hotel restaurant. Walking back to the car afterwards, we peered over a parapet wall and looked down upon layers and layers of dwellings that appeared to be glued to the rock face like a giant's staircase of ever-descending pantiled roofs.

Passing Nontron and the bridge, the road continued to descend to the valley bottom, passing great flaky-barked maple trees on our right. These great trees line many kilometres of French roads and are an utter joy to see, but with the continuing accident rate and subsequent mortality involving roadside trees, there are rumours that the government is considering the removal of these roadside avenues of trees for safety reasons; something wrong here somehow!

A weak sun was doing its best to raise the temperature as we entered the outskirts of Perigueux.

"It won't be long now," Jenny says to appease my fidgeting body, "Another hour and we'll be there."

Another hour I mused, but she of course could visualise how close we were but to me the journey was endless.

I offered to drive again to give her a break, besides it seems quicker if I'm in the driving seat but she insisted that it is better if she drives because she knows the route so well. The truth is that she was probably right and she wouldn't relax and let me drive in case I got lost!

So again I dozed off into a half sleep and missed the beautiful scenery that I later came to appreciate; then I became aware that the car had turned left as I was rocked from left to right. Along a lane I opened one eye to see woodland rush past, closed it and dozed again. I could smell cows and imagined we had just passed a farm, and then suddenly the car lurched to the left and stopped.

I had been deeper asleep than I think, and before me now was an overgrown drive, barred with a plastic red and white chain which announced *"Propriété Privée-Défense D'Entrer."*

My first reaction was that Jen had taken a wrong turn and ended up at a farm, I turned to look at her to find a knowing grin.

"Well…" she said, "…you better get out and undo the chain then."

I was astonished and all I could say was, "What...are we here then?"

Struggling from the car with stiff limbs I then fell over the clumps of long grass; I undid the chain and slipped quickly back into the car, now wide awake with childlike anticipation. I had never seen any photographs of the house and pictured in my mind some small holiday home badly in need of repair; that is, if I had any mental picture at all, but nothing could have prepared me for what was in front of my eyes and all I could muster was "WOW". I had arrived at 'Prieu'.

3

We descended the drive in the car and then stood outside of the house stretching our stiffened limbs.

"Well, what do you think?" She hesitantly enquired, standing with the aged key in her hand.

"Do you like it?"

"Like it," I replied. "I love it, it's beautiful and nothing like I expected it to be."

She opened the main entrance door and a narrow arc of light flooded in bringing life once more to a house that had slept unused for nearly six months. As she groped her way towards the windows to open the shutters I heard her exclamation.

"Ugh…Oh my God!"

It transpired that the house *had* been occupied during her absence and the squatters had spun a blanket of fine silk in every direction.

I entered into the lounge and walked across the original handmade quarry tiles. The room was nearly six metres square with walls of exposed stone and above me an oak-beamed ceiling with timbers that had been blackened by years of wood smoke. The original open fire place now housed a wood burning stove. I heard a solid sounding 'Click' from the far corner and the ceiling light burst into life; the power was on.

I followed Jenny through a low doorway into another large room where I could almost hear the spiders scurrying away as Jenny opened the shutters. I squinted against the sudden light but could see it was a dining room with a big table and four chairs; they looked small in such a large room. The room was divided and beyond a high peninsular unit was the kitchen, and then as I turned back around I noticed a double bed that I almost missed in the far corner. A door led to a compact bathroom.

I felt quite inadequate watching Jenny prime the water pump from the well, but we soon had the kettle on and then together we set about removing the cobwebs and cleaning six months' worth of neglect and soon had the place habitable if not warm!

I started a roaring fire in the wood burning stove which was now heating everything within reach; but despite that, the thick stone walls that had been cooling since the summer wouldn't give up the fight easily and it took two or three days before they started to radiate anything resembling warmth.

While our supper was cooking we set about making up our bed and I was most reassured to find that it included an electric blanket. I've never before experienced getting into a heated bed, but later that first chilly night it was bliss. We snuggled down in the warm and I slipped into sleep with a smile on my face.

I slept late, and woke to find a winter sun shining through the gaps in the shutters and making patterns of shadows on the window panes from the overgrown garden. I made tea and opened the shutters. That first cup of tea is always nectar but looking down the valley through the window that first morning gave it a whole new perspective. I couldn't wait to wash and dress and go exploring like some eager child.

The morning was fresh, but the sun at that hour was warming as I carefully edged my way through the unfamiliar overgrown terrain to investigate the pond. It was lifeless and still but I could hear a faint dripping of water which I later discovered came from the piped spring waters that feed it; it was heart-shaped, a hidden mystery to me, a sleeping promise for warmer days.

Now with the obligatory pot of tea under her belt Jenny felt equipped to show me around the rest of the property. To the left and outside of the house was the well – the sole source of our water.

We turned back across the front of the house and then past garage doors before we descended four steps and passed two huge barn doors; we stopped at a small door at the end of the building where she produced a key, and as she opened the door I began to see the immensity of the space within and it appeared that it had changed little since the cows moved out.

She struggled with the door as it grated across the concrete floor of the milking parlour. Inside I could feel the dampness as we ducked under a low beam to the side of the cow byres and entered the main area with a floor of rich soil from years of overnight stabling of the small herd.

The huge barn doors creaked and groaned on their wooden hinges as we struggled to open them, then as our eyes adjusted to the light Jenny explained how the barn had been extended during the nineteen thirties to accommodate a further seven cows; it was easy to see the once smaller barn accommodating four animals which had now become a workshop and a garage.

The garage stored tools and mowers, tables and chairs for summer days, steel boxes for rodent proof storage of materials, all draped in plastic sheeting to keep the spoils from the resident Barn owl from fouling everything.

Leaving the barn my tour took us around the side between the barn, and the small outbuilding - two small stables which might have housed chickens or rabbits for the pot.

To the rear of the house, the roof sloped down to within shoulder height and housed the *Chai*, a place where wine from the small vineyard still owned and worked by François the previous owner, would have been made and stored. A rudimentary wine rack stood rotting and worm eaten against one wall, tied for support to the beams above with a length of old and fragile string. The floor was the earthen and measured twelve paces by four; it was so damp that great clods of it stuck to the soles of my shoes and made walking difficult.

Prieu had seven underground water sources within the grounds; two ran under the house passing through the foundations of stone which were two metres deep, two had been tapped into to feed the pond, and three fed the well, a stone-built tube sunk four metres into the ground and rising one metre above which was covered over with a pan-tiled roof.

Now I'd had the whole tour my mind was buzzing with questions as we returned inside for mid-morning coffee, and I was amazed how much history Jenny had absorbed from François.

After coffee we went to the village for a few provisions. Cancon was not a village that would have featured prominently in any tourist book, but that day my first impressions of the few people I met were of warmth and friendliness; little did I know then that I was destined to become part of that community.

Returning to the hubbub of England made me appreciate the peace and tranquillity I had experienced in France, and although the remaining days of that first week I spent at Prieu dissolved into a haze of pleasant memories, I felt that a seed was beginning to grow inside me and I hoped that I would have an opportunity to return.

4

Jenny was still asleep as I slid from under the warmth of the duvet and quietly left the cabin.

Crossing the single-lane road onto manicured lawns I could feel the warmth of the early morning sun on my body. Springtime was advancing quickly towards early summer days and I relished the change within the club grounds as the summer beauty of it all unfolded once more.

Descending the pool steps the water felt sharp enough to warrant a few brisk lengths before I lay floating on my back looking at another clear blue sky. I wondered where else I could do this, and reflected on the changes my life had taken over the last few months.

I became more involved assisting Brian with the small restaurant at the club, giving him well-earned days off. He was approaching retirement and still holding a full-time job working nights with the Post office; how he coped with the lack of sleep I don't know, and eventually his health began to suffer.

Cleverly he planted the seeds over the months, and as they grew Jenny and I began to consider taking over the catering franchise. We knew we had something to offer and the ability to provide good food.

Together we fixed a change-over date with the club management and made the commitment. Apart from the one or two who popped in for a coffee or lunch during the week, it was mostly a week-end and bank holiday affair; in bad weather we rarely saw anybody.

But it was a big commitment of our time, one of us had to be there from eleven in the morning until five in the afternoon, and additionally we also covered refreshments for the mid-week sauna evening.

Sundays were the best and the busiest day and I usually started preparing the vegetables and meats for the traditional lunches around eight o'clock in the morning; it became a weekly social event for us, and although it was hard work we enjoyed it immensely.

Some members arrived at ten o'clock and spent the morning in the lounge with a newspaper or chatting with friends; others came later and shared a drink at the bar, some came very late and found nothing left. Our list of pre-booked lunches was constantly growing!

By twelve thirty all the tables would be full with diners, and as the hubbub of conversation quietened to the chink of cutlery on plates we would clear the sinks and load the dishwasher in readiness for the later onslaught of dirties.

Some people had special dietary requirements and some just wanted the crunchy bits of the meat from the end of the joint. Some wanted more gravy, others more roast potatoes, and we learned to accommodate them all.

By late afternoon as they slowly drifted away we washed the last of the pots and pans then collected, cleaned and stacked the plates. With our arms full of tea cloths for the wash and a full till, we eventually walked home across the lawns and crashed; too tired even to change and wash off the odour of food and cooking.

We drifted through the long summer days thoroughly enjoying it, and when it was quieter one of us would return home for some chore; for Jenny the washing or a little maintenance on her garden; for me it was some small further advancement on the cabin.

There were frustrating days when the daily call from my sales manager would reveal an appointment mid-afternoon and I had to quickly shower and change, leaving some engrossing job unfinished. Generally I had to leave for work late afternoon or early evening during the week, and sometimes it was a real struggle to have to leave knowing I wouldn't return until after dark.

When the rapport was good with clients the conversation after the sale invariably moved to more general topics, and the inevitable question would always arise, where did I live?

If I felt comfortable doing so I used to have some fun with receptive clients, painting an idyllic picture of my home and the grounds; then just as I could feel them assessing my income to be able to afford such a property I would drop the bombshell of where my home actually was.

People's reactions were rarely one of disapproval but more of interest in a way of life they knew nothing about but were convinced they would never test for themselves. It was an education for them to realise that it was not a way of life for perverts but one enjoyed by ordinary people from all walks of life; just like themselves. I could imagine the conversation being passed on to their friends at some later dinner party.

Warm summer days were cooling and the numbers of daily visitors dwindled to a trickle as autumn rounded the corner. Spielplatz was an entirely different place outside of summer and the first fall of leaves placed a magic golden carpet everywhere.

It is the residents with green fingers who devote their time freely to lovingly tend the club's flower beds and borders. Now there are many hours of work ahead to winter over their precious plants in warmer places. The only professional gardener was a retired policeman who trimmed the lawns one last time in preparation for the coming winter.

Bare trees, hedges and shrubs once again reveal secret gardens and lost cabins. It is a sad time and seasonal friendships are again put on hold until next year.

As Christmas approached we began to plan for the annual Dinner Dance. The club social committee had told us of the budget allocation for the buffet and we were determined to equal the event's reputation of previous years and put on a good spread.

Scheduled again in mid-December we knew it would be a lot of work and it was, but none the less it was a great success with everybody complimenting us on the achievement.

It had turned out to be a busy and eventful year for us, and so we arranged cover and took our Christmas to France to relax for a while.

The car was always packed tight on such a trip and this trip was no exception. Customs at Dover pulled us out of line for a spot check and asked the usual string of travel questions. A pleasant female official was satisfied with our answers and then proceeded to inspect our cargo through the windows. A boxed Christmas tree and a box of decorations, two sacks of coal, clean bedding, presents, clothes and tools, all bar the kitchen sink.

With a look of disbelief on her face she smiled and said, "I'm not going to attempt to look in there, go! And have a nice Christmas."

We laughed together at the relief as we ascended the boarding ramp.

Prieu like Spielplatz is very different in mid-winter but still to be back lifted our hearts; it felt like the house was pleased we were warming it with our presence and two sacks of coal.

One special evening during that time in France, we sat on the rug before the warm glow of the fire enjoying the last of an excellent bottle of Cahors. We were just talking like couples do about nothing in particular.

Jenny said, "Can I ask you something?"

"Of course you can." I replied wondering why the mystery.

"Can we get married?" She asked.

Without a second thought I replied. "Yea ok." Just like that.

"No…" she said, "…I'm serious, can we get married?"

Again I replied, "Yes, I'd like to marry you."

Then obviously pleased with my response she added, "But you answered so quickly, how come?"

I explained that in a the short time we had known each other Jenny had become that someone special in my life, and I had concluded that we were definitely going to stay together for the future; what I hadn't decided was what I was going to do about it.

I answered her question saying, "I always knew we would be married one day, it was just a matter of when so it was natural to answer as I did."

So we went back to England to make plans for a wedding.

5

The drive back to England seemed to take much longer, as we were eager to be back and announce our plans to family and friends. We talked about where and when, who to invite, wondering what the cost would be and slowly some sort of plan evolved.

The club restaurant out of season was quiet and my conversion work was progressing well with Jenny's help and our conversations regularly touched on our future together. One major question that arose planning a life together was where were we going to live that life?

Whilst my cabin could accommodate two, it was only practical for one; Jenny's cabin was no bigger and it needed a lot of repairs. Besides we both had too many possessions to make either option viable. I broached the subject with Jenny and discovered that she had been mulling over the same thoughts. Neither of us wanted to give up the privacy and beautiful surroundings that we now enjoyed and we knew we couldn't afford to duplicate it in a property outside of the club.

Then during a lull in our inconclusive conversation while going round and round in circles looking for the solution, Jenny quietly said, "We could always go and live in France."

I had never considered this but together we very quickly decided it was an excellent idea, and one that excited us. We were both divorced and the six children we had between us were grown and had their own lives and we felt there were no ties to stop us. Every way we evaluated it we could only see benefits. It was a large house capable of absorbing all our possessions and with room to expand.

Excellent weather prospects in a warmer climate giving us extensions at both ends of the season and within a community we could identify with. In tandem with our plans for a wedding, we now had plans to emigrate to France.

Weighing up the situation for our immediate living requirements, Jenny decided to sell her place and move into mine. It proved to be a good move not only because she made a small profit on the sale, but additionally because her cabin later manifested itself to be a can of worms, and the new owner spent a considerable amount of money on it.

Jenny is a past master at planning and organising any event and everything has to be perfect. We wanted to have the wedding ceremony and reception in the beautiful grounds where we lived, but although it was possible with an official registrar attending, to organise such an event was rather complicated.

We didn't want to be married in a registry office and so we talked about churches. As a child I attended a Baptist church with my parents until I married and moved away, so we chose the same church which greatly pleased my father as he was still a member there.

However we could think of no better place to hold a reception than within the club grounds, and as the list of invitees grew beyond the capabilities of the clubhouse, we gained the permission of the management and made plans to have a Marquee erected; we would also be able to use the facilities of the club house licenced bar.

Timing was also very important. While our friends and relatives knew we were naturists, we felt it would be inappropriate to subject them to a full display of nudity during an afternoon in June, so we planned for a late afternoon wedding so we would be arriving for the reception when most sun seekers had left.

During the following months we spent many hours preparing and freezing our chosen cold buffet. Courgette and peppercorn terrines with heart shaped scones, five whole spice-glazed salmon served with coriander and mango mayonnaise. We made duck and turkey pies and also a vegetarian pine nut and parmesan strudel. All accompanied by a marinated cucumber salad and Couscous niçoise.

For dessert there was a choice of lemon syllabub trifle, or pear and raspberry compote with cinnamon cream. Planning the guest list was not the easiest thing while trying to keep the budget tight, but still the number soon grew to ninety.

Designing the invitations, order of service, menus for the tables and place names, Jenny returned to her old office and enlisted the help of her previous colleagues in the print room. At home later she then spent hours filling in names and addressing envelopes ready for the post.

We were amazed to realise that we had spent two hours in the hire shop where we chose all the table ware and platters. The choice was immense and we congratulated them on their patience with us.

For the tables, Jenny constructed a central display with a perfumed candle surrounded by blue and white silk roses, then tethered and floating one metre above were matching coloured helium-filled balloons. She had sewn ribbons at four places around the circular tables and then pulled them into pom-poms to complete the effect.

Included on the tables for each of the ladies was the white netting Bomboniére bag. The long standing tradition of giving Bomboniére to celebrate special occasions such as weddings was started centuries ago in Italy. Each little bag contains five top quality sugared almonds, because five being a prime number cannot be divided, like the bride and groom. They symbolise, health, wealth, happiness, fertility and long life. They are a lovely way to say thank you to your guests for sharing the joy of your day. I just hoped the fertility part wouldn't be very strong!

Jenny had been searching all the local market stalls with her ideas for flower arrangements in mind, and now armfuls of silk flowers began to appear on a weekly basis. She produced a large display for the marquee, and then her own garland and the posies for her bridesmaids and finally two smaller ones for the two younger bridesmaids, daughters of our friends.

We booked a day trip to Calais to purchase the wines for the event, taking an empty car this time and looking forward to a day out on French soil. As the port of Calais approached in the dull early morning light, I left the warmth of the saloon and went up on deck. I stood alone on the prow feeling the sea wind on my face and I shivered. Then as the ferry approached the dock a feeling of deep emotion came over me, and a sense of belonging like I was coming home welled up within me and I was glad to be back.

Searching the shelves of the Calais *Hyper Marche* for wines that would suit our menu soon had our trolley overloaded and difficult to steer and as usual I managed to find the trolley with the squeakiest castors and uncontrollability, much to the mystified gazes of the French shoppers.

I just about picked up one comment from a jolly old fellow who said "The oil is over there". With a knowing grin I replied, "*Ah Oui, merci beaucoup*."

Struggling with the loaded trolley back to the car became a major tactical event across the potholed tarmac; I imagined some wicked and grinning maintenance engineer secretly watching his attempt at wheel sabotage through a crack in the door. Eventually we headed off to service other needs.

Lunch was simple, sustaining, and very French with probably a little too much wine. Sleepily browsing the other shops during the afternoon, my imagination drifted longingly to a cosy armchair by the fire and a nap before our return back to the port.

If I was surprised by my feelings when we had docked at Calais, I was even more perplexed with my emotions when our ferry left the docks for our return to England. I felt as though I was being pulled in two directions; from my existing home on one side, and a new home where I wanted to be on the other. I was glad of the time during the crossing for my head to make the transition.

Four days before the wedding day we received a call from the owner of the marquee company to confirm their arrival on the Thursday morning. Yet one more carefully planned part was falling nicely into place...well almost. Dropped nonchalantly into the tail-end of my conversation with him, the owner had stated that the blue chairs that fitted perfectly with Jenny's colour scheme were not available and would be replaced by red ones. I did tell him she wouldn't be happy.

She was immediately back on the phone to him pointing out very strongly that she didn't care about his problems with supply, she had chosen blue and blue she wanted, how he got them was his problem. It did the trick and much to Jenny's relief he reported back saying that he would be able to supply blue after all.

A very apologetic team arrived Thursday morning and before lunch they had erected the marquee on the lawn in front of the clubhouse. They lined it internally with white drapes and laid the blue carpet, and then set out the tables and blue chairs in place for ninety. Two chandeliers set off the whole scene which looked ready to receive a royal banquet.

Jenny spent all the day preceding the wedding laying the tables and adding all the planned wedding décor and trimmings, and adding light blue ribbons to the top of the walls to break the all white linings. At the far end a wooden floor dance area was laid, and upon it stood a table displaying Jenny's three-tiered cake on a spiral stand.

Everything was now ready, we even had a chef to help serve the buffet, but we suddenly realised we had made no provision as to how the tables would be cleared after each course and we couldn't expect guests to jettison their own plates.

Fortunately Andy who would be providing the bar came to our rescue by telling us that his son had had experience of waiting, and he was sure that together with one of his pals they would be glad to help. They were of course pleased to have the chance of earning a bit extra so we now had two waiters to clear table.

"Just pile it all up neatly out of sight at the back of the marquee", were the instructions we gave them, and then we would deal with it all later. In black trousers and crisp white shirts they moved unnoticed around the tables, clearing the debris and topping up glasses like true professionals, and we don't know what we would have done without them.

By eleven o'clock in the evening, the excitement of our day and all the preparation had taken its toll on us and we were ready to leave for the grand hotel and our overnight stay, to be on our own as husband and wife, leaving them all to it.

Although for June the weather could have been kinder, it was a magnificent wedding. We deserved the full English breakfast the following morning at the hotel and the attention of the staff that waited on us. Being centre stage the previous day neither of us could remember eating much so were glad of a hearty breakfast before returning to the club and the preparation of the Sunday lunches for all.

We took a quick look inside the marquee.

"Oh my God." Jenny exclaimed, and then closing the entry flap we caught sight of the catering boxes at the rear, piled high with all the dirty dishes, inclusive of all the leavings. Some friends had salvaged all the edible food to their freezer, but the rest was left for us and with our Sunday commitment to the club that would have to wait until Monday morning.

As members drifted into the clubhouse that Sunday morning we received a constant flow of best wishes from all, and a few surprised looks that we were even there instead of on our honeymoon.

We convinced ourselves that the hire company would probably hot wash every item before re-hire, and as the weather was fine and the kitchen was small, we drained the hot water cylinder into two great tubs on our lawn. It was a family effort forming a very efficient production line; two people were scraping off the plates into a bin liner and stacking them into the dirty tub to soak a while, then one washing and rinsing in the clean tub and stacking to dry on the make-shift rack. Jenny did the checking, counting and re-stacking back in their boxes, and after four hours between us we eventually finished. The hire company happily returned our deposit, despite the one and only breakage, a wine glass.

Later we tackled the marquee, bagging all the rubbish and neatly folding the table cloths for laundry, an hour with the vacuum cleaner and the carpet was returned to what it was.

We have a box somewhere that houses all the ribbons and table decorations along with one of each of all the printed matter, Jenny's souvenirs. The album of impromptu photos from the disposable cameras that we placed on each table is priceless. We are still searching to find the identity of the bare bottom with flashy boxer shorts and likewise the owner of the adolescent male genitals.

Once the marquee was taken down and driven away and we had replaced the plastic tables and chairs on the lawn, the only witness was the flattened grass underneath, but our memories will last forever.

6

During the months we spent excitedly preparing for a wedding, a discovery brought us firmly back to reality; Jenny had found a small lump in her breast. I reassured the best that I could and we made the necessary doctor's appointment to start a process that would almost consume us during the following six months.

Following many investigative tests, we were devastated to learn that it was what we both feared, an active and aggressive cancer and prompt surgery was very necessary. Checking his agenda and with a manner of utter sympathy and compassion to us, the consultant surgeon wanted to operate the following week.

"But I'm getting married", replied Jenny in a tone that pleaded help me here with this decision. Back to his diaries he agreed to postpone the operation for a week, admitting her on her birthday. The surgery was successful and she retained her womanly attributes, the ensuing chemotherapy and radiotherapy were hell. Nobody can tell you what you will feel as each person reacts differently. Some say it was hell, others say it wasn't as bad as they expected.

Each time we arrived at the oncology unit Jenny was weighed first. The drugs dosage was relevant to body weight so they had to check each time. With her weight verified, we waited again while the drugs were made up fresh each time because they do not keep.

Time in the waiting areas passed slowly, as we re-read the same tired magazines. Candidly, we looked at the other people who were waiting in an effort to determine who the patient was, and who the spouse or supporting friend; we also wondered how long they had been coming or how serious they were.

Some spoke openly, anxious for any snippet of information to help them cope, ourselves included. Some seemed to adopt the attitude that they have a disease which needs to be kept private, that friends and relatives will disown them if they knew. Most of us there were somewhere along the normal course of six treatments. Some waited for the second time around. During the waiting period one morning, we left the hospital to buy a few bits and pieces in the local town, and started what was to become a regular habit.

We had rushed out with only a meagre breakfast, and only realised this when we passed a small Italian café and became hooked on the aroma of grilled bacon. We found a table and sat pondering the menu with a splendid cup of fresh coffee when we became aware that the waiter was, in fact, waiting.

Sporting a crisp white shirt, black tie and pin-sharp creased trousers, he spoke with a heavy Italian accent. "*Do you see somating you lika?*" he enquired as if he had always been our best friend.

As we struggled to make a selection he ventured. "*You lika maybe some bacon and egg, with a leetle sausage and some beenz and fried bread, maybe some musharooms?*"

The reply from us was spontaneous and in unison. "Yes Please!"

And so it was that we found something so pleasurable and simple to alleviate the distress of our visits.

It varied, but normally it took two or three days for the full effect to take hold. The drugs were aggressive, they had to be, but they also killed normal healthy cells. The body can recover but it takes three weeks before you are strong enough for another bashing. Each time Jenny returned, her body's ability to cope was a little lower. Then there was the all too familiar hair loss.

After the third session we began to identify the people who were the patients; they were the ones wearing a wig or for some a scarf or hat that looked out of place. Jenny was offered a special cap to combat the hair loss. It looked like a boxer's training helmet that was filled with a gel. They came straight from a freezer cabinet to be fastened over the head. Jenny lasted about ten minutes before she demanded that it be removed.

"I can't be doing with this." she said, "I'll take my chances with the hair loss against the pain of this bloody thing."

Some it worked for with varying degrees of effectiveness, some it didn't.

When it was ready, the concoction of three different drugs was hooked to the pole above, from where it dripped slowly into a vein via the flow monitor, and as we sat in easy chairs for two hours, we watched the staff moving and monitoring from patient to patient.

Nurses in general offer varying degrees of sympathy to a hospital patient, but we both agreed that the nurses in the chemotherapy unit were in a league of their own. They moved between the dozen or so people sitting there, in a calm relaxed manner of true professionals; they seemed to instinctively know who was coping and who was not, offering the latter much needed support. They found time to answer any questions about our unfamiliar ordeal, then later when their schedule allowed them to chat a while, we were able to swap backgrounds and interests

Leaving the treatment suite that first time, we walked apprehensively back to the car. Jenny was smiling, feeling a little weird but in good spirits.

"I feel like my head is about four feet behind me." She commented, "If this is Chemo, no problem, I can cope with this." A few days later we left for France to prepare the house and garage to receive us and all our worldly goods.

As the therapy sessions proceeded, Jenny's ability to cope with the chemotherapy rapidly declined. Racking stomach pains after the first days were getting worse, and earlier relief with a small meal before it started seemed to be having little effect.

Part of the drug mixture was a steroid, and her oncologist had concluded that the high dosage of this had deteriorated her stomach lining and caused an ulcer, hence the relief after food. With a reduced dosage it had improved a little but by the fifth session Jenny was ready to quit. It took some serious persuasion by her oncologist and a very caring husband before she agreed to complete the course. Then approaching the fourth session her hair was thinning quickly so taking advantage of the help and advice available, we met the 'Wig Lady'.

It was an enlightening experience with a true professional and after spending an hour roaming through the samples and catalogues for style and colour Jenny had placed an order. In my opinion, unless one spends an absolute fortune, most hair pieces are detectable, but I have to say when it arrived, it wasn't bad.

Then one morning a few days later Jenny showed me her pillow and how much hair she had lost during the night. Then resolutely she announced, "I'm going to cut the lot off - grade one!"

She locked herself in the bathroom and I could hear the clippers busy at work. She eventually emerged and gave a twirl saying, "Well... what do you think?" She stood there with an expression of uncertainty waiting for my reaction.

It was a dramatic change and I stood there looking while Jenny formed an anxious look on her face, until finally and truthfully I said, "I love it!"

Jenny had the sort of head shape that really suited a very short haircut and I thought it was really sexy. But however much encouragement I gave her, I don't think she was ever very comfortable with the cut because she worried what people would think of a grey-haired woman of her age supporting a much younger cut. I wanted her to keep it in the style but when her hair re-grew a woman's vanity won.

The following radiotherapy was a breeze in comparison; the only drawback was the tiredness. Six months later, when sudden bouts of extreme fatigue would overtake Jenny, I had to remind her confused mind of what her doctors had said; that she could expect this tiredness for months and out of the blue for no apparent reason.

When leaving the chemotherapy suite for the last time we said our grateful goodbyes to all the staff. They all knew exactly what Jenny meant when she said, "I hope I never see any of you again."

I accompanied and supported her through it all, every consultancy, every treatment and I've never felt so helpless. Such was her state of mind that she offered to release me from our proposed marriage but even if I had wanted to escape this traumatic situation I could never have done so, but I didn't; we were in this together, for better or worse.

Over a decade later we are lucky to be still free from this disease that shows no mercy or discrimination of its victims and their families. To me, every day is a bonus.

Before Jenny became ill we were fully occupied making plans for the wedding and the move to France. In addition the restaurant had eventually become a twenty four hour a day occupation for both of us, seriously depleting my love of food and cooking, and robbing us of quality time together. Every waking hour revolved around planning, buying, cooking and serving food and we found we had to consciously stop ourselves from talking about it.

I had sales meetings every Monday morning and appointments with customers every evening which usually meant I didn't return until after ten, and sometimes later. Jenny spent the time covering the opening hours when I couldn't, and frequently became frustrated as once more she had to leave something unfinished to open for business.

Wedding plans were well advanced but she had a lot of preparation still to complete and now we had a major packing task ahead. With so much to achieve the distraction away from her illness was probably a good thing but eventually when the full implications presented themselves something had to go and it was an easy decision to give up the restaurant.

After our wedding we spoke to the club's management who were very sympathetic. They had no idea of what we were going through and could see it was our only option, and they asked Brian to come back as a stand-in while our replacement was found, a decision that later left us very much out of pocket.

During the time that we ran the restaurant, Brian showed his true character and it wasn't nice. Intent on boosting his own ego he often spoke about people behind their back, frequently embellishing the truth, but now we learned that he was saying some really nasty things about us and our involvement with the restaurant. We had considered him a friend and were devastated at this betrayal, and therefore we decided to rescind his invitation to attend our wedding celebrations.

When later we broached the subject of our investment into stocking the restaurant freezers and cupboards we were told that Brian said to clear it all out, he didn't want any of it! We had to remove it, condensing and storing all that was possible at home and unable to store it all we had to throw away some good food and felt angered to be out of pocket with no recompense possible.

We had heard many stories concerning his negative opinion of us, he was a strange fellow and we subsequently discovered that it was his detrimental input and opinions that affected us financially. I should have been wiser before the event as I had seen his same fantasy gossip affect other people and indeed had felt it before myself.

Now it was all history that we couldn't change, we had to look to our future.

7

In my twenties I had an ambition to buy and convert an old barn or similar building, and my enthusiasm was fired by the various magazines available that showed these awe-inspiring projects. But in reality I knew these grand ideas were beyond my financial capability.

The purchase of my cabin and the following concept of design with the conversion work gave me great satisfaction and partly fulfilled this desire, albeit on a far smaller scale. Always having practical skills, I felt gratified in my continuing ability and achievements.

Our conversations were regularly returning to the subject of living in France, and Jenny revealed that she had often considered what to do with her barn. Between us it didn't take long to formulate the obvious; we would create a modern contemporary new home within the barn and then when it was finished and we'd moved in we would let the original house for a holiday Gite.

The beauty of the idea, we had a furnished house ready to move into and live, the garage provided storage for all the boxes and household items not immediately required, and we had space - lots of space to work within. In addition the income from a Gite would be welcome.

A provisional date for the move had been set, and we excited ourselves sketching our plans for the barn conversion. We dug out all the photos we had showing the barn interior and started to plan a layout and design, but with the experience of my cabin design and the renovation, we soon discovered that photos were not supplying us with enough information; I needed firm site measurements to work with.

Springtime had gently eased into summer as we prepared for and enjoyed our Wedding and the restaurant was now in the past. The club grounds and gardens were resplendent once more in full colour and the sound of mowing and the sweet smell of fresh cut grass turned our thoughts again to France.

We knew from past experience how quickly the garden there would become overgrown, and I needed to take the site measurements for our planning so taking a belated honeymoon we left for Prieu.

The early spring rain had been excessive, and as we descended the drive we could see the top stalks of the grass and weeds above the bonnet of the car. The path to the house was unrecognisable and creepers had entered under the old poorly fitting door, to wind their way inside.

The Horns of Plenty had grown way above the pergola and up onto the roof and the whole plant, still covered in little red trumpets all over it, was now lying on the ground where the wind had flipped them back over breaking the pergola.

Jenny's lovingly tended flower beds had given up to the weeds and it was difficult to see any distinction between the grass that was a lawn of sorts, and the flower beds. It was far too long for the sit-on mower with some grass lying almost flat; what we needed was something mechanical and aggressive.

The gardening section of E.Leclerc supermarché displayed four likely strimming tools; the one with a four-stroke Honda engine looked to be exactly what we wanted, but unlike the others it wasn't displayed with a support harness. With few linguistic skills it's easy to just make a choice and go to the checkout, but we now had to summon an assistant.

A weary looking chap dressed in a store tunic three sizes too big arrived promptly and became immediately baffled by our meek attempts of explanation.

I was standing centre stage in the aisle of a French supermarket doing my best impression of a contestant on a charades game show and speaking Franglais to an open-mouthed shop assistant while Jenny looked on in horror.

Bless him, he quickly cottoned on and removed a harness from one of the others that were on display, and clipping it to the one we wanted he said, *"Voila, bon Journée"*, and then he disappeared. We had bought an industrial Strimmer - a mechanical scythe.

It was supplied with a circular steel blade that was capable of cutting down a small sapling, but we thought that might be a little too aggressive for our needs, so I fitted the interchangeable head that took heavy-duty nylon strimming thread, and then I adjusted the harness to fit me comfortably, which was no easy feat.

I filled the tank with petrol and after priming the carburettor I pulled the cord and it started like a dream; I clipped it onto the harness and began. I quickly fell into a good rhythm and by holding the cow-horn operating handles and advancing like one of those plastic toys that waddle down an incline I managed to make a clean sweep from side to side.

After a few hours I had cut a sizable area which now looked like a field of hay ready for baling. Unfortunately we did not have a baler. Traditionally the French tool for the collection of hay is a wooden rake that has 10 centimetre teeth, and a handle that is set at forty five degrees. The first sight of this implement as Jen brought it out from the barn sent me scurrying back to look for a proper rake.

Undeterred I soon found it clogged and useless, reluctantly conceding to her demand, I tried the wooden thing, brilliant. I had to admit it was the tool for the job, and was surprised to learn that what looked like some old tool found under aged rubbish in the barn, was still sold new.

I have since discovered that basic French tools across the board do not look pretty, and appear unrefined, but they do the job very well and in many of cases they have developed better suited to materials and work here than their British counterparts.

Neatly raked piles of mini hay stacks then littered the garden and necessity surely became the mother of invention. Hooking the car trailer to the back of the sit-on mower, we began our very own mini harvest. With pitch fork and wooden rake we piled high the trailer for numerous journeys around to the back of the house with our impromptu tractor and hay wain, and eventually we built a stack of hay three metres long that we couldn't see over.

It had turned into a busy week but I did find the time to take the measurements I needed from within the barn.

Autumn back in England gave us mixed feelings. The sadness as another summer of warm sunny days gave way to the splendour of fall and the golden carpet of leaves.

Research into the official paperwork necessary for the move led us into a bureaucratic mine field. Banking, social security, pensions, medical, pets, all had to be investigated. Eventually sourcing the correct department at Newcastle, the National Insurance office gave us a wealth of information on what to do and how to do it; the friendly staff seemed to identify with what we were trying to do.

The ever increasing stack of packed boxes for France quickly filled my garage. All neatly taped up and labelled, from floor to ceiling when the fragility of the contents would allow. Apart from our personal items, we were merging two households into one, having duplicates of many things.

With our own home, and a Gite to furnish, it made sense to keep it all, doubling the packaging. Packing boxes for a move, as anyone who has done it will quickly tell you, is a nightmare. Why is it so difficult to make objective decisions concerning what to keep and what items really are redundant?

We remove things that have been stored and unused for years at the back of our cupboards, wrap them in tissue paper and carefully pack inside a labelled box; then on arrival at their destination we carefully unpack the contents of our boxes into our new cupboards, where again they remain, unused until the next relocation!

I frequently arrived home to find a scene of utter chaos, with Jen assuring me she knew exactly what she was doing. There were half-packed boxes and tissue and bubble wrap, all covering the floor alongside yet another stack of sealed cartons to find storage space for.

The entertainment value for our two Siamese cats was priceless, but we had to do something to create more storage space and the solution presented itself in the columns of the local newspaper. While browsing the "Items for sale" columns, Jenny had noticed an ad for a second-hand self-assembly steel shed, and at a very reasonable asking price.

We paid a happy man his asking price and drove away with it in the back of the car, all neatly labelled and with the original assembly instructions, and a plastic bag filled with the nuts and bolts.

We laid a level base of paving slabs and proceeded to make the assembly just like big boys Meccano and soon had the sides ready to receive the roof panels. On completion we were surprised to find every nut, bolt and screw accounted for, without the expected need to make additional purchases. It must have taken the seller hours of painstaking work to present it for sale so well and we congratulate him.

We now had nine cubic metres of extra storage, watertight and mouse proof. Amazing what simple pleasure is achievable from a tin shed! Amazing also how many times it became necessary to remove and re-pack the contents to gain more rapidly depleting space as the number of boxes grew still more.

Ten months seemed a long time, but the acceleration as days whizzed by towards our moving date was beginning to worry us. Applications for the export papers for our two cats were in hand with the required authorities, but we now found we needed to increase this by one.

Arran was a four year old highland Collie and family pet officially owned by Jenny's daughter Lynsey. Lynsey was moving from the family home into her own flat and with daily work commitments she felt it unfair for Arran to be cooped up alone all day and asked if we could consider giving him a home with us in France. We just knew he would love the wide open spaces and constant company with us, so he was gladly added to the ever increasing list.

Quotations from two companies proved decisive in the conclusion to move ourselves. They also told us that a seven tonne truck would suffice; the maximum drivable on a standard United Kingdom car licence. Making further enquiries for hire prices and terms led us to a local company allowing fully insured international usage. Excitedly we booked it; after months of intense preparation we now knew for sure that we were moving.

As the number of packed boxes began to stop growing, the pile of unwanted items for the dump grew bigger and wetter upon the drive, and the time available to take it to the dump became less and less. We distributed unwanted but still useful items to likely recipients within the family and friends, and eventually paid the club gardener to dispose of the rest for us.

With all moves to a new home there are always the last minute items, the vacuum cleaner, cleaning products, plants from the garden, and of course, the kettle. Our last minute items went a bit further than that.

Jenny's sixteen year old son Richard was a very knowledgeable and enthusiastic naturalist, with a keen interest in fish and pond life. He worked weekends at the local garden centre - within the aquatic section, where his expertise became invaluable to customers, and us. The large pond in our garden was home to his many fish including his Koi Carp, and unable to find them a new home he asked if they could live in the large pond at Prieu. Of course, so they had to join the list along with the two cats and now the dog!

We drew the line at the Umbrella Cockatoo, known to be one of the most destructive pets as we had discovered to our cost. During one of her escapades, she managed to remove two steel bars in the base of her cage, gaining the freedom of the lounge.

Not content with that she proceeded to remove the material covering and stuffing where she sat at the top of the couch, moving then to the doorway, up one side, across the top and down the other nibbling all the plaster off, and finally stripping the plastic sheathing from a length of aerial cable she opened the rear cover to a hi-fi system. We are not sure if it was live at the time - but she also stripped off the outer covering of the mains cable.

We consider ourselves lucky that she took no interest in the wall to wall boxes, but the ensuing repair time necessary we could have well done without. A friend, who had always had affection for the bird, rapidly declined our offer to give her a new home, so reluctantly we sold her back to the breeder, who we knew would maintain her best interests and his own, as we lost half of her true value in money during the transaction. *C'est la vie.*

Confident that we had now completed every preparation possible, we contacted the van hire company to ensure the booking we had made months in advance was still in place.

"Yes" they assured us, "Although the truck originally set aside for you does have a mechanical problem and is now not available, we will be able to supply a vehicle."

Suddenly alarm bells started to ring, as the offered truck was a refrigerated one. They assured us that it was the same internal capacity with the additional benefit of a wide side door, and the necessary hydraulic tail lift.

They promised to deliver it to us the evening before loading day, and with the assurance that the refrigeration unit would be turned off we relaxed. As expected they phoned us mid-evening for final directions to our location which was a little unusual, and we took delivery of the truck and received a quick résumé of its workings and documentation. I walked back from the club car park to the cabin with mixed emotions; this was all highly exciting but at the same time we were very conscious of the enormity of the task in front of us.

The number of packed boxes had eventually grown beyond our storage capacity, and we had managed to half fill a neighbour's garage with the overflow. It consisted of a complete flat packed kitchen, including fridge/freezer, double oven, dishwasher and washing machine. We had taken advantage of some excellent offers on pricing because we knew they would have cost far more in France.

Taking advantage of the remaining daylight, we decided to load what was stored in the neighbour's garage; then we re-loaded it all for better distribution of the weight. I then reversed the truck into our narrow drive, gently reshaping the hedges and the overhanging branches not used to accommodating such high vehicles.

Jen stood watching as I raised the rear shutter and as we looked inside our hearts sank.

There was no way the space was ever going to swallow up all our boxes and we rapidly came to the conclusion that a second trip was going to be required. We started to use the last available light of the day; anything that could be loaded tonight would gain us valuable time tomorrow.

Jenny - with her intimate knowledge of contents and weight, directed the loading and we quickly began to fill the space above the heavier kitchen equipment. Tired and with depression looming because of the second trip, we reached a joint decision for food and a good night's sleep as the best option.

We awoke fresh and in renewed spirits. My son Greg and daughter Emily had offered to help and make the trip with us, and then they would see where we were going to live. The bonus for us would be the extra two pairs of hands at both ends.

Friends and well-wishers came and went in a constant stream as they passed the drive, some spent time giving valued assistance to us. Jenny's son meanwhile, was busy netting and bagging fish from the pond. All he could find were eventually put into plastic bags and packed into stackable plastic storage boxes.

With Jenny they made a swift journey to the aquatic centre to fill the bags with oxygen and seal them before they were ready to be loaded; last on - first off and into the pond on arrival. Every safe available space had now been filled so the fish went on, and the shutter was secured. The first cargo was ready.

Last minute clean-up of the house became unnecessary as I would be returning in a week, so we prepared to load ourselves. My son Greg joined me in the truck and Emily packed herself into the car alongside Jenny. In the rear of the car with all the 'first night' necessities, were a Highland Collie dog and two bemused and caged Siamese cats.

We left early evening for the first stage of the journey to Deal, and an overnight stay with my Aunt. Pauline - my father's sister - is a jolly widow who still resides in Dad's home town; a convenient ten minutes' drive from Dover. She's always pleased when we arrive and she chats incessantly, anxious to receive all our news, and give us hers!

Her small terraced house always seemed to enlarge itself to accommodate us all. This time she gave up her own room to the girls, and Greg and I were to double up in the other room. Therefore Aunt Pauline was to squeeze her ample size into the box room on a camp bed.

There is something very special about Fish and Chips from a seaside town, especially so as it is likely to be the last dish of the kind you will eat for a very long time in the foreseeable future.

We relished the grease on our fingers, preferring to eat from the newspaper with lashings of salt and vinegar. What simple pleasure we enjoyed that night. All washed down with a proper cup of English tea made by someone with years of dedicated practice. Although filled with excitement and trepidation, sleep came quickly to us all after we had attended to the needs of the animals.

At four thirty we quietly roused ourselves so as not to wake our host and walked through the sharp morning air to the awaiting vehicles, grateful that nobody had shown any interest in their contents during the night.

We settled the animals and I climbed up into the lorry cab and fired the engine once more. We moved off knowing we had plenty of time yet still Jenny was refused embarkation. It transpired that at five thirty in the morning in late April very few cars were making the crossing, and therefore loading was completed in minutes and now the ramp was closing and the ferry was ready to sail.

My mobile rang. I was queuing at the freight terminal and instead of the expected last minute instruction from Jenny I soon learned of her plight. She would have to wait two hours until the next sailing.

We quickly revised our plans for a convoy and agreed that I should continue en route and then Jenny in the faster vehicle would catch up somewhere along the way. I pulled onto the freight weighbridge at check in and handed over my documents, and nearly had a fit; the weight registered at nine and a half tonnes. Oh Shit!

The expected refusal and the horrendous consequences of it didn't happen. I was given the ticket and waved through. Greg and I shared a look which to me said, "What now, Dad?" I parked awaiting embarkation and we considered the implications of a very long journey grossly overweight.

Landing with a two hour advantage on the car, I gently proceeded onto French roads, firmly of the opinion that straight roads would be ok, but that I should take extreme care of my speed on anything other.

Your sight tells you that a road is basically flat; flat that is, until you feel the frightening sway of a top heavy lorry behind you, but whilst I was still very well aware of the weight, I was reassured when watching other trucks swaying the same in front of me. So I learned to avoid the areas of tarmac likely to cause the vehicle to sway, and I slowed to an almost stop when traversing roundabouts.

We were safely advancing southerly through France and successfully negotiating the route without Jenny's directions, so Greg decided to contact the girls. After the two hour wait at Dover they had finally made the crossing and were heading in our direction, and they were pleased to know that we were proceeding well.

Conversation was difficult because our thirteen-year-old Siamese cat Sulin was objecting violently to the indignation of a caged journey of unknown duration and destination; probably thinking that the vet had moved!

Seven hours at the wheel of an unfamiliar heavy truck was enough for any one, and so we pulled into a wooded layby confident that the car and our lunch were almost upon us. It was a welcome stop for us all, especially the Collie because for the past hour he had been lying with his legs crossed.

The whingeing cats, well they would have to suffer the further indignation of the dirt tray within their cage. Most cats make a terrible row when they're miffed, but that noise palls into insignificance when you hear a very pissed off Siamese. Now - as Jenny related the events of her journey to Greg and I, we were suddenly glad we had been in the truck instead of the comfort of the car.

Minka the male and the younger at three, had decided his primary necessities outweighed the indignation of using the cat tray. Then while travelling on a fast road in traffic, he had ventured into the cat tray and deposited a disgusting turd. The smell immediately filled the whole car causing chaos amongst the occupants which resulted in an emergency stop. People inside the passing cars looked on mystified as all doors were flung wide open to relieve the offending odour and Minka promptly curled up and contentedly went to sleep.

We drove on; Greg was dozing intermittently to my left and the car was now many miles in front as dusk began to fall. A lonely solitude crept over me as I stared into the darkening road before me. The effects of sitting in the same seat for most of the day were radiating painfully down my left leg sciatic nerve from my buttock to below my knee.

Two or three stops during the night for a quick stroll in the fresh night air temporarily relieved the growing agony, but eventually I had to give in. Curling my legs to a new position around the steering column and with a pillow on the steering wheel, I managed a light sleep for about an hour with dreams of a rocking sensation and headlights.

I awoke a little refreshed to see a faint dawn; I left Greg sleeping and crept down from the cab. Cobwebs hung draped in dew among the trees of the woodland stop-over, in a silent reverence I had a reluctance to break. Lighting a cigarette I ventured to stretch my stiffened legs and take the pee that had awoken me. I explored the area nearby, its unspoilt beauty lifting my spirits in preparation for the final push.

Greg awoke with drowsy eyes as the engine once more fired into life and the familiar drone returned, and then like a child, Greg asked…

"Are we there yet Dad?"

We both burst out laughing at the phrase from his past, which spurred us on with returned determination.

As we neared the last thirty minutes of our travels his adult logic returned and he said, "How much effing Longer!" Finally, gratefully, safely, we parked at the top of our drive at six thirty in the morning.

Knowing that Jenny and Emily had arrived well past midnight, and being reluctant to attempt the hazardous task of backing down the drive before we rested, we walked the final 150 metres down the drive and crept into the house to find Jenny her normal bubbly self and Emily still fast asleep and looking lifeless upon the couch.

Finally the realisation that here was where I hoped to spend the rest of my life sunk in, unfortunately I also realised that I was destined to do this journey three more times, twice back, one more coming.

8

Four days!

That was the time available for my aching body to recuperate before starting the return journey to collect the balance of our possessions. During that time we had a lorry to unload and a home to find for the contents.

We knew the necessity of secure storage so during the previous trip to France we had cleared out the garage to accommodate the load, and we also knew that most of it would stay boxed for a long time. Now it was just a case of reversing the truck as close as possible to the doors and then emptying it.

From the lane, all you can see of the house and barn is the pantiled roof with the one chimney standing proudly alone. When turning off the lane, our drive descends like the slip road from a motorway and before the first left turn the lane is already way above head height. After this turn the descent continues straight and is flanked on one side by impenetrable woodland and on the other side by a tall hedge. At the bottom of the hill a gentle left curve opens the view to the garden and the front of the house, twenty five metres lower than the lane.

The available space and soft ground where the drive ended was not conducive to turning a truck, so reversing all the way down was therefore the only option. I climbed into the cab and fired the engine, and then very slowly, inch by inch, nine and a half tonnes began to descend aided by my mirrors and two sets of outside eyes.

The grass verges on either side of the compacted white stone drive loomed menacingly close; an error here would mean an inevitable loss of traction and no chance of forward movement to retrieve a straight line without probable entry into the flanking ditches. Accurate steering with no mistakes was essential.

It took forty-five minutes of extreme concentration and when I stopped the engine and dropped from the cab a great relief and satisfaction washed over me.

Having supervised the loading, Jenny of course took immediate charge of the unloading with her intimate knowledge of the boxed contents. Firstly the fish and they didn't look very active in their travelling compartments. One by one each oxygenated bag was carried to the pond and then opened and lowered into the water.

As the waters mixed the fish rallied and swam off to explore their new home. Some of the larger fish didn't survive the journey and one of those was a semi-tame Koi carp affectionately named Madonna. Richard had trained her to swim towards and nuzzle his fingers under the water; it was some months before we truthfully answered his enquiries as to the welfare of his fish because we knew how close he was to them.

Next we attacked the rest of the load with a vengeance and box after box was restacked inside the garage. The flat-pack kitchen and electrical goods we placed safely towards the back; it would be quite a while before their installation. Surprisingly it didn't take too long and at last I closed the roller shutter of the empty truck and walked away, grateful to be free of the encumbrance for a few days.

Four days of relaxing quickly passed as we introduced my family to some of the local sights and the delights of French cuisine and all too soon it was time to leave for the return trip. We said our goodbyes and the empty lorry eased forward for the ascent to the road. This was no adventure; I just wanted the journey behind me as soon as possible.

I could see Jenny standing abandoned in the rear view mirror waving us off, and I knew she didn't relish spending the following week on her own. I also knew that she would soon have some of the boxes open and spend her time busying herself giving the house a homely look ready for my return.

Three in the cab this time we headed north in jovial moods, confident that without the weight we would have an uneventful, although long journey. Not so. Twenty minutes from home we were stopped at a lay-by for a spot check by the Douanes; the French Customs and Excise authorities.

They were looking for concealed drug shipments on route through France and Spain and they required my papers. A United Kingdom driving licence seemed to present no problem to them, but understanding the truck hire document with its combined insurance section took them a while to decipher, as four of them offered various opinions as to its validity.

Somewhat frustrated they must have decided to give us the full works. Into the back of the truck they all climbed, looking first at the neat row of our cases, then back and forth to each other while exchanging grunts.

Out came the bottles of wine, the Jack Daniels and the tobacco. Out came all the dirty clothes, out came the toilet bags, contents all shaken and smelled, every item lay exposed for inspection on the floor when suddenly another officer appeared with a sniffer dog.

Frantically searching my pocket dictionary for the French words for moving house, I hoped to defuse the situation. The dog seemed satisfied, but the officers were obviously not as then one of them produced a long-handled mirror and started checking under the chassis for hidden packages while another produced a dipstick to check for a false compartment in the fuel tank.

Eventually satisfied, they guiltily repacked all our possessions neatly, if not by our standards, and wished us "*Bon Voyage*".

Standing on the roadside experiencing the false feelings of guilt displayed for every passing motorist, one wonders to what length drug runners go to warrant such procedures, but back en route after nearly an hour's delay, we settled to the drive, and the eventual returning aches and pains and boredom.

We made better time without nine and a half tonnes behind us, so we stopped during the early evening at St. Junien to stretch our legs and look for a meal to keep us going through the night.

In a small side street we found just what we wanted; a nice-looking restaurant with an uncomplicated menu. We settled in an intimate alcove by the window to make our choice.

Greg and Emily took the easy option and ordered steaks, but I was looking for something a little more adventurous in French cuisine and ordered *Andouillette*, and I was very pleased that the waitress had understood my questions and informed me that it was a speciality sausage.

When it arrived it was three times the size of the average English banger, very tasty and beautifully presented, but I was a little suspicious of its contents and resigned myself to later consult a dictionary and understand what the filling was.

I subsequently confirmed my suspicions and discovered their description as; "*...being made from pig's intestines contained in knobbly lengths of gut, for which they are none the less delicious*".

This is where my English heritage takes over and although I ventured to try the dish, I think I shall not repeat it. To my knowledge there is no part of the pig that is not edible and the French Charcutier and Traiteur has made it an art form. From region to region the recipes vary with each having their own specialities. The brave seekers of gastronomy will find endless delights to try, and shop owners readily offer samples before you buy.

Back in England safely, and with the balance of our home ready to leave once more, this time an older pal offered to keep me company on the trip and have a few days off. This time I was definitely not going to attempt it in one.

Rodney is excellent company at any time, his intelligent conversation is always stimulating and we have regularly indulged in our joint hobby of eating good well-presented food with fine wines. Both of us looked forward to sharing this experience together in France, as we pulled off the road and booked into a hotel for the night.

Shaved and showered, we ventured into reception and discovered that on Sundays their restaurant was closed. Then eager to use his latent French, Rodney skilfully asked if there was another restaurant locally that could be recommended. A cordial receptionist explained again that being a Sunday evening the choice was very limited but that there was just one.

So the long-awaited gastronomic pleasures in a country that boasts its expertise in food, led us through the doors of McDonalds! In consolation, we promised ourselves that we would stop for a blowout the following lunchtime, (and probably a nap afterwards) and so we surrendered to Big Mac and Fries.

On the road again the following morning in bright sunshine with a clear blue sky, we were refreshed and relaxed and the final haul became a visual pleasure with springtime unfolding slowly the further south we travelled.

Arrival and with the second safe negotiation of the drive behind me, once again I was able to relax for a few days. Air France had my booking for the final return journey to my new home; when I had safely delivered the truck and Rodney back to the UK.

Plagued by the usual dilemma with my sciatic nerve, the only real satisfactory event of this final trip was our promised blowout. Again we decided on an overnight stay to break the journey and keenly sought out the hotel's restaurant.

We crossed a wide hallway towards two magnificently carved oak doors and entered the immense dining room as an ear-piercing squeak shattering the silence and the aged hinges announced our arrival. The Maître d'hôtel appeared and seemed astonished to find us there, and we concluded that perhaps he'd been down in the cellar checking his wine stocks!

Moving towards his booking lectern to welcome us, he weaved his way through the tables, the epitome of a waiter honed from years of professional service. Had we booked, he asked when we requested a table for two people, and as we confirmed his suspicions he pointedly checked his bookings and then politely showed us to one of twelve tables; the others remained empty all evening.

Attentive to our every wish he patiently coped with our command of his language, explaining the intricacies of each dish enthusiastically and further suggesting that we should try an alternative wine cheaper than the one we chose, because in his opinion it was superior.

He was probably correct as it was superb.

Little conversation had passed between the two of us as we ate and now as we sat contented and soporific, sipping two very large glasses of excellent Cognac, we both agreed it was the best meal either of us could remember for a very long time.

During the flight back, I lowered my book and reflected upon the last two weeks.

Anyone contemplating moving house themselves to the continent, think again! During a fourteen day period, I had loaded and unloaded nearly twenty tonnes of our possessions, transported it in total one thousand four hundred miles, and travelled myself by fair means or foul, a total of nearly three thousand miles. We probably saved in the region of fifteen hundred pounds, against a removal company's quotation, but I think I should have earned double that?

9

That first week after the move we did very little except allow our aching bodies' time to recover, and our minds the time to make the adjustment. In England the constant drone of motorway traffic was always audible, and now here we relished the peace and quiet.

After I landed at Toulouse airport, Jenny whisked me home and gave me a tour of the house, and as predicted, she had spent the time during my absence changing the previous holiday home into something more comfortable and permanent.

I was concerned that she had moved the heavy furniture by herself because she could have had an accident in my absence, but that aside she had done a superb job unpacking our clothes and creating a warm homely environment.

Most items for our daily requirements were there already, but occasionally we sought an item of necessity from the mass of stacked boxes in the garage; something to make a job easier in the kitchen or a table lamp to give more light somewhere, but we tried to make do where possible because invariably it took over an hour to find anything. The labels worked well in locating the box we sought which was invariably on the bottom of a pile, it was getting them out that took the time.

With springtime firmly established Jenny was now focusing on the garden to tend her precious plants, removing their lovingly wrapped packaging and placing them in a temporary new home to revive and flourish. I spent my time changing electrical plugs, freeing reluctant hinges and bolts, and arranging my tools and stock of fixings into some sort of workable order within the lower barn.

Eager to investigate the viability of our plans for the barn, we started to clear some of the aged debris and spent many hours discussing and looking, trying to visualise this vast expanse of space as we wanted it to eventually be. We regularly returned to the plans I had drawn, to verify some point or, as was more often the case, to redraw an improvement in the design; a process that would continue for quite a while.

Full-time residency now showed us some of the problems rainwater could cause outside. Roof guttering had never been a part of the property as most water from the roof fell to the rear and was taken away by the ditches and in heavy rain this could flow in a torrent. We discovered that a small subsidence of earth had raised the level in the rear ditch and rainwater was flowing through the stone wall into the lower part of the barn every time it rained.

This was originally the area where the cows were milked, and because it was the only area with a concrete floor, it had become a temporary home to my numerous boxes of tools and fixings. Now all the boxes had soggy bottoms and quickly required lifting and stacking upon pallets out of the wet.

When I lifted the boxes the wet cardboard frequently gave way spilling the contents over the floor. Precious tools, many with sentimental value that had been handed down from my father were now showing signs of rust, and my screws, nails and drill bits were now all mixed together and sopping wet.

We had to do something quickly to rectify the ditch, so we spent the following day ankle deep in soggy clay with a constant flow of water passing our feet and temporarily lowered the ditch, knowing full well that very soon a more permanent and mechanical solution would be needed.

Reluctantly each shovelful gave up the fight with a sucking noise like somebody drinking soup straight from the bowl. Then once on the shovel each clod stuck like glue and had to be removed with a trowel, but although painfully slow we managed to lower the ditch enough to achieve a good flow of water at a much lower level so that the floor inside the barn would eventually dry.

Showered and clean later, we reflected on the task that had taken most of the day instead of the couple of hours we had anticipated. We had also learned some small insight into what country life was like for previous generations on our land; the struggle of daily life that moulded and shaped the landscape by hand to what it was now.

I am told that the origin of pantiles is that they were made by forming the wet clay over a maiden's thigh. This method achieved the required rounded shape tapering from one end to the other and gave the optimum required length. What truth there is in this I am unable to verify, but we knew our pantiled roof was well past its sell by date and had taken steps for its replacement during one of our visits before the move.

Old houses are roofed with old tiles, and old tiles deteriorate. The danger with a poor roof is of course water penetration, and that danger increases dramatically when the stone walls are held together with a clay mortar, because its strength relies upon it staying dry and hard. A leaking roof means wet walls, and wet walls will eventually collapse.

Enquiries to our French neighbours had produced a recommendation for an artisan roofing contractor named Monsieur Albige, and so we met him on site during our summer break the previous August. He was a short stocky man with a permanently worried look upon his face which was shadowed by his beret.

An inspection of our roof produced lots of ums and ahs from him and precious little else in the way of intelligible words. He retrieved a pencil from behind his ear and while he searched his pockets for something to write upon I suddenly had this mental picture of him fast asleep in bed with his pencil still there behind his ear!

He began a private conversation with himself making various notes on a piece of aged paper that he found in the bowels of his pocket and we could almost feel the cogs of calculation turning within his head and then suddenly he stopped, turned the grubby paper over and wrote a figure. The sudden change in his unmoving expression took us by surprise as did the unexpected smile that creased the whole of his face like a deflated balloon; he would commence the work before our arrival in April. We agreed the price and promised to sign his printed quotation when it arrived.

In February we excitedly telephoned our French friends for a progress report.

"How is the roof coming on?" We asked.

"Well," they replied, "He hasn't started yet, but he will be soon."

Happy with their confidence we awaited the next report, but we didn't have to wait very long.

About three weeks later our friends phoned and after the usual greetings and news they came to the reason for their call.

"We called you…" they began, "…because there's a problem with the roof".

With little time left before the move we were worried and pressed for more information.

"Well…" they said, "…he's done a quarter of the roof over the barn, but unfortunately he's had a massive heart attack and died!"

We were devastated at this terrible misfortune for his family especially his son Fabrice who worked alongside him, then we slowly came to terms with the implications for our roof. Our fears subsided because our friends informed us that in situations such as this with a contract to fulfil, the office of the Marie invite other local artisans to conclude the work in hand.

So as events unfolded we considered ourselves fortunate that one of the best local tradesmen had agreed to complete the contract and for the same price that we had originally agreed, all that remained to be decided was when?

The ground during May should normally be beginning to harden under the increasing heat from the sun, but with the unusual amount of spring rainfall it had not had that chance, which had delayed the start of the work. Loss of traction and the safety aspect of lifting heavy loads and then maintaining them at roof level was a worry for our new contractor on the soggy ground, and hence we still hadn't got a starting date.

Since the move we had slumped into holiday mode and I sat in the lounge one morning nursing my second cup of coffee and willing the caffeine to bring some order to my sleepy head. As the fog cleared I started to think how best I would tackle the day's as yet undecided project, when I heard a distant, bleep-bleep-bleep-bleep, gradually becoming louder.

"Jen," I said, "I think there is a lorry coming down our drive."

Slowly two great wheels appeared from behind the cover of the hedges, followed by a great red vehicle and two further huge wheels.

Unable to postpone the work on our roof any longer Monsieur Lafour had arrived in his Manitou, a giant of a machine capable of lifting great weights to the top of our roof with its extendable arm. Leaving the great machine parked on our lawn, he explained he would be back to start the very next day

True to his word, he arrived sharp at eight in the morning with two apprentices crammed within his pickup truck, which was towing a cement mixer which looked brand new. One other lad arrived in his car and as this lad appeared we were pleased to recognise Fabrice - the son of the unfortunate Monsieur Albige who had died.

It later transpired that our new roofing contractor had employed Fabrice and agreed to continue his apprenticeship; there was no doubt that this would provide a welcome income for the family. He showed himself to be a most attentive worker and we soon realised why Monsieur Lafour owned such a brand new looking mixer.

At the end of each day's work, Fabrice would delay departure while he meticulously cleaned off every last speck of cement from the machine, both inside and out, and he applied the same attitude to all of his work and was an excellent testimony to Monsieur Lafour's long-standing good reputation.

Each day a section of tiles was removed and sorted; the good ones were stacked elsewhere on the roof while the unusable ones were stacked on a pallet to be lowered back to the ground.

Twisted and warped with age the tile support battens were then removed and discarded. The oaken framework inspection found a few suspicious looking beams which were replaced and levelled with new ones to give a flat area for the new tile battens.

Finally towards the end of that day, the new under tiles were accurately positioned before a mixture of the old tiles was laid over the top to fill the gaps and complete the lay. Using the old tiles gave a mixture of colours and shades and visually the effect was a roof that didn't look brand new.

Each day during the following two weeks they completed another section by repeating the same process until the whole roof was replaced, and then a week of hard boring work to cement the ridges, eaves and hip tiles in place.

On the final day of work just after lunch, our valiant workers were on the roof putting the finishing touches to the hips and ridges under a blue sky with a few patchy clouds. Within thirty minutes a lovely afternoon had developed into something very different. Fluffy white clouds were replaced by threatening black ones as a chilly breeze grew in strength, a warning of the approaching storm. Very soon large plops of rain developed in a full scale downpour sending our valiant crew scurrying off the roof.

Frantically collecting their tools they descended from the roof drenched and moved undercover while I threw a great sheet of plastic over their truck to cover the sand and open bags of cement. Fabrice was soaked to the skin but still insisted on cleaning the mixer before he pulled the wheeled machine under the cover of our barn canopy.

Grateful for our towels they exhibited smiles of resignation to the weather, and returned the next day to repair the minimal damage and clear site. The finished roof looked magnificent; to say we were pleased would have been an understatement. It was only fitting we should share a bottle of champagne together and toast our roof, but of course we had to wait while Fabrice finished cleaning the mixer one last time.

Every silver lining has a grubby cloud around it and after the champagne with much shaking of hands and goodbyes we looked upon the state of the garden. It looked like an army battalion on manoeuvres had passed through.

The Manitou's great wheels four feet high and a foot wide had churned great troughs wherever it went and the hydraulic stabilising feet had pressed great holes a foot deep into the soil. With necessity it had habitually covered the same ground between our roof and the stack of new tiles, the stack of old tiles and the piles of old wood, eventually churning it into a bog.

One of our underground springs runs through the Chai at the rear and the water is collected by buried perforated pipes before it flows into a silt trap outside. There it is joined by rainwater from the largest expanse of our roof and together the waters run into a ditch and then underground again through sections of concrete pipe set under a grass track which gives vehicle access to the rear of the house and garden. On a rainy day this constant trickle can become a torrent.

The colossal weight of the Manitou with its cargo of tiles passing back and forth over the soft ground and the pipe sections had split them apart and left them broken and sticking up out of the ground at all angles, and now the water flow was flooding the quagmire where he had habitually turned the vehicle. Even the dog refused to go there to retrieve his ball which was just as well because a wet and muddy Highland Collie is no joke.

Inside the grubby cloud though was a silver lining. Apart from our spanking new roof we had an enormous pile of old battens and planks which was about fifteen feet round at the base and probably eight foot high, and buried within it were a good many of the old and twisted oak beams.

Later that same year as winter approached, we spent countless hours outside wrapped up in warm clothes, and determined to remove this eyesore from the garden we cut and stacked it all into three covered rows of three feet high and twenty feet long. It lasted all that winter and half of the next.

10

Necessity had forced us to make a temporary repair to the broken pipes and by digging a shallow trench we diverted the escaping water and returned it to its original route instead of flooding the garden. Before becoming broken and uprooted the concrete pipes brought the water underground where it then flowed into another ditch which was once the border between the garden and the adjacent fields. Additional land bought during the purchase of the property had placed this ditch centrally through the lower part of the garden.

We had been searching intermittently for a solution here because the growth of grass and weeds within the ditch couldn't be controlled without a major time-consuming effort. Now something permanent had to be done with the pipes before the winter rains, and it seemed a good idea to try and combine the two; but how?

Jenny had met Lynn, one of our neighbours, who had moved to France from England twenty five years ago and married Jacques – a French farmer. It was to them that we turned when in need and Jacques's experience and knowledge was invaluable.

Approaching sixty, he had a close-cut greying beard which framed a ready smile and a glint from his gold-filled teeth. His fingers looked like pork sausages as they rolled another cigarette which he screwed into the corner of his mouth while he spoke. His advice on building work and materials was immense and he seemed to know how and what to do in any event.

The four of us were standing in the garden, and with Lynn acting as translator, we were discussing various options that might rectify the problem, when Jenny offered yet another idea.

A little unsure about the idea's viability she said, "Instead of the spring running along behind the barn and then turning right along the side and through the pipes and the ditch, why don't we continue it in a straight line through new pipes underground, and then dig a new ditch on the boundary and fill in the old one?"

I quickly realised this was the solution that we had been searching for which would repair the pipes and re-route the ditch, and I could immediately visualise the beauty of mowing the lawn in that area without the ditch bisecting it. Lynn made the translation for Jacques who could see the obvious benefit straight away and gave us his approving "A*h Oui*"; Jacques approved!

We sat with drinks outside the house while we discussed the details; Jacques shared my whiskey and together we lowered the level in the bottle very easily, but that was often the case when we got together and it usually produced better spoken French from me without the fear of embarrassment whilst under the influence of alcohol; I was pleased to be able to communicate with him direct instead of through Lynn.

Nevertheless, after surveying of the area one last time with Jacques, we felt confirmation was required from Lynn who eventually said…

"Oh yea, he says he'll do it - but he doesn't know when."

Neighbourly assistance in France seemed to be a reciprocal arrangement, so I was not surprised Jacques asked for my help to lay drainage pipes in the paddock where Lynn kept her horses, although the call at 8-30 in the morning a few days later to meet him at 9-00 was a bit of a scramble. He had arranged for a pal with a JCB digger to come over and lay his pipes during the morning, and then he would come to us after lunch to lay our new pipe run and dig a new ditch.

Great! We now knew the when and we were looking forward to seeing the how. In preparation we had purchased a number of one-metre-lengths of concrete pipe, and were embarrassed to learn that they were not the material for the job because of the clay sub-soil. Plastic piping was recommended as it would sustain flexing whereas our concrete ones could come apart underground, giving us problems in the future.

Bringing the plastic pipe with him, Jacques's driver quickly dug a trench and laid the pipes to the boundary in what seemed like thirty minutes; he then changed the bucket to one with sloping sides for the ditch and turned right to continue along our boundary.

Meanwhile, using his farm tractor and front bucket, Jacques filled the trench over the new pipes, and then taking all the earth dug from our new ditch, he filled in the old one before repairing the ground by the fractured and broken pipes. Long after the JCB had left, Jacques continued to flatten and level the ground over all the whole area until he was satisfied that he had achieved an acceptably flat surface.

We knew we still had a lot of work preparing the ground ready for a new lawn, but this major advancement and solution to a potentially big problem with the water had left us both very happy.

The next time it poured with rain I put on my wellies and waterproofs and rushed outside to inspect all our revised waterways, like a child on the beach waiting for the tide to fill the moats around a sand castle. Stepping back inside the house drenched and with a big smile I was pleased to report that it all worked well.

11

Before the move, our planning had included many exciting aspects but there was one that stood above the others; the eventual installation of our very own swimming pool.

We researched the variety of systems and prices available and slowly we built a dossier of facts and gradually formulated an idea of what we wanted against what was affordable. We had settled on an English company who were firmly established and expanding within our area of France and who also had English speaking representatives.

We discovered that the company would be exhibiting at a forthcoming London trade fair and so we decided to go along to verify a few points and discuss our ideas. Their system along with the technical facts and figures made good sense to us, and it was available fully-installed or in kit form. We decided to place our order immediately and benefit from its use during hot days working on the house, so we chose the liner pattern and looked forward to installation after our arrival.

Now, as with all things in France you never quite know when; and once again one quiet morning another machine arrived. We thought Monsieur Lafour's Manitou was big; this new arrival was huge, but the all-important difference was that it ran on tracks not wheels.

The driver was horrified when he saw the damage to the lawn and the quagmire that was our pool site, so while he waited for his colleague to arrive he repaired the ruined and churned area and the access route, and by scraping the immense bucket across the ground and flattening with the tracks he achieved in ten minutes what would have taken us weeks.

Extracting his ample body from the cab, this gentle shy man gladly accepted a steaming cup of coffee while awaiting the arrival of John-Jacques.

While the machine and driver are all important, John-Jacques was the technical side of the pair. In complete contrast to the digger driver he was so petite we amused ourselves privately that without his beard, he could at a small distance have been mistaken for a child.

He introducing himself in near-perfect English and quickly disappeared inside the back of his van, re-appearing energetically with laser level, string, spray paint, and hammer and spikes.

His long-standing experience was only too apparent as he quickly marked out the figure eight shape with fluorescent paint spray, agreeing that our chosen area was perfectly situated. With a puff of black smoke the great digger fired into life, taking the first cut with such accuracy that he almost dissected the marked lines.

We were so excited we couldn't tear ourselves away, and bringing our coffee to the garden we sat and watched transfixed. The huge bucket removed a cubic metre at a time and soon had one half of the dig to depth. John-Jacques jumped inside the hole and took measurements with his revolving laser, checking the depth and level to his story pole. We could only see his head and shoulders and were amazed when he just sprang back out.

Once again the driver descended from the cab to meet John-Jacques poolside to discuss the depth. Obviously not quite sufficient as he took a final cut, so fine and accurate it could have been programmed by a computer.

Repositioning his machine for the second half, he soon achieved the whole dig. Spreading out the spoils, he raised the lower half of the surrounding ground, and adding some to our errant pipe site; he then rolled back and forward on the tracks to compact all that was newly laid. The pool dig was complete and as we sat together over the last of the lunch we provided, John-Jacques explained that we had time spare with the machine and driver, so would we like him to straighten out the damage on the back lawn? Would we? "Yes please!"

So again he scraped and flattened back and forth as we watched the foot-deep tyre trenches returned back to a grassless lawn. Later when the huge machine was mounted onto the low-loader parked at the roadside above, we looked again at this miraculous transformation of our garden in awe of what had been achieved in just a few hours.

We listened to the last sound of the lorry as it disappeared from view down the valley road, and Jenny quietly spoke.

"We could never have done that in a month of Sundays."

Still unable to comprehend the change, I replied. "I know, and we have the garden back also."

Retorting immediately she exclaimed, "That's what I'm talking about."

So we laughed at my insensibility to her garden and went indoors to get the camera, discussing when we thought they would give us the date for the next stage and installation.

The Fish collection brought with us had not fared very well in the move and those in the pond who had survived the colder months were fair game to the Heron. This wily bird was emptying the pond before our very eyes and we were unable to keep a constant vigil. We were alerted to the problem by finding numerous carcases on the lawn that the bird had found too big to swallow and we had to resort to a wire fence to stop his entry. The duck weed was also becoming a problem.

Jenny's daughter Lynsey had come for a break and she also had seen the weed problem, so upon Jenny's instigation they had both set off one morning to find a solution. I was enjoying a quiet read when they arrived back from market with a box containing five fluffy yellow ducks at five weeks old. They were no more than ankle height but they sat quite comfortably on our laps chirping while we hand-fed them with tit-bits.

We kept their box as a familiar bedroom and housed them in the garden tool shed overnight with copious amounts of clean straw. The next morning we rushed to confirm their welfare and were saddened to find one had died. Upon inspection we discovered bite marks and nasty wounds along its neck and back and concluded it must have become victim to a rat. We were quickly learning the cost of a country life and the precautions necessary to maintain our increasing livestock.

The remaining four ducks progressed well and were all given names by Jenny; as mother duck she adopted a method of calling them like the girl in the film with her geese. "Hey hey hey", she would call and off they would waddle following her towards the pond.

They all quickly found their genetic skills in water and became a delight to observe as their little legs paddled like fury after an errant insect and the duckweed began to disappear. Up tails all, they sifted the mud from the bottom, disappearing sometimes underwater, to re-emerge on the other side.

As they grew we began to see the emergence of their adult feathers and determined that they were a cross between the Barbary duck, and the Mallard, much favoured by the French for the pot, but somehow I knew that for Jenny this would not be an option.

Daily their confidence grew as they explored the garden, until one day they all went missing. We spotted them in the middle of the meadow at the front of the house, happily hunting any insect that moved within their lightning response.

Our naivety told us that ducks feed in water or graze; it came as a surprise to learn that in fact they eat, or will try to eat anything. Constantly hungry we realised that kitchen scraps and what they could catch was not enough. In a rural area animal feed suppliers are plentiful so we soon found a suitable feed from the picture on the sack and they thrived on it. Their full plumage developed and allowed us to determine that we had two pure white females and two males in varying designs of black and white with a sprinkling of the Mallard iridescent dark green. They were too immature this year, but we looked forward to next spring for the outcome!

We became ever-vigilant for their safety, making a visual search for where they were every time we went into the garden or arrived back home. Returning home on one occasion I came down the drive and could only see three. Though not yet unduly concerned I wanted to verify their whereabouts for my own sake. Standing under the horse chestnut tree in front of the house I still couldn't locate the second hen until I heard the faint throat-orientated clucking they make way above my head.

Looking up I found her sitting on a branch quite happily surveying her terrain. It seemed they still had a few surprises in store for us as I didn't know ducks sat in trees, but I do now!

Walking back to the house we simultaneously heard the telephone and like two silly children we barged at each other to be first to pick it up. Painfully stubbing my toe and hopping on one foot I received one last barge from Jenny which sent me sprawling over the grass as she beat me to the phone.

"Hello….. Oh! What a surprise." Shrieks of delight gave way to the silence of an intent listener.

"Of course you can." Jenny excitedly replied. "When?"

I couldn't decipher who the caller was so I waited anxiously for the call to end, trying to piece together one side of a conversation I couldn't hear with the one I could.

"Come on then, who was it." I demanded as soon as the call ended.

"Keith and Margaret are coming." She replied, overjoyed and unable to contain her excitement.

"When, how long for, come on, tell me all?" I said now sharing her pleasure that we were to see again these dear friends.

"Where are we going to put them?" I questioned, visualising our lounge turned into a temporary bedroom.

"Don't worry; they said they would be more than happy to sleep in the tent." A part of the conversation I had missed while nursing my toe and I agreed that the large frame tent we had was more than capable of becoming a comfortable bedroom for two weeks in summer and we both looked forward to their arrival in the coming weeks.

The following weeks flew by; the vacation following the move had come to an end and eventually we organised ourselves and started to work. The barn was still much as it was when the cows left plus the usual gathering of junk that was all disappearing under a blanket of cobwebs.

It needed a good clear out. The earthen floor was rich from years of overnight manure and was covered in broken tiles and wood fallen during the removal of the old roof and it all had to be removed and dumped on the pile outside.

Eager to put our plans into action and do something progressive we started removing the front half of the feeding stalls which were attached to the wooden cow byres. We intended to keep the byres and incorporate them as a feature later, but once again what we expected to be a simple job turned into a struggle as aged six-inch nails were very reluctant to release themselves from the solid core of the oaken beams.

Eventually this vast open space materialised and with excitement we laid our drawn plans on an old camping table and walked into imaginary rooms through imaginary doors. Some changes became immediately apparent as it was obvious that something wouldn't work or an idea on paper looked totally impractical in reality.

The enormity of the project began to dawn on us during one evening when we sat indoors ruminating over the changes to the plans. It didn't deter us, but we realised it was to be a long time before we would ever live in it.

Besides, our regular planning conferences had shown us that we needed to attend to more urgent topics within the house to create a few more essential creature comforts. The gas hot water heater was complaining now that it was in constant daily use and we found that there were insufficient power points for our everyday appliances, and in the evenings we struggled to see in the inadequate lighting.

We made a list of jobs. It didn't help much because it kept growing, but it was a list.

Dusting and pitching the frame tent on a flat portion of ground, we aired the blow-up mattress in readiness for Keith and Margaret. We sat in the garden later, excitedly awaiting their arrival and half rising from our seats every time an infrequent car passed on the road above.

Eventually one was heard descending the drive and we rushed towards it to embrace the occupants as the doors opened.

Keith and I shared a warm greeting and words evaporated while he drank in the view.

Eventually the girl's squeals of excitement died down as Margaret commented to Jenny.

"Wow, it's so quiet here - and bloody hot." And they shared hugs, overjoyed to see each other again. Later after dinner, we all sat naked in the garden catching the last rays of the sun, finishing the wine and catching up on the news from the naturist club and all our friends we had left behind us there.

We received many good wishes which always provoked yet another mini conversation about how they were and what they were now doing. Jenny and I both agreed later that it was nice to receive all the good wishes and realised affectionately that nothing had changed much in five months.

We spent the days together lazing in the sun or larking about in the splash pool and in the evenings we went exploring the tourist sights and the many good restaurants available there. Margaret read in the sunshine or chatted with Jenny, and Keith rekindled an old hobby and sat behind the pond with an easel and water colours painting a most professional picture of the house, which now hangs proudly in our lounge.

François nearly caught us all naked one day when he descended the embankment from his orchard into our garden with a huge bowl of fresh cherries from his annual glut. I think he has become used to our outdoor habits and now he usually makes plenty of noise upon his arrival.

Later while dinner was cooking, we sipped apéritifs together and stoned cherries to make a pie for dessert. It had been an unforgettable evening which left many empty bottles, and a huge bowl of cherry stones!

Very reluctantly we eventually had to say goodbye to them both, and waved furiously as their car disappeared from view at the top of our drive. We knew we would see them again very soon, as they had fallen in love with our dream, and wanted one of their own. A dream that had started when they had agreed to buy the barn they had found, twenty minutes away from us.

12

The move had paled into insignificance, the roof was complete, the damaged ground had been repaired and now the pool was underway; everything was going to plan except the hoped-for quick sale of my cabin in England, the repercussions of which would go on for nearly a year.

It was not a property you could put in the hands of an Estate Agent, and the club management required that prospective buyers should be club members of one year's standing or at least satisfy the directors in their ability to become responsible residents. Past history has shown that for obvious reasons some folk are not suitable for residency in a naturist environment encapsulating a family atmosphere, and they are declined.

The clubhouse notice board or a chat with the secretary will reveal what's coming up for sale, while the grapevine quickly reveals recent purchases and prices. Evaluating recent sales and trends, and in consideration of my renovation outlay, I had offered my Cabin for sale at a price that reflected its high comparable condition.

Word went around and we initially had a lot of interest shown, but no offers. In a situation very rare, two additional properties were offered for sale shortly afterwards, and a third was pending, all three substantially cheaper because they required renovation, as mine had done when I bought it.

Assured that the coming summer season would bring more serious enquiries we had to leave England with it unsold. We never expected to retire from working, but we budgeted that the sale of the house would clear the all too familiar credit cards and mortgage, and give us a small equity for a head start to fund the barn conversion and free time to do it, while we settled into our new life and sought out a new long term income. Suddenly we had two houses to maintain and what little capital we brought with us was disappearing fast. An income had to be found and a hold put on non-essential capital expenditure.

We telephoned the pool company and explained our situation. They understood our predicament and kindly agreed to put things on hold until the house was sold. Assured that it did not inconvenience them our embarrassment subsided; at least the final payment for the pool was ours for the time being.

Our lounge had one small window and a half-glazed door which led out under a small veranda roof. Little light penetrated from outside and the ensuing gloom was in need of a solution. To the left of the door was the alcove which housed the old stone sink and the wall above was only half thickness and ideal for the installation of a window for much needed light to brighten the room.

We had a second-hand window frame in good condition that would fit once I had created the opening and it only needed one glass pane replaced and a lintel above. I found a likely beam in the barn and removing sufficient stone, the beam slid neatly into place. The following day was hot when I began to create the opening under the beam and I welcomed the shade under the veranda canopy.

I found that removing stones from a wall is an occupation that requires extreme concentration, because until it yields from the clay mortar you never know how big it is going to be or in which direction it is going to fall, hence gentle persuasion with a crow bar is preferable to a big hammer. There is always the possibility of the unexpected, but when it came it was not from in front of me; but from below.

The aluminium steps I was using had developed an unseen fracture around the holes where a tie rod passed through and eventually they buckled and disintegrated under me, sending me sprawling onto the pile of stones. Trainers and a pair of stout gloves offer little protection when you're naked and I considered myself fortunate to only get away with damage to my ego and not to life and limb.

Undeterred I found it preferable to continue from terra firma and soon removed the last stones save one. I had eroded the mortar around it and could see that it was big, with as much still inside the wall as that which protruded, but like a wobbly tooth it wouldn't come out. Eventually it decided to give up the fight and I was prepared to just keep clear and let it fall.

Instead of sliding gracefully to the ground with a thud it held one last surprise and flipped over and crushed my finger; the same finger that Jenny had lovingly repaired after a previous incident with a circular saw blade. I was learning new and expensive lessons, but I persevered and soon acquired a flair for laying stone which had begun when I installed the new window. It had become a joy to work with and my new-found skills were soon to provide a welcome income.

It began when I assisted some friends who were repairing and rebuilding their garden wall; they were impressed with my efforts and when the English builder who renovated their house called by, they proudly showed him the wall. He too was impressed with my stone work and wanted me to make contact because he needed my skills to assist on his team.

I summoned up the courage to embark into this unknown area and I made a call to James and learned that he had recently purchased a new house and his plans were to raise the height of the stone walls by one metre and create additional height within the loft space for more rooms.

I met James and he took me to the site so that he could acquaint me with the project, and then we returned to his current home to discuss the details. I was extremely pleased with my good fortune and I left with a job; in fact I left with two!

Just before I left James' house I had noticed an old banjo on his mantle shelf and I ventured to ask if he played.

"I'd like to," he shyly admitted, tentatively adding. "Do you?"

"Yes, I do." I modestly replied, and gesturing towards his instrument I asked, "May I take a look?"

It was an old and battered Zither banjo with only three of its five strings and a copious covering of dust.

He was embarrassed by its condition but passed it over explaining that it had been given to him and that it had sat on his mantle shelf unloved for a very long time.

"Can you teach me to play it?" He enquired.

"Not in that condition I can't." I explained, but I continued by offering to bring the instrument back to a condition where it could be played. I admitted to him that I was not very proficient myself having just learned before leaving England; but I added that I would be pleased to pass on what I did know and perhaps we could have some fun together on the way.

Thirty years in metalwork and welding and I was now going to be Bob the builder and teach the Banjo!

The building pay wasn't great but it was an income. The job, he explained, wasn't scheduled to start for two weeks because his team were completing an existing project, but he said that if it suited me, I could start right away clearing the ground of vegetation from around the property before building work could begin.

I agreed despite the pay being less than that which the eventual stone work would provide, and I spent two days armed with my new strimmer and a chainsaw, working in temperatures that were in excess of thirty degrees, wearing full overalls and gloves, full face visor and ear defenders. I was drinking four litres of water a day to replace what I was losing and I went home knackered.

In my youth I boasted that without a job I would willingly sweep the streets if that was all I could get, but I had the distinct feeling after those first two days that I was being taken advantage of, and I telephoned James that evening to voice my misgivings. I explained that I thought the work was far more involved than he first thought and that in consideration of the effort necessary to achieve what he wanted, my reward deserved to be more. He was unwilling to increase his offer so we parted amicably.

However, subsequently viewing the neatly cleared site ready for building work to commence, and still in need of assistance with the stone work, he quietly spoke to Jenny in the bar one Friday evening saying that on reflection he had been a bit miserly, and did she think that if he paid me more in keeping with my value, did she think that I might return?

"Yes I think he might…" she said, "…but you need to talk to him yourself." Then she added that I was not previously very impressed. Well done Jenny for planting the seeds and it was a few days later that James and I made a new agreement and thankfully I returned.

I'd never been at my best while working at height, and I found myself three metres above the ground on two warped scaffolding planks, hauling up buckets full of wet cement mortar by a rope and catching large stones as they were lobbed up to me. I was reluctant to stand hands-free while moving, always preferring to keep one hand on something solid, which caused great amusement amongst the lads as I wobbled to and fro bending up and down for stones.

The Team were great and accepted me as one of them and I gradually gained more confidence in their company and with my newfound skills. Lunch times, James and I played Banjo together to practise what I had taught him during his weekly lessons at home. On the advice of my own teacher back in England, I taught this left-handed man to play right-handed, and he learned quickly, enjoying the rewards of his efforts.

After three weeks the stone work for me was complete, and while not as fast as my employer, I was pleased at his approval of my work, and especially with the remunerations. Pleased also that I had found a Blue Grass banjo enthusiast.

James sometimes had enquiries for smaller projects he was unable to undertake, and from his recommendation they filtered through to me bringing a steady flow of work and increasing my reputation. I built a garden wall to hold back an embankment above a newly created bog garden, it took three hundred blocks and was fifty metres long and finished in cement render afterwards. The client was very pleased and paid me promptly on completion.

I fitted windows where windows didn't exist before, created bedrooms from stud work and plasterboard, built and conceived more garden walls in stone, erected first floor balcony terraces in decking, and concreted and laid slabs for a large pool terrace. I built a minstrels gallery inside a converted barn, and I built a staircase from stone to provide a private entry to a suite at first floor level. When completed it looked like it had always been there - complete with moss.

As my reputation grew so did the work load allowing me to choose what projects I undertook. Never happy working at heights, I declined any roofing work always preferring where possible to keep both feet firmly on terra firma. Although irregular the income was welcome and we managed to scrape along. I can turn my hand to most things and have built up a wealth of experience over my life of how to, and how not to. If I wasn't sure, I would ask builder pals first before I started, and I owe them a debt of gratitude for their unfailing patience with me.

All the building work for earning a living had fired my enthusiasm to get on at home, so one evening Jenny and I analysed what we could do that wouldn't cost us a fortune in materials. With just the two main rooms, the dining room had doubled as our bedroom as well. Now as more boxes were being unpacked space was reducing and we wanted a bedroom.

The *Chai* to the rear was the planned obvious choice. It backed onto the house and it had two further walls that each had a small window opening. The fourth side comprised of two rotting wooden doors and in total enclosed an area thirteen metres by four and a half.

By knocking a doorway through from the dining room, and then creating a small hallway, we would be able to create three double bedrooms. Then by replacing the rotting doors with new patio doors and glazing all the rest above a small wall, we could create a large room for ourselves and have two good-sized guest rooms.

Removing the old rotting doors and framework safely was not an easy job as the roof above them had sunk over the years, trapping the doors and stopping them from swinging freely. At this end of the building, the roof overhung by a metre, which allowed us to extend the room a little and still keep a small overhang.

Footings were laid followed by a low block wall which was stone faced on the outside to retain the character, and then we were ready to construct the frame work for the patio doors and the windows which would enclose this now open end. I then began to level the earthen floor, removing earth from one area and transferring it to another with the invaluable use of a newly purchased laser level; although I found its use difficult in bright light and so chose to continue as the winter evenings closed in, when the fading light made this much easier.

Although it seemed an arduous task by hand, a much flatter area soon began to appear and we could visualise the final concrete floor on which I would construct the dividing walls for the rooms. Unfortunately, actually laying the first two metres of this concrete on our own proved more time-consuming than we thought; we were mixing at the front of the house and then barrowing the wet cement all the way around to the back, before running each barrow up two plank ramps and into the chai.

We needed to cut the doorway through the wall from the dining room to shorten the route, but before the Chai was added it was an exterior wall, and it was half a metre thick. So in consideration of the mess it would cause and how little thought we had put into it, it could wait for now.

13

Winter had hardened in the New Year, and as the temperatures plummeted lower we stoked up the log fire in the lounge trying to keep the house warm. The lounge was snug but little of the heat penetrated the other rooms. The electric towel rail kept the chill off the bathroom but a shower was still a brave venture. The bottled gas heater on low kept the chill off during the night in the dining room which was also our bedroom, but we preferred the three bars alight during the day to combat the heat loss and draught from the poorly fitting original oak door to the outside.

The lowest outside temperature we recorded was minus 14C and it came as a bit of a surprise to us living in the south west of France; we didn't expect it. Although it was well below freezing it was not unpleasant outside and most days it was often sunny with clear blue sky, or just a few fluffy clouds, but a hat, coat and gloves were essential. It allowed us to continue with some of the chores without being chilled to the marrow.

The pond froze except the small area where the sources dribbled in from the pipes, which pleased us immensely in consideration of our re-piping work.

Jenny awoke one morning and desperate for the first tea of the day, she made her way with bleary eyes towards the sink to fill the kettle. Within the bed in the adjacent dining room, I buried my head under the bedclothes trying to blot out the day's commencement noise but drowsily I became aware we had a problem.

"Wake up, the water's frozen!" Jenny demanded.

Still half asleep I desperately tried to engage my brain and logical thinking. Reluctantly I threw back the duvet allowing all my preciously guarded warmth to escape and planted two feet on a chilly tiled floor and made a grab for my clothes.

The water pump under the sink in the kitchen draws water from the well via plastic piping. It had never been necessary to bury the pipe because it was always drained of water after a summer holiday. It runs over ground before it enters the kitchen wall two metres away, and we had overlooked the implications of minus fourteen degrees upon an exposed water pipe.

It was frozen solid and we had no water except what was left in the kettle, thankfully just enough for Jenny's early morning tea. Disaster loomed as one cup of tea is never sufficient and I had to do something soon or face divorce.

With tussled hair and a mouth that tasted like a Sumo wrestlers armpit, I was now fully awake. I wrapped up in warm clothing and ventured outside to investigate what could be done, anxious to defrost the pipe soon before it split, and the ensuing further implications.

Necessity surely is the mother of invention and I found a solution in the barn. Among the two truckloads of possessions we brought with us was a space heater that burned paraffin; although quite why we thought it necessary when moving to the south of France to bring with us a space heater I don't know, but thankfully there it stood in the barn, and with fuel in it. All I needed now was inspiration for a means of retaining the heat around the pipe.

Again the answer presented itself. No wonder we needed to make two trips when we moved because in addition to the space heater, I had brought fifty sheets of two inch thick insulation board, eight by four feet which were left over from my cabin conversion. I must have thought that this originally free material would have become of some use – somewhere!

It had. Cutting it into strips a foot wide I constructed a box tunnel over the length of the frozen pipe and left an opening for the space heater to blast into. Thirty minutes later we again had running water, and Jenny thankfully had her second, and a third cup of tea!

I closed off the heat entrance and left the unsightly box in place until the temperature improved, later laying the entire pipe safely underground.

Nothing was moving with the sale of my Cabin and we were getting some pressure from the UK. The frustration of not having access to the equity we needed here to get on with our plans, and the continuing cost of two houses was beginning to tell on us both.

When you are doing all you can to further a situation, I tend to accept things as they are and not worry about what I cannot change. Jenny on the other hand was worrying and allowing the stress to affect her. As hard as I tried, I was unable to convey the senselessness of her worrying.

During one particularly bad day for her, she decided to find something to do outside to take her mind off it and donning suitable clothes she hoped to walk the garden and find some occupation worthy of her time. I preferred to stay in the warm reading a good book.

Alarm suddenly roused me as I heard a faint crying of my name. I jumped up and looking from the window I saw Jenny walking back across the lawn sobbing profusely with something white in her arms.

We both met at the door and I immediately shared her grief as she held the lifeless body of a dripping wet duck she had rescued from the pond under the ice. Foolish bird had trapped itself under the ice and drowned.

The joy that she gave us before she died was immeasurable and we were both deeply saddened by the loss. She would sit after bathing and preen on the grass above the pond, and it was here I dug her final resting place. As I laid her to rest gently layering the earth to cover her lifeless body the emotion overcame me and I cried for her saying, “Bloody stupid Duck!”

Later that same day, we sat remembering with fondness some of the times we had witnessed her antics. How cross we had been at the time when we came back in from the garden to find all four ducks happily sitting on the carpet, the cat food gone and duck shit all over the floor. Apparently they had asked the dog and he had said it was OK! Yea right! The look in his face when approached on the subject said it all. “WHAT?”

14

François is not only our neighbour but also the previous owner of our house; he said the house name 'Prieu' means, to pray. He said his ancestors rebuilt it circa 1800 using stone and timber which came from a much older house on the land close by. At its completion the new house consisted of one main room with an enclosed wooden stairway leading to the *Grenier* - roof space. In addition to the entrance, a small door led into the attached barn for four oxen and one other opened to the rear.

The original fireplace was open and was used for heating and cooking, its great chimney is now blackened by generations of wood burning and it did have the supporting chains for the cooking pots still hanging inside. There is still a shallow stone sink built within a recess in the front wall, and it still had a rounded stone in place to prevent water from draining away through a hole in the wall.

It was home to a man and his wife who worked the land with the oxen, but soon a growing family would have necessitated the addition of further space for living and sleeping in later years. The stone work to the rear of the house testified to this extension and recent discussions with Francois had confirmed my suspicions.

He explained how he lived there as a boy and recalled facts easily in answer to my questions in stunted French; his affection for his past home was only too apparent. Then seventy three, he said he was retired and I interpreted that as meaning that he no longer farmed for an income, but despite that he was always busy doing something around and about his land, content to leave the farming to his nephew.

His stature was small and upright and he had a full head of grey hair normally covered with one of his black berets which varied in quality according to his present occupation; when we would meet him at market it looked brand new, but the working one had a white sweat line around it and was nearly devoid of nap.

He was always pleased to stop for a chat when I saw him tending the hedges and ditches surrounding our house or while he was trimming back the woodland to add to his enormous stock of winter fuel which was stored in neat rows everywhere. He must believe he will live to one hundred, and probably will, enjoying more energy than I had at twenty years younger.

His ready smile displayed his browning teeth, and his guttural French flowed affectionately to my struggling ears. Words flowed one into the other and as he registered my lack of comprehension he gesticulated with his gnarly hands to offer some vain assistance for my understanding. It worked, and eventually I got the gist of things.

Annually he lovingly tended his vineyard to the rear of our house; using skills he learned from his father he produced six or eight vats of superb red wine to see him through another year. He said he took a small glass with his breakfast every morning; coffee?...never!

His wife Rene was harder to understand and spoke as if she had a mouthful of toffee. A rounded lady who now suffers from diabetes after years of gastronomic abuse, she was always smartly dressed displaying the crisp clean pinafore of the day. Like François she was always busy; cleaning, cooking or preserving the many fruits and vegetables he grew in his gardens. What little spare time she had was devoted to her flowers and borders, winning prizes in the village for her displays.

Winter was shedding its frosty mantle and zero night time temperatures were giving way to warmer sunny days. The sort of days that inspire time spent outside again.

The pool dig was just sitting there waiting for the next stage and the sides were beginning to suffer from subsidence. We were not unduly worried at this stage, but we were not looking forward to removing the fallen earth and stones back out again. What did worry us though was the increasing constant dribble of water that was seeping through the side wall nearest the barn. It was gradually filling the deeper end and when it later rained all day the depth increased to at least half a metre over the whole floor.

The Ducks loved it and in the mornings when we let them out from their pen, they took off straight for it and landed in the water and scattered the now resident frogs. We would watch them as they bathed, but soon tired of the pleasure as afterwards they would cover the surrounding lawn in feathers as they preened.

During another of my fragmented conversations with François, I showed him the problem with the water source leaking through the side wall of the pool dig. "Ah Oui," he knowingly ventured and quickly indicated to us the route of yet another unknown spring.

Apparently it ran under the barn and right through the centre of the pool dig en-route to the pond, and we had disturbed it. Our best plan was to find the pipe within the wall of the pool dig and re-pipe it around the dig, and then re-join it in the far wall to continue its route to the pond.

The next day we explored with a trowel and revealed a short length of broken piping, so we dug and pulled out stone after stone, until the hole was a metre wide and a metre back from the pool edge. We worked for four hours until we were knee-deep in sucking mud looking for a pipe we couldn't find despite that each new stone we removed promised to reveal it.

When at a loss as to what to do next we heard François's tractor on the road above and I ran up the drive to hail him and hopefully glean some further insight into the whereabouts of the pipe.

Perplexed at the sight of us covered in wet mud he parked his tractor and came to investigate. When he understood how we had been searching all afternoon for a pipe, a wry smile appeared and he explained.

The water source had been re-routed underground by his father during the 1930's when the barn was extended. They had formed a long tunnel by using a continual build of one stone each side and one on top and all the stones we had been digging out were in fact what we had been looking for, not a pipe at all but a man-made underground water channel. We had to share with him the humour of the situation and I expect he enjoyed a good chuckle when he later related it to his family.

We subsequently built a collecting sump underground and successfully piped the water away around the pool to continue its flow into the pond.

It didn't seem long before buds again started to appear and snowdrops were bringing some life back to the garden. Last summer the hedge to the side of the drive had grown so much that it was reducing the width of the drive and the brambles from the woodland opposite were trying to meet them and engulfing the ditches.

That spring we'd decided that although technically it was not our property, we would take it upon ourselves to harshly trim back the woodland overspill from the side of the ditch to prevent the same colossal job every year.

It was a mixture of saplings and blackthorn with damp-loving creepers, brambles and ivy, and along with the grass it all required an assortment of tools to remove it and clear the ditches. It took two days but after a final sweep with the strimmer for the grass, the result would suffice for a couple of years.

The other side of the drive was mostly hazel so we cut and trimmed back everything growing inwards and upwards to thicken the lower growth. The resulting drive looked loved and manicured and worthy of our labour and I pledged to not allow it to become so overgrown again. François was impressed because it saved him a job and I think he could see that we had the right attitude to the land that he loved.

In the naturist club grounds in England and our own garden there, we were privileged to see some extraordinary sights of the resident wildlife. I believe that we witnessed a tameness of birds and animals unusual elsewhere. The calmness and security seemed to extend to them and they seemed to have little fear of humans. Blackbirds foraging the undergrowth or borders would stay put as you walked by, and rabbits grazing the lawns in daylight would just move aside as we passed by.

Coming to France we thought we would miss the abundance of garden wildlife so rarely seen here during our summer visits, and we wrongly assumed that with the vast countryside available there was no need for them to visit the humble garden. Birds and animals are opportunists and they will come for food, and now that we were resident we were feeding the birds through the winter months, and now they keep coming back.

Without the necessity to be getting all the jobs done during a summer break, our times of relaxation in the garden had now revealed over sixty types of birds, some regular and some a rare treat like the Kingfisher we unmistakably sighted over the pond.

During late March and early April before the trees leaf, we had discovered a wealth of bird activity. Resplendent in their mating colours their courtship displays were a delight to see and I watched spellbound as Black kites performed their aerial displays. Daily we would look towards the valley for a sighting of these magnificent birds of prey and we were rewarded on one occasion when we heard the female calling to the male. We watched him arrive and copulate, then return again when she called; we felt a sense of privilege to witness nature so free.

We have heard the faint trumpeting calls and looking to the distance we have seen the approaching cranes and watched them getting nearer and nearer as they passed high above us migrating to and from Scandinavia, sometimes spanning two or three days.

Buzzards circled overhead on a thermal to gain height, then almost disappeared from view before gliding for miles to a new hunting ground. We've seen them sitting on overhead wires waiting and watching as we pass by in our car; and if we are lucky they will take flight and reveal their full splendour. Feeding Lapwings flocked together in the fields on either side of the road, so close we could see their plumage colours in detail.

An early Dragon fly settled to rest on a leaf of our Kiwi plant. As it sat motionless I drew closer until I was within a few inches and I could see every detail, from the filigree wings to the wondrous eyes that make it such a voracious hunter as it flies over our pond. It is also about this time of year that we hear the first Cuckoo, and we search endlessly in the leafless trees for a sighting with the binoculars. Then one day as I walked into the lounge, I glanced through the window and saw an unusual bird sitting in a small tree very close to the house. The binoculars are always close and I soon identified my first cuckoo sighting.

The unmistakable "Hoo-Poo-Poo" call filtering across the valley signals the arrival of the Hoopoe. This summer visitor is a delight to see as it probes the lawn with its long beak in search of food. Light pinkie-brown plumage and a striking black and white wing pattern identify it at a glance.

Four Deer have trotted down the drive and crossed under our single wire boundary to continue down the valley towards the river. Through the secrecy of my binoculars I have observed their natural interaction at the edge of the woodland, less than a hundred metres from our front door.

In country life there are always mice, the trick is to keep them out of the house. Here we also had the Garden Dormouse, *Eliomys quercinus*; the black stripe passing their eyes made them look like little burglars with masks on. They have a body length of up to 147mm, and a tail that adds an extra 135mm with an end like a small paint brush. This delightful animal had nested in our roof but unlike mice they did little damage. They were nocturnal and would emerge at dusk to traverse a wall like they were walking on the ground. At dawn we could hear one of them 'chick-chicking' in the bushes near the wall we thought was their entry, calling the other family members back for sleep after the nights foraging.

15

Chris who taught me to play my banjo was disappointed to be losing a student when I revealed our plans to immigrate to France, but we promised to keep in touch and did indeed exchange news by telephone every couple of months.

Of course I was delighted with his latest call although Jenny wasn't so sure. With a few days spare holiday to use up he wanted to visit and asked if we could put him up. The thought of four or five days of constant banjo playing didn't exactly thrill Jenny, but I reassured her saying that of course we would hopefully play some banjo, (never one to pass on what I hoped might be a free lesson), but that it would definitely not be constant.

In England Chris and I got on very well, but it was I felt a Student/Teacher friendship. Now he was coming here and neither Jenny nor I were sure how we would all gel together.

Unfortunately without the benefit of a bedroom to offer Chris we had to make up a camp bed in the lounge. Breakfast that first morning was an eye opener to Chris's enormous appetite as Jenny related the possibilities saying, "I don't know what you prefer Chris, but we have cereal, toast, eggs and bacon, jams and marmalade, tea – coffee?"

"Oh..." says Chris, "...egg and bacon sounds great, but I'll start with some cereal if I may."

So while Jenny cooked eggs and bacon much to my delight, Chris polished off a bowl of corn flakes and a cup of tea.

That we thought would take the edge off of anyone's appetite but the plate of toast served with the eggs and bacon quickly disappeared, and a second plateful soon followed as Chris sampled many of our jars of preserves. It must be the French air we thought, but could we keep this up?

I of course enjoyed a few free Banjo lessons which were very beneficial to me as I had not played with another musician who stretched me for a long time, and James my banjo student was very keen to meet him so off we went one afternoon to meet James at his house.

After the initial introductions and conversations died down, Chris asked to see James's old and battered banjo. He verified it was in tune and expertly brought it to life with an old-time fiddle tune. As the fingers of his right hand picked the strings in a blur, his left hand accurately found the frets for the right chords.

I have never seen James with such a big smile on his face as he could now hear and see what he was trying to achieve himself under my tuition. By complete contrast James's wife has a discouraging dislike of the instrument which shows in his progress, but I do believe I saw her smiling also.

When I knew of Chris's imminent arrival, I had made a few calls to local musicians I knew; they played a variety of instruments between them so I arranged a jam session at the local bar. I also told many friends so I was hopeful of a good crowd to swell the evening.

It started slowly but the bar was soon packed with people hoping for a good evening. As the word went around I had no idea who might turn up to play and I was later surprised when French, English, and Dutch musicians all started to appear.

During my search for blue grass musicians I had met a chap called Jim who played guitar; although we had played a little together his interest was in blues and ragtime. Chris was proficient with many instruments, and the guitar was no exception and he soon latched on to

Jim when he started to play. Borrowing a guitar, Chris soon picked up the tune Jim was playing while I struggled to add some backing on the banjo and suddenly the evening took off.

The bar was located in Monflanquin, which is home to a brass band called *Les Vert à Pied*, and I was pleased to see some of the members had joined us for the session. Joel played bass guitar while Dick, a rotund Dutchman offered the odd break on the trombone. In addition one of their trumpet players got in on the act as well, providing an unusual but melodic ensemble.

Later somebody produced a Beatles song book after we had all drunk a considerable amount of beer, and the ceiling raised a little as I led the chorus with an awful rendering of 'Hey Jude' which probably kept the neighbours awake when everyone eventually joined in.

As the evening neared its close Chris came under pressure from James to return to the banjo and play the tune every aspiring banjo player aims at; 'Duelling Banjos', which was made famous by the film 'Deliverance'. Many people know it, if not what it's called or where it comes from, and every time I hear it or watch the film it raises goose bumps on my skin. I can play it but my poor old fingers do not have the speed to do it proper justice like Chris and Jim did, much to James' delight.

All through the evening I had kept the players fed with drinks from the bar and as things came to a close I went to pay the bill. Catching our host Didier's eye I summoned the damage and he asked me for 4 Euros! I was bewildered at this meagre amount and as I handed him the coins I questioned him why so little when I had expected nearer fifty. Although my French had improved impressively it was still not brilliant, but I understood his meaning alright.

"Well..." he said, "...You've provided the entertainment and filled my bar tonight." I was quickly learning that a community spirit I thought was lost did still exist, and I appreciated his gratitude and he certainly received mine.

Chris returned home with a new perspective on jam sessions and a few good tales to relate to his music pals at the pub. We looked at our empty larder and looked forward to his promise of another visit, another year.

Seven hundred miles north and a little later in the year, springtime was reawakening buyers' interest in my cabin. We had heard that someone was showing a keen interest and wanted a second viewing.

I was anxious to tickle this fish a little so I gave him a call. He was already the owner of a summer residency and therefore he would have satisfied the management criteria which was essential, and he now wanted to live there all year. We had found a price that sat well with us both, but my experience with buyers was telling me that something was not quite right, so I gently pushed.

He opened up and told me that his purchase was entirely dependent upon the sale of his own summer cabin. I had chatted with him during the work he did improving it and so knew it was desirable; it was just a case of waiting for enquiries.

Springtime was bringing members back after the winter months so I took a calculated risk and made him an offer. Upon a gentleman's agreement, I would accept the lion's share now, on trust of a concluding payment when his sale finalised.

It worked and after a day spent in consideration he finally agreed to go ahead. The relief for us was enormous, lifting the pressure from us immediately; at last we could see an end to the nightmare that had plagued us for months.

When confirmation arrived that his payment transfer was in our joint account we jumped for joy, and later that day we settled to the serious business of concluding our financial ties with England. We sat with a list in front of us next to the telephone and then disposed of two thirds of the money within two hours.

My cabin had now been empty for over six months and therefore had accumulated additional community charges for the local authority and ground rent for the club management. Then there were the final accounts for the electricity supply and the credit cards which we had been partly living off. The finance on my car, sold for a song to my daughter, and the remainder of what I owed my father on the original purchase.

British banking has changed dramatically over many years but my bank was another story in itself. Bank managers who knew you and your circumstances personally have long been a thing of the past. They now act on directives from higher up the chain of command and there are no grey areas for flexibility any more, it's black and white and if your requirements do not fit into laid down criteria, then that's it pal.

When your account is buoyant they are only too pleased to offer help and advice; taking more of your hard-earned cash to pay for it. But when you are trying to negotiate a financial tremor, their ears are closed.

The computers that now seem to run the industry however, remain very much alert to penalising you heavily for the slightest transgression. I concede that banks are in business to make money for the shareholders who own them, but they have lost track of the fact that I am a customer, and not the other way around. Unfortunately in today's high technology world we all need them, and boy don't they know it!

I'd kept my bank informed over the months as things developed around their uncooperative attitude and I informed them now that I had the funds to clear my account and close it. I gave them a date three days in advance and asked for the exact required sum that I should transfer on the said date. Not a vast amount, but clearing a small loan and overdraft facility and closing the no longer required account.

I transferred the money and looked forward to receiving the final statement showing zero. It took three months and many phone calls back to UK before they got it right and refunded the overcharges, and the beauty of it all, they still didn't get it right because when the final statement arrived it was accompanied by a refund cheque.

The cheque will never be cashed as it is framed, hanging on my wall, proudly displaying its amount….2 pence!

We reflected with sadness at what was now left from the proceeds of the sale, against what we had hoped to do with it, but we happily consoled ourselves that we didn't owe a penny to anyone; and that was a great feeling. Gratifying also was the trust I placed in my buyer who later justified my trust when I received his letter expressing his thanks and enclosing his cheque for the full balance.

16

The 'Vide Grenier' is the French equivalent of the English car boot sale, and rough translation means empty loft. Locally to us they are a simple affair and most events have not yet realised the big money potential of attic relics, excepting the larger towns and cities and the inevitable traders. A small commune may offer a few stalls huddled together in the church car park, while a larger village can host a considerable display of residents' junk spanning many streets, which they hope to sell and make what could be a small fortune.

Of course it rarely happens and most of the goods are carefully reloaded and taken back home, but in reality a lot of what is on offer should be deposited at the *Déchetterie* (the local dump). But of course it depends on what you're looking for; if you're a young mother with children who quickly outgrow clothes – then it's a good opportunity to find good quality clothes in a size larger.

Likewise if you're looking for something just a little quirky to finish off the decor within a room then there are plenty of good relics to choose from, but avoid the traders who will always ask for top-dollar. If your favourite cafetière has fallen foul in the dishwasher then a replacement can usually be found.

Other stalls specialise in electrical goods; old plugs and sockets, ancient telephones and hi-fi systems.

"Does it work?" you may ask.

"*Mais oui*", will be the reply coupled with an indignant expression because you've had the cheek to question its credibility. If you are lucky an early perusal will find the stall selling homemade cakes by a pinafored Madame and for a few Euros you can be assured of a gastronomic treat.

Before I learned to find some worthy excuse to stay at home, I used to accompany Jenny during many morning forays at the *Vide Grenier.* One such morning I had dutifully followed up and down countless stalls on a bright Sunday morning, and having made all the right comments when required I had drifted into a quiet corner trying to analyse the bizarre expressions upon people's faces as they passed in robotic lines. Suddenly my attention was drawn to some lunatic performing semaphore two stalls away and realised it was Jenny and my presence was required *tout suit.*

Summoning my best 'I'm really interested' expression I listened and discovered that she had spied an old chair in an awfully sad state, then pointing it out to me she quietly asked my opinion as to whether I thought I could do something to bring it back to a reasonable condition that she could re-upholster.

A feigned expression of bankruptcy from the seller followed acceptance of our low offer and we carried it, very carefully back to the car.

Back at home we carefully lifted her fragile prize from the car and laid it on the lawn. For the chair the effort seemed to be the final straw and the seat parted company from the back as the covering material's meagre threads finally gave way to its age, as the joints had done years previously. The aged cloth covering came away like tissue paper amidst a cloud of choking grey house dust and revealed that the chair had been home to many mice over many years.

She saved the horse hair under-padding but the rest went straight into the bin along with the bent and rusting tacks that had proved so difficult to remove. Now she had reduced it to the wooden frame Jenny passed it over to me.

It had obviously stood on a damp floor for a lot of its life, and previous owners had cut off the eroded and worm-eaten stumps. A quick look through Jenny's many books on the subject soon directed us to what it should have looked like. It had two straight legs at the back and cabriole legs at the front. Amazingly our search of local shops subsequently produced two similar cabriole legs that I could work with, the rear ones I could make from timber at home.

Cutting, shaping and grafting the wood for nearly two hours and I had the front legs ready and by the end of the day the frame again looked like a chair as it sat festooned with clamps waiting for the glue to dry within the re-dowelled joints. Jenny also waited, watching my progress and anxious to start the re-polishing.

When it was dry she gathered all her materials together; the springs and padding, the sacking and calico covering, and all the precious horse hair stuffing and in a short while her fingers were red and sore from pulling and stretching the webbing over the springs, but eventually she was ready for the final upholstering with a modern but classic fabric, showing a period design of pink and cream that she had chosen. When the wooden frame was rubbed down and re-polished it looked loved again, but now the re-upholstery was complete the finished chair again looked elegant. Wrapped and sealed in plastic sheeting it was carefully stored to await its placing in one of our new bedrooms.

Jenny's friend Lynne and her husband Jacques make their living from dairy farming. Their income is further supplemented by the yield from the land, and they grow a rotation of maize, wheat, and sunflowers. Like all farms there are the resident chickens to provide the eggs, but Lynne and Jacques's hens were about to increase a little. They had a large poultry house sitting empty and had ventured into raising chickens on a large scale. They were awaiting delivery of five thousand hatchlings but European regulations are stringent for such breeders and do not allow other fowl to be on the farm for protection against cross infection. So the few egg-laying farm hens they already had were destined to go.

We had planned to have our own chickens eventually but hadn't at this time done anything about it, so when Lynne approached us we gratefully accepted four hens and Lynne assured us they would integrate well with the ducks.

Now fully grown, our ducks had the run of the garden which had become a bit of a problem.

Knowing that food came from the kitchen they were soon tapping on the glass door begging, and walking on the outside path was a hazardous occupation through their crap. Unattended they had also begun foraging within the flower beds and as far as Jenny was concerned that was the last straw.

The imminent arrival of the chickens now meant that a stockade was essential. A speedy modification to the small stone outbuilding had created a small entrance at ground level and inside we installed roosting poles and laying boxes. With a few posts and some chicken wire fencing we created an enclosed area outside and we were ready. In their new home the hens readily accepted the ducks and vice versa, and once settled the hens became good layers and we started to enjoy the benefit of our own fresh eggs.

A few days later François arrived with a bucket full of French beans topped off with some of his tomatoes. He grew abundant amounts in his vegetable garden and often appeared with an aged wooden basket filled to overflowing with his surplus. The taste of his produce fresh from the ground was wonderful, a taste I had never experienced in commercially grown.

Sitting him down for the customary whiskey we proudly told him of our newly acquired flock. His face brightened at our increased entry into French country life so we invited him to have a look to seek his approval.

He did, and two days later he returned with a handsome cockerel in a box with its legs tied, ready to be released into the chicken house at dusk an hour later. He explained that a new bird added to the flock will integrate better when given a night roosting together this way. Uncertain as to how we would cope in the early morning with a cockerel, we were pleasantly surprised to find his crowing quite acceptable.

He was quite a compact cockerel and when not feeding he stood quite upright with a biscuit crown and rust coloured ruff giving way to a mixture of white speckled with black and chestnut on his chest. His wings were white with black bars and the high tail feathers arched over were jet black and white.

He quickly became master of the flock of chickens, scratching and scraping for insects then announcing his find to the others who would speedily run over to peck this new food supply. Whenever we or the dog approached he called to the hens to convey the potential danger. I loved to sit and watch them and I listened with interest at their interactive clucking as they communicated between themselves.

None of the hens had shown any instincts yet of becoming broody but we knew from the evidence in our eggs that there was no doubt that Cockie was doing his job!

Like all birds at this time of the year, the two drakes had become quite amorous, but there didn't seem to be any rivalry between them because all their attention was being diverted towards the duck. We could see this when we looked at her back when her wings were folded and all we could see were the quills, all the feathers had been worn off from the constant attention of the drakes' feet.

Her neck also was red and sore looking from pecking. Drakes hold a duck firm by standing on her back and taking a firm grip to the neck with their bill. Their webbed feet have sharp claws as we had found to our cost previously.

While one of the Drakes fed happily, the other would sneak off and find her, do the business and return as if nothing had happened. She never seemed to complain and our fears of male aggression never materialised to our knowledge. Just as well because it would have been difficult to isolate who her real mate was and who wasn't.

She began to lay; first one, then two, then three until finally she had sixteen eggs and soon she was sitting on them constantly, and we watched her body weight decrease dramatically.

Then one evening about a month later, as we gave the others a small feed to get them all in for the night, she came off the nest for a quick top-up, giving us an opportunity to inspect her eggs. We found one with a small hole in it and a distinct "cheep, cheep" coming from the inside and excitedly we returned later for another look before turning in for the night.

Mum was not happy to be disturbed by a torch shining in her eyes as we tried for a proper view, but we saw more eggs with holes or cracks. During the next few days we were thrilled to find thirteen fluffy little chicks, all perfect little miniatures with beaks like a baby's fingernail.

After two days she took them from the nest box in search of the pond and to water. We were amazed at their resilience to injury as one by one they followed mum down the step from the chicken house, tumbling and rolling at the bottom of the drop; one big white duck followed by a long line of thirteen little yellow and black fluff balls all trying to keep up with mum as she made her way to the pond, tripping over grass blades, righting themselves and scurrying back in line.

Genes are a wonderful thing and we delighted at how naturally they entered the water and bathed for the first time while still keeping close to mum. Back on dry land they all stood and preened together, with the chicks exhibiting all the skill of their mother.

One exuberant chick, showing he could do it better than the rest, overbalanced and rolling over and over back down the concrete slope he again entered the water in a most ungainly fashion. With a quick look to make sure nobody saw him, he hastened back to re-join his brothers and sisters.

During her childhood Jenny had developed a very early affinity with animals. At eight years old she arrived home from school one day proudly leading a pony.

Unable to believe her eyes her mother had ventured, "Where on earth did you get that?"

Excitedly she had replied. "It's mine… I found it by the side of the road."

It used to be the custom, rarely seen nowadays, for gypsy travellers to tether ponies for grazing on roadside verges. Seeing one such pony Jenny had assumed it had been abandoned, so she had decided it must have a home; and where better than with her.

Unprepared to comprehend the gravity of the situation, she was forced to return the pony in floods of tears accompanied by her exasperated mother who feared for the repercussions. Today Jenny is still a sucker for animals, especially injured birds and recently rescued an ailing collared dove, probably mauled by one of the cats. It was unable to fly with an injured a wing and it looked shocked, so it was placed in a cage with food and water and affectionately named Beryl.

Most wild birds when caged and injured rarely recover, but after a couple of days its wings rose to normal position and it looked quite perky. Jenny released it and it flew to the roof of the house where it sat to regain its location. The local Farmers would not have offered the same assistance; nesting in barns and cattle sheds their numbers have increased to pest proportions, costing them hard-earned income to scare them away with explosive devices.

We didn't see it leave our roof only that it had gone, so we presume it survived, or at least we hoped so.

17

Since moving to France my banjo had spent most of the time within its case while I had been searching for like-minded musicians in France so as to further my experience and enjoyment of playing. I'd heard about a chap who played guitar and whose wife had a market stall at Villeréal on Saturdays, so I sought to make his acquaintance and that's how I came to meet Jim. It started a long standing friendship that has survived some awkward times, but which I hope will always be there.

After I met him, I heard on the grapevine that Jim was struggling to find work, so when by chance he appeared in the bar one Friday evening I approached him.

I explained that I had a long standing project constructing a terrace around a large swimming pool. It was heavy work and it was taking its toll on my back so I was anxious to finish it and I needed help.

Despite me not being able to pay him much money, Jim readily agreed to work with me to finish the job and I soon discovered his ability to accept the most mundane manual work and take it as a personal challenge to reach completion.

He was a quiet, deep thinking man with a gentle nature and a wicked sense of humour, and while working we would regularly amuse ourselves with mini competitions to test each other's musical knowledge of songs.

We attacked the final base concreting like two men possessed and soon found our joint skills were complimenting each other. With the base down we started to lay the slabs on the largest side of the pool first and checked our lines frequently to maintain accuracy.

Leaning awkwardly sideways to eye the latest line right next to the pool edge, Jim lost his balance and fell into the pool fully clothed, cap and gloves. He surfaced with a huge grin and recovered his composure before moving to the pool side and eyeing the line.

"Yep, that's fine", he said, and hauled himself out of the water sporting that special Jim smile as if it was an everyday occurrence. This was a foretaste of many such incidents that I would later come to expect from Jim.

One rainy day, we were unable to continue with the work on the pool terrace and unwilling to lose the momentum I had suggested that we could attack the wall at home to produce the opening through to the bedrooms. After half an hour of levering and removing stones, we saw the first daylight through the wall into the dining room.

A further two hours produced a huge pile of stones behind us within the chai and a pile of old clay mortar to the side. It always amazes me how reluctant stones are to give up their setting in a clay based mortar; and it further amazes me how large some of them are, and how high and accurate they have been placed within a wall, some of them as big as a bag of hardened cement.

One such stone was at ground level in our new opening, half above and half below the finished floor level. Reluctant to open the hole any lower, and keen to avoid the ensuing extra repair work, we jointly agreed to cut away what was necessary with the diamond disk cutter; a big Mistake!

Rushing outside choking and gasping for air we turned to watch the fine dust produced by the cutter billowing from the open doorway like smoke. When eventually after fifteen minutes it cleared sufficiently for us to re-enter, Jenny was not amused.

The whole area had been bathed in fine white dust, which was eventually settling on anything remotely less than vertical. While pleased with this advancement to the bedroom project, any pleasure was quickly crushed by the cleaning task now ahead of her.

Jim and I fitted side profiles to the opening, and after levelling the oak lintel beams we started to re-stone above them, and finally the sides were finished before we called it a day. The drawback was that we had opened up a doorway to an unheated area which had to be closed off temporarily, then still allow easy access though when required. We blocked it off when not in use for building with a curtain in front of a large sheet of insulation board; it did not exclude all the draughts but certainly made a significant difference.

Working together, Jim and I soon had the pool terrace well advanced and ahead of schedule, allowing us time to react positively to a new enquiry.

Our new client was a retired actor from a very well-known English soap and he was desperate. He had a holiday home close by which he also let as holiday accommodation. It was a month before the arrival of his first paying guests and his French builder was nowhere to be seen. We agreed to meet on site and discuss how we could help.

Flapping about like a headless chicken, he showed us all the unfinished work, and explained what had happened. He had felt sorry for his worker and so to assist him through a difficult personal crisis he had paid him in advance and gone back to England confident that the duration of the winter months was plenty of time to complete his specified work. I made frantic notes on a pad as he related his sad tale of woe, seldom stopping for breath and generously spraying us with saliva from time to time when the exasperation overcame him.

In the background like some actor in a comedy farce, his wife flitted from room to room clad in a skimpy top and shorts that would have looked better on her daughter. In one rubber-gloved hand she held a tin of paint festooned with drips, and in the other a paintbrush worn down to stubbly bristles from years of abusive use.

He calmed visibly when after analysing my scribbled notes we offered our services for two weeks, and confidently assured him we could bring it all back on track in the time available; but we were totally unaware of what we were letting ourselves in for!

We dismantled the wrongly assembled staircase kit, and quickly had it re-assembled and fitted correctly. It led up to a bedroom via what was to become minstrel's gallery, but the five beams that were to support the gallery horizontally were still awaiting fixing within the walls and the whole construction was in danger of collapse.

We secured all the beams and laid the flooring and then the fun started when he produced all the materials for the balustrade from his barn. There were thirty five balusters of differing lengths and designs that he had collected at various English car boot sales. I laid them on the floor and arranged them many times to form some sort of pattern and finally cut them all to the same length ready to be installed along with the hand rail and centre support post which was an old dining table leg.

He gave Jim a sink which he installed in one of the bedrooms. It was fully fitted with gold taps and a waste, and when Jim turned the water on it leaked like a sieve through the broken interior of the mixer tap. Additional instructions to remove an old pipe that he told us was no longer connected soon had water spouting up the wall, and created a frantic search for the stop-cock.

We dug stone from an earth covered pile to build a staircase outside, then reluctant to buy proper treads which would have saved him money on our labour costs, he arrived with varying types and lengths of metal for us to use, retrieved again from the bowels of his barn. He later admitted that he had brought most of the materials out from England having purchased his bargains at car-boot sales. We left him after our two weeks work very happy with the progress achieved and the payment he made for it, and now we affectionately refer to him as 'Car boot Ken.'

During working with Jim, I got to know him a lot better. It transpired that after a sudden split up with his wife of twenty five years, he had hit rock bottom and was very depressed. As a thinking man, he was aware of his depression and was trying hard to come to terms with it, learning and reading how to control his thinking.

Searching for a new direction to rebuild his life, I suggested that his music was perhaps the building blocks he was looking for. I knew before I met him that he played the guitar, but I didn't know how skilled he was. Following his preferred style of blues and ragtime, he has developed a style of playing all of his own, listening and learning from artists like Reverend Gary Davis and Marcel Dardi.

I had heard of a café in a nearby village that welcomed amateur musicians on a Friday night. So I suggested we should go to see what the venue was like and perhaps play. He readily agreed so later that week off we went.

I started to learn the Banjo just before I left England, and according to my teacher, I was one of his better students, which of course encouraged me greatly. I used to go to pubs and clubs, seeking out other blue grass players and I learned a lot from them.

Here in France I missed this contact with other players and in consequence my playing suffered. So for me the chance to rekindle playing with like-minded musicians was welcome.

Arriving at the café we found a ready smile from our hostess and exchanged warm handshakes with the two after-work drinkers who eyed our instrument cases with interest. Ordering a couple of beers we sat chatting expectantly waiting for musicians to enter and my fingers to de-frost; I began to wish I had ordered coffee instead of the arctic temperature French lager. “Sod this.” said Jim, “I’m going to play.”

Out came the guitar, strings tickled for tuning and off he went into a well-known blues number. Following with Eric Clapton’s “Here in Heaven,” the chaps at the bar rallied an appreciative applause, while the bar maid’s smile towards Jim broadened.

Not to be out done, out came the banjo and while Jim picked up the tune and quietly backed me, I picked out Cripple Creek, a well-known blue grass fiddle tune. Just as the applause from our mini audience died away a well-dressed lady appeared from a room out back.

Carefully approaching she explained to us that there was a committee meeting in progress until ten o’clock when she would happily listen to our music but for now could we please stop.

We all saw the funny side of it, sharing the joke with our new drinking pals and our hostess’s gesture said, “Well…this is France!”

Unusual the meeting was, but not unusual for musicians to appear after ten thirty. So we waited, drank a few more arctic beers, and were rewarded when in walked a chap with a guitar. Placing his guitar in the corner like a well-trained dog, he crossed to the bar with an acknowledging nod towards us and made the expected greetings to all.

Taking the beer from Françoise behind the bar he came over to our table.

He was not tall and his build displayed none of the usual signs of gastronomic and alcoholic abuse, but his firm hand shake confirmed a strong physique. Grey and wavy, his shoulder length hair framed a worn face with a nose that barely supported his half-framed glasses which were perched right on the end. Behind his glasses his bright eyes sparkled with warmth and friendship. He wore a thick shirt, skin tight jeans with a tobacco pouch and wallet bulging out the rear pockets, and Jesus sandals.

"*Bonsoir*," he said with interest, "*Ah, deux nouveau musiciens*?"

Our introductions promptly elicited his reply, "*Ah, vous et Anglais*? *Je suis Jean-Louis*." and a quick statement that he spoke no English at all.

Jim's French is always better than mine and a rapport soon developed as we assisted each other overcoming his lack of English and our feeble French. Jim explained our transgression with the committee in session and much to his amusement he said, "They are old, what do they know about music?"

A few additional musicians came later and we received the same warm greeting and interest from each of them. An added bonus was Roland who spoke reasonable but rusty English. Jean-Louis called him over regularly amidst rapturous laughter of our pronunciation attempts.

Eventually an amplifier was set up with a microphone stand and a few chairs were set together facing the small audience that had filtered in; and music flowed. Unaccustomed to Jim's style he quickly became the attraction for the evening, I took a back seat to listen and watched this sunken man find something within himself, as his spirit visibly lifted, and Jean-Louis watched in awe, recognising this talent. We came away tired, just after midnight, leaving Françoise still serving drinks to the stragglers, and glad that we had ventured into French social life musically, and Jim found his building blocks.

We drove home through the unlit winding lanes in joyous mood reliving the experience and promising ourselves that it would become a regular haunt, and it did.

A few months later during the same journey home, Jim said, "Its pitch black beyond the lights of the car, spooky isn't it; it reminds me of when I nearly killed myself."

"What…" I said, "…when was this?"

"Oh…" he said, "…I didn't tell you about that did I" Then he continued.

Attending another such venue to play guitar, Jim had left sober in the early hours of the morning and was driving home through the pitch-black French lanes. Staring into the blackness beyond his headlights, there was an awful BANG, and his car suddenly took off! He had hit an unseen curbing stone that was sticking out at the roadside and his car launched itself under the impact.

A hard landing had burst and shredded all four tyres and damaged the steel rims. Somewhat shocked, and then seeing a light in a nearby farmhouse, Jim tentatively knocked on the door looking for assistance.

A bewildered look from the occupant in his night attire soon vanished when Jim's predicament became clear, and with the use of the telephone quickly offered, Jim telephoned his estranged wife for assistance. Learning that she was soon to return home, he left a message with his twenty-year-old son explaining where he was, and that he would start to walk to shorten the rescue distance.

Expecting that help was on its way he set off with the only items of value from the wrecked car - his two guitars. Walking the entire distance of thirty five kilometres, he arrived exhausted at his wife's home, bewildered as to why no one had appeared to rescue him. As dawn broke he woke his son - the message bearer, to inquire what had happened.

"Oh yea Dad, sorry, I forgot to tell Mum when she came in!"

Jim hasn't had much luck with cars. When visiting a pal one evening he had parked outside of the remote house on the farm track. Leaving the house hours later he was unable to find the car and after the first thoughts of theft, both Jim and his pal realised that nobody would want to steel his car, such was its condition. As their night vision improved in the darkness a ragged hole in the hedge downhill from the house began to appear.

Further investigation revealed a dark shape in the middle of a field, downhill from the track leading to the house. Carefully treading the wet grass, he made his way towards the car and discovered that apart from the front which was displaying excellent camouflage foliage, it seemed undamaged. Unable to return uphill in the wet grass and back through the hedge, he transcribed the field for twenty minutes before finding an alternative exit.

On another occasion Jenny had accepted a lift to somewhere, and on entered his car had immediately registered a gagging smell. Searching for words in preference to abandoning the idea she pleaded, "Jim what on earth is that awful smell?"

"Oh yea, it's my dustbin bag in the boot". He replied apologetically.

"Well how long has it been there?" She again asked.

"Err… two weeks; I keep forgetting to take it out!" Such was the pattern of Jim's life.

The Gendarmerie has the power to levy fines immediately when necessary. Stopped for a normal spot check, Jim was asked by a female officer to produce his documents.

"Papers please." She asked.

"I'm sorry," he apologetically replied, "I don't have them with me." (*Offence 1.*)

"I see, and why are you not wearing a seat belt?"

Submissively he again replied, "I'm sorry, I forgot." (*Offence 2.*)

While Jim was shrinking lower in the seat, the Gendarme viewed him with great suspicion and asked him.

"Is this your car?" Meekly he confirmed it was.

"But it's registered to another department, how do you explain that?" she asked.

Swallowing hard he replied, "I've only just bought it and haven't had the time to change it yet." (*Offence 3.*)

With an expression to convey her full authority she assessed the situation.

"I see... you're driving without a seat belt in a car you can't confirm is yours, you have no drivers permit to show me and no certificate of insurance or vehicle testing."

"No... I'm sorry." he quietly confirmed, and waited while she digested what action she should take. Expecting to be marched off in handcuffs, one of his pleading smiles appeared across his face as she made her deliberation.

"Buzz off…it must be your lucky day!" The Jim smile had saved him again.

18

Occasional problems with my lower back were not a new experience. Thirty five years in engineering, working bent over benches that were far too low, and lifting heavy materials had weakened the spinal joints over many years, but fairly regular appointments with an excellent chiropractor had kept me in trim and I quickly learned how to protect my back with revised working practices.

The move had of course aggravated it and likewise my building work both for customers and at home. I knew an appointment with a chiropractor was well overdue and I had been putting off the obvious language dilemma to make the search in France to find one when with perfect timing Jenny had found an advertisement in a local newspaper.

'English Chiropractor in Eymet.'... thirty minutes away and a godsend!

I met Simon and warmed to him at once confident that he would soon have me 'clicked' into shape. It must have been at least eighteen months since my last adjustment in England and hence it took a few sessions of manipulation before my spine was returned to working order.

Revaluating any physical work to lesson any risk was frustrating as return visits soon told me what aggravated it. When the warning signs presented themselves every few months, I'd make an appointment for a service and rest it a while and slowly the time between visits lengthened which allowed me to achieve normal progress with my revised methods.

On a good day our thoughts had turned again to the pool. The sides had collapsed over the winter and the whole thing had become a disaster. The company with whom we had placed our order also provided the pool in kit form for self-installation, and with a full agenda for their team of installers they happily accepted our change for self-assembly. We decided to put the cost they would have required to better use elsewhere

Initially we thought we would remove the collapsed soil and fallen stones by hand, but now as we stood within the hole we could see the enormity of it and once again Jacques offered a solution. He knew of a chap across the valley that had a digger, so asked him on our behalf to come and take a look to see if his machine could cope.

In comparison to the original '*Pelle méchanique'* it was tiny, but with it he admirably returned the dig to its former shape for a nominal amount. Great, we were back in business and with Jim's help we laid the base rings on pads of concrete, going round the outer edges again and again with a water level to ensure the best possible accuracy to within two millimetres.

The weather in early July was hot and after we had pumped out most of the water, the clay base had then dried giving us an opportunity to work towards having a useable pool. We needed to order lots of soft sand and cement for the base and then take full advantage of the two extra pairs of hands that would soon be arriving for what they thought would be a holiday.

Midsummer is the time for the 'Bodega'. This annual tradition is a street party and most villages organise one. Our local village was no exception and as you passed through the streets during mid-July you could see the banners and signs appearing in preparation.

Unaware of how to proceed at such a grand village event we were pleased to be accompanied by Lynn and Jacques. The '*Place de le Halle*' with its ancient wrought iron covered market place and adjacent street had become an enormous function room for the evening. Across the street from the walls and balconies above, many strings of coloured lights and bunting had been attached creating the illusion of a high ceiling.

Beneath, the rows of chairs and tables covered in crisp white paper cloths were already being taken by families anxious to secure a comfortable position and a hubbub of happy conversation was filling the air. There still seemed plenty of room so we perused the stalls of the various vendors of food and drink.

We recognised and greeted the two brothers who own the huge beef farm directly behind our house. They were busy within a haze of smoke rising from a sizzling barbeque, cooking their beef steaks and speedily cutting each piece into bite-size pieces - to be eaten with the aid of a cocktail stick - while their wives were trying to keep up with the demand for the accompanying *frits.* The aroma reminded us how hungry we were so we quickly made the circuit to discover what other dishes were on offer.

Mussels and chips, spicy sausages in lengths of French bread, pieces of delicious barbequed chicken and great round pans sizzling with paella. *Tarte flambée*, a speciality from the *Alsace* region, is a wafer thin dough base spread with a mixture of soft white cheese and cream, which is topped with fine pieces of smoked bacon and sliced onion, and then quickly baked in an oven to serve sizzling hot. It is absolutely delicious and the couple behind the counter were working like fury to keep pace with the queue.

Crêpes and waffles with an assortment of *confiture* for dessert. *Aperitifs* were served with some food, for other drinkers two open sided tents served the liquid requirements, beer and an assortment of wines.

Our salivary glands went into overdrive as the aroma from the many dishes available percolated our noses. Jacques is responsible at the Mayor's office for the *Jumelée*, the twinning of our village with another in Alsace; his familiarity with the locals soon introduced us to many characters we know by sight only. Feeling a little like outsiders, we were glad to be accompanying them as we relaxed into the atmosphere, and together under Jacque's vast gastronomic experience, we sought a suitable aperitif.

As he was waylaid by yet another local he hadn't seen for a while we chatted with Lynn in English. We questioned the puzzled expression on her face which brought forth the revelation that her familiarity of the English language had diminished over the twenty five years she had lived here and she was now struggling to find and recognise the words once so familiar.

It was still early in the evening by French standards as more and more people were appearing with ribbons tied somewhere on their clothing signifying that they had paid the pittance for entry.

Among them was a small assembly wearing white dungarees with green gingham shirts and red neck scarves. As we watched they grew to their full complement and we realised that one of the bands had arrived; *Les Vert à Pieds*.

An ensemble of cornets, trumpets, saxophones, clarinets, horns, a tuba, flute, snare drums, and a base drum to hold them all together with the double time beat common to French brass bands. We watched with interest as they formed into a rough circle and began to play. Suddenly the atmosphere came alive as they paraded through the swelling crowds, stopping at intervals to again form into a circle and entertain in a different area.

Conversation near to the band became difficult and Jacques indicated towards the food stalls for our first course and a second aperitif. With nods of approval and full mouths we soon demolished *moules frites*, and a bottle of Alsace white wine purloined by Jacques from one of his pals.

Looking around us we soaked up this electric atmosphere. All ages were there, babes in pushchairs, toddlers in hand, youngsters roaming free - their high jinks freely tolerated. Teenagers parading in their latest fashions as they played the courtship game; young married couples joined as equals with their parents, as they joyfully attended to the grandchildren in the tradition of family sociability that are so evident here. Some of the retired couples were wearing traditional French costumes, and they were a delight to behold.

Unseen behind us a second band had formed and Dixieland Jazz then filled the air around the tables and I was delighted to hear a banjo playing among them.

Under the huge wrought iron market canopy a collection of happy children were playing under watchful eyes, and a man was busy upon a lorry trailer. He had in front of him an array of lighting boxes and loud speakers and above him a gantry supported more. The disc jockey was quietly in preparation for later in the proceedings when the covered market place would become his dance floor. The strings of coloured lights came to life as darkness slowly descended upon a party in full swing, enhancing the party atmosphere as the brass band made another pass on its circuits.

Conversation would have been impossible were we not enjoying our second course which was the paella, then suddenly a great cheer erupted as the band swung skilfully into '*Bon Anniversaire*' - Happy Birthday to you. Close by, an elderly Lady was blushing with embarrassment as the rest of her family pointed towards her in appreciation of her birthday now shared by all.

We bumped into friends Ann and Regis, an English lady and her French partner who we greeted warmly, but Jenny felt the need to go one further.

"Ah bonsoir monsieur," she said and warmly embraced the elderly gentleman with them, kissing him on both cheeks. Only after the bemused faces of us all did she realise that it was not who she thought - the father of one of the local restaurateurs that we know so well - but a total stranger - Regis's father. Sharing the joke warmly he told us via Regis that he hadn't had a lady in his arms like that for years. She was of course suitably embarrassed like the birthday girl, but we placated her by agreeing that there was a very close likeness.

With years of tradition, French people have perfected how to enjoy themselves at such occasions. Eating and drinking go hand in hand and span the evening through; the bars stop serving when people stop drinking. We have never seen anybody under the influence of alcohol to the point where they become a nuisance or an embarrassment.

As late evening approached, the bands were drifting away and the volume from the dance area had increased as people started to take to the floor. It hadn't developed yet into a young person's disco and strict tempo music floated over the dancers as they displayed their skills. Skills practiced by all ages, young and old alike, Foxtrot, Waltzes, Quickstep, Latin American, they knew them all. The joy of watching some of the older couples glide in perfection around the floor put us to shame. We ventured once or twice to join with them but without the same history of enjoyment in our background we were definitely outclassed and preferred to gain our enjoyment from watching from the side.

I was really enjoying this immersion in French society, relishing the use of the language, stunted as it was but becoming more fluent after a few drinks. Jenny and

Lynne however had decided that it was time to call it a day. After many years of attending official functions with Jacques, Lynne was pleased to leave early with Jenny who was just plain tired.

After returning on my own and relocating Jacques, I suggested a little something to eat and drink, just to top us up. He gave me one of his mischievous grins and tapped his nose. In a quieter corner we were welcomed by a group of his cronies sitting at a table. Unlabelled bottles containing various liquids adorned the table and I was introduced to "*eau-d-vie*". Moonshine French style. Made from fermented fruit and then distilled twice into a clear brandy it can vary in strength and character. As we sampled each in turn I found that while some took the lining from my throat, others were smooth and full of the flavour of the fruit, likewise the alcoholic content varied according to distillation.

This after dinner '*digestive*' is normally accompanied by coffee, as I was soon to find out when someone appeared with a tray of syrupy black liquid in plastic cups and a dish of sugar lumps. Unaccustomed to this combination I was ill-prepared for the effect.

Relishing the thought of a warm coffee, a huge sip only intensified my burning throat and confirmed my thinking that this was definitely an acquired taste. My fellow drinkers were greatly amused at my reaction as they displayed warmth to me with smiles of contentment that they had had done their bit towards '*entente cordial.*'

A bleary look at my watch confirmed that I also had done my bit, and that one thirty was a good time to leave, but my new found pals had other ideas. "*Encore*" they demanded, and I considered myself lucky to escape with just one more tot.

Relieved that the car was parked on the outskirts of the village and pointed in the right direction, I managed to safely walk the distance relishing the now cool night air and aware that I should not be driving. I concentrated hard, but somehow it didn't stop me missing my turning and arriving at the next commune. Retracing my route and making the correct turn I passed a familiar post box, it took a further half a kilometre before I realised it was mine and I had just passed our house. Eventually lying safely in bed, my churning stomach reminded me that I don't drink strong liquor late in the evening and I resigned myself to a restless nights' sleep fraught with indigestion which would continue for the next twenty four hours.

19

We have four days to polish the house and garden before Jenny's daughter Lynsey and her partner Nick arrive for two weeks, camping on the lawn. For Jenny it had to be perfect, as furniture was rearranged and dusted, carpets vacuumed, old ornaments replaced with different ones giving the whole house a makeover. Then she attacked the garden, weeding the flower beds and sweeping the paths before attending to the climbers which had gone rampant and needed to be trimmed back to make access to the house a less hazardous affair.

On the tractor mower I was allowed, even encouraged, to cut the grass over most of the garden, except that which was adjacent to the house where Jenny felt that her efforts with the smaller motor mower gave a finer neater cut, so I always concede to this area which she will leave manicured to perfection.

As we sat ready and waiting, their car came to a halt on the drive and Arran's one good eye was on the doors. Once Lynsey's dog, he was overjoyed to see her again and for a full five minutes he got all the attention. Finally arms were flung around as the girls hugged and Jenny was close to tears with the relief that they were again here with us. We men, tough and unemotional, contented ourselves with a strong hand shake, as Nick demanded. "I could murder a beer!"

This was the second time we had met Nick, and we were pleased at Lynsey's choice of partner. She was particular in her choice of guys but he obviously fits the bill as we could see a changed girl, one who was very much in love. Likewise, Nick obviously adored her and we could see that there was a strong bond between them.

For Jenny, this was special and as Nick and I sat with a beer chatting, I watched her happy face and saw the joy within her.

Instigator of the ducklings, Lynsey couldn't believe how much they had grown, and while she was delighted to see then she asked why we were two short. In answer to her queries we revealed that one had died, accidentally flattened under a fallen plank of wood used to make the chicken house rat proof, and another had died of shock. During an early expedition of the garden it had strayed a little too far, and Arron doing his sheepdog bit had gently returned it to the flock, unaware of its fragility. Later questions from Lynsey concerning the eventual welfare of the adult birds horrified her as we revealed that they would be destined for the pot.

The weather was glorious and we spent many warm evenings outside enjoying the smell from the bar-be-cue while our dinner cooked. As dusk approached after our meal we still sat, talking in competition with the evening chorus of frogs coming from the pond. The noise grew progressively louder as each one joined in until suddenly it stopped, and we could converse again in the silence of the frogs.

Not content with the pond, they had become squatters in the mini lake within the pool dig. Fortunately the flooding had now ceased after the provisional re-piping of the source, and their usurped territory had dried out ready for laying the base, so re-housing errant frogs back to the pond was becoming a regular occurrence.

Now that the base ring was set and hardened in place, the galvanised steel side sheets came next and at last a recognisable shape appeared as the ten sections were bolted in position. I slid the bolts through from the inside and Lynsey worked outside fixing the washers and nuts with her slender body wedged between the dig sides and the sheets.

Delivery of a huge pile of soft sand and a pallet full of sacks of cement had been delivered, bringing us to the conclusion that we definitely needed a few extra hands to accomplish the mixing and laying of the base. With Jenny's daughter and Nick here, we enlisted the offered help of two other friends and we had a pool party!

With a scaffold plank strategically placed like a diving board over the edge, I tipped barrow after barrow into the hole. Michele one of our helpers was running relays with me back and forth from Lynsey who fed the mixer, without stopping all day. Below ground-level within the dig, Michele's husband Richard and Nick together spread and levelled all the wet cement, smoothing with floats until a satisfactory surface was achieved; while Jenny kept us all supplied with plenty of cold drinks and food, and constant encouragement towards the finished shallow end of the pool.

The deeper half with the diving pit presented different problems and would be a job for another day. Still rather boggy, it needed to dry a little more.

The youngsters worked in shorts and tee shirts while the rest of us hardened naturists worked taking full advantage of the August sunshine. Much to the amusement of the others I took my chiropractors advice when at risk, and wore my back support belt; I looked like a cigar with the wrapper still on, a comical sight as the photos now reveal. Later when we were all showered and clean, we anesthetised our aching muscles with the obligatory alcohol and I profusely thanked the team for this major step forward.

Once experienced, an evening at the 'Pizzeria Le Saint Pierre' was one to be repeated, and we were always happy to accompany friends there to eat. Our hosts Gerard and Marie offered a personal welcome and excellent food in a simple and colourful restaurant.

When we first went there a year ago, we discovered that we were similar ages to them and we had both remarried at the same time, and they always greeted us like friends they have invited to their home, and I'm sure that this formula was what kept their tables full. Gerard never forgot a previous conversation, and despite the fact that it may have been months since our last visit, he would recall these conversations asking with true interest how things were proceeding. After welcoming us he would return to his preparation area in front of the wood burning pizza oven, while Marie disappeared into the kitchen where she was unseen until later in the evening when her orders were fulfilled.

She was a shapely petite woman of Spanish origin and produced the dishes alternative to pizzas; salads, pastas and desserts. But her specialities were the Friday night fish specials. The arrival of her dishes was a feast for the eyes before the gastronomic pleasures. Our fidelity was obviously appreciated, because when as often we were part of a larger party than us four, it was not unusual for a bottle of wine to appear during the meal with a knowing wink from Gerard that said, "On me."

Lynsey and Nick loved it and bathed in the atmosphere, then as we waited for the arrival of our dessert Nick turned on hearing the "Happy birthday to you" theme then being playing on the sound system. The answer he sought was revealed much to his embarrassment, when the candle-lit cake Jenny had made, a replica of a bottle of Jack Daniels, was placed in front of him, and in joint language, the restaurant sang to him.

When the dimmed lights were brightened again and the other diners resumed their meals, he asked. "How the hell did you sneak that cake in here without my knowledge?"

Then Lynsey replied, "It's amazing how blind you can be with your mind on the first glass of lager." Now on his fifth he was obviously enjoying his birthday.

The next morning however, he was a little delicate and was looking forward to a quiet day; Lynsey had other ideas, and pestered him constantly to aggravate his hangover. Feeling sorry for Nick I diverted Lynsey's attention to assisting me with the construction of the pump house for the pool, which she was keen to become involved with, Nick visibly relieved, returned to a good book.

James my first employer and Banjo student had lived in France for ten years. Coming originally for a holiday, he liked what he saw and stayed. On a building project in his early years here he met Vanessa, the daughter of a client and they have been together ever since. They had sold their small home in Monflanquin and with vision had bought a wreck of a place in the country; the conversion, where I assisted with the stone walls. It was now complete and after settling into their new home they felt it was a good time to become married and we were thrilled to be invited to the wedding.

They are very much integrated into French life so we knew their day would be an interesting event and we were looking forward to seeing a marriage – French style. We arrived in the picturesque village square of Monflanquin and joined the assembling family and guests outside the *Marie*; pleased to see some old friends there we had not seen for a while.

Eventually we had to break this happy gathering as Tom, James's best man ushered us up the stairs for the ceremony. The official room, dignified with its oak panelled walls and magnificent ceiling was packed to overflowing, with a quarter of us who arrived last spilling into the hallway. Taller than most I managed to see some of the proceedings through the open doorway, and in the silence we could all hear their vows.

The Mayor wearing a dark suit and his official sash of red, white and blue stood with two other dignitaries behind a long oaken table, reading the necessary words to evoke the response. Although it was an official ceremony the atmosphere was very cordial and relaxed punctuated with occasional bursts of laughter? When complete it took ten minutes for us all to file back out into the square, where the happy couple had to be torn away from well-wishers by the photographer. Leaning from a high wrought iron balcony, he eventually gained everybody's attention and made the shots.

The tradition in France is to carpet the route from the Marie with laurel leaves which is a lovely idea. Tradition also has it that when a cavalcade of cars leaves en-route for the reception, headed by the bride and groom, it is a noisy affair. In this cavalcade we were about forty cars, many adorned with ribbons and balloons as car horns sounded off throughout the whole route, in this case to James and Vanessa's house some five kilometres away. As we passed from the centre of the village through its outskirts then through two other lesser communes the snaking line of noisy cars was attracting quite a lot of attention. All along the route residents and passers-by were waving their good wishes to the couple, and sharing their happiness.

Following the signs we parked in the designated field, strolling the few metres towards the house in the scorching August sun. The last time I saw the house it had no roof, doors or windows, and the surrounding area was still a building site with piles of unused sand and building blocks sprawling around the courtyard. Today the courtyard had been laid with fresh new white gravel, and its central garden was now resplendent in summer flowers.

Overlooking the courtyard the house looked magnificent and the adjacent jungle of a garden looked loved once more, a credit to all their hard work for this special day. Opposite the house a splendid Marquee sat levelled on stilts ready to receive us all later in the proceedings. I peeped inside as the caterers went to and fro from the house laying the tables; it looked ready for a regal banquet. I looked once more to the happy throng of guests chatting in groups, apératif in one hand leaving the other free to select a morsel from the circulating trays of delicious nibbles.

The scene was perfect; in the background a reduced complement of the Monflanquin brass band played quietly to entertain us as the happy couple circulated amongst us receiving our best wishes. Catching up on events with friends we had not seen for a long time, and making new acquaintances soon dissolved the time before an early dinner was served. The meal was French style; *Pintade* (guinea fowl) and delicious. All credit to the caterers who although very experienced in their trade did an excellent job with the facilities at hand.

Behind us a low stage was set ready for a band and a disco. A band I discovered later, I knew. I had previously received a call from a chap called George. Hearing I played banjo, he wanted to invite me to an evening session of mixed amateur musicians and I gladly accepted. It was a very professionally organised affair with a high stage in front of numerous tables full of expectant guests who knew George's reputation for a good night out. Jenny's positive encouragement and a few glasses of beer did nothing to forestay my increasing nervousness as the evening approached eleven o'clock, worried that my ability could not match what I had seen so far. Jim played a solo spot with a few of his numbers and by then the time was approaching midnight, well past our usual retiring time. Eventually I capitulated to my fears and thinking I had been forgotten we left for home. However George stayed in touch, even apologising for not giving me a spot and so another friendship was made.

Now at the wedding it was George and his pals who were to entertain us with their music. Quiet melodies as we finished eating were soon replaced by waltzes and foxtrots encouraging the more proficient strict tempo dancers onto the floor to display their skills. Changing the pace they soon emptied the tables onto the dance floor with first-class renditions of rock, blues, country and western, current chart toppers, they played them all, reading accurately the mood and changing to keep the dance floor full. Just to sit and watch they were obviously totally enjoying themselves and I noted the base player skilfully plucking the strings melodic finger style with three fingers, playing a base tune rather than a steady beat, his body gyrating and absorbed within his music. Their vocal harmony together brought the songs alive and I hope they charged in keeping with their professionalism.

20

Michele and Richard we knew from the naturist club in England, in fact we were the prime moves in getting them together as a couple.

Michele had been divorced for some ten years and had struggled, on her own, bringing up two children, the younger of which had learning difficulties.

Richard came to the club with friends who were helping him to rebuild his life following the death of his wife after a long illness. They were perfectly suited and all of us who had become friends with them recognised that they would be good for each other. There was an obvious attraction between them, but both were very shy and reluctant to make any moves. Whenever the topic came up with Michele, each of us in turn would receive a regular barrage of questions in the vein of, “Do you think he likes me, perhaps I should ask him out for dinner?” It left us all who had her best interests at heart, pulling our hair out with her uncertainty. Something had to be done so we organised a dinner party, inviting them both, and not telling the other. It worked, and they were soon dating regularly, much to the relief of us all. They are now very happily married and inseparable.

Fate had led them to our door here in France one Christmas and New Year break. They had booked a chalet at La Rochelle and experiencing awful stormy weather during the drive down, they had thought it prudent to phone ahead and check on the local weather conditions. Devastated, they had learned from the owner, “Don’t bother coming we’ve been flattened by the storm.”

Knowing that we were not so far away they telephoned us. They readily accepted our offer to 'camp' on the lounge floor - as at that time we hadn't even started the bedrooms - and we occupied the only bed in the house in the corner of our dining room.

During their stay with us they showed their appreciation of our hospitality at a local restaurant and as we left they were soon showing interest in the window of an estate agent. They now have a superb second home thirty minutes south of us and when family commitments allow they hope to reside there permanently. Likewise our friends Keith and Margaret did the same thing, preferring to buy an old barn and convert it themselves. We are blest with four very dear friends locally, and we look forward to their coming out. Sometimes we even manage to all be here at the same time and can enjoy many pleasant evenings at each other's home or the many restaurants nearby. One such time we talked a restaurateur into cooking us a fish and chip supper and we all shared the humour of the occasion that we wanted fish and chips in a country famous for its food.

Summer heat can sap your energy and we realised we were subconsciously avoiding the issue of laying the concrete for our bedroom floors. Keith and Margaret had taken a prolonged summer vacation to advance the progress of their barn conversion, and recognising our dilemma had suggested that we all pitch in and push our bedrooms on a bit more because the September weather was in our favour. A good idea and in no time we had most of the floor done for the first bedroom, and time left to eat and drink, again turning a work party into a social event.

Fired by the progress Jenny and I did some more a week later. By planning where the walls would eventually be so as to make provision for the electric cables under the floors, we completed sufficient concreting to enable us to start constructing a wall for the first bedroom, which had now become a priority. Chris, my banjo teacher had arranged a second visit, and additionally Jenny's son Richard was coming with his girlfriend a few weeks later.

Anxious we did not want any more guests sleeping in the lounge, we switched all our efforts to the one room where walls were at full height and the door and frame was in place. Leaving the other two rooms as a building site we isolated them by constructing a small lobby from insulation board.

With time running out, it soon became clear that our efforts were not going to provide Chris with a bedroom this time and once more he would be sleeping in the lounge. His stay was only to be for a few days, but he asked if we could again get together with my new-found musical pals. Jim was looking forward to meeting Chris again, and I spoke to Jean-Louis who invited us to spend the evening at his house for dinner and music.

I don't quite know how I did it because a conversation with Jean-Louis was not an easy thing. He spoke quickly with an accent that somehow reduced words in a sentence to one long variation of sound. Sometimes I could pick up a key word and fill in the rest, a process which often gave me the completely wrong end of the stick. These conversations usually evoked from him either an expression which said, are you mad; or explosive laughter with a friendly slap across my shoulder as he registered my dilemma.

Jim's directions led us eventually to the house and a warm welcome for us all. A short gravel driveway opened up to an array of outbuildings opposite his house. One houses his collection of Kayaks; we guessed about fifty, and one his open fronted workshop. Others were crammed full of what seemed to us to be all the props from Steptoe and son. His stone-built house was grand, but externally it showed all the signs of a man with little time to maintain it.

We climbed a stone staircase to the door which led into a large kitchen. Inside the arrangement was typical to what would have once been a farmhouse kitchen.

On one side there was a great open fire place, burning two great oak logs and flanked by two worn easy chairs that looked very comfortable. The mantle above was covered with a collection of outdated calendars and pictures all covered with a layer of dust that portrayed many years of habitation by a single man and an open wood fire. A large table that once would have seated a family of fourteen separated the room from the modern well-fitted kitchen units.

The table itself was surrounded by a collection of different chairs and excepting an area at the end where he sat to eat, it was covered with an arrangement of old newspapers, books, pots and pans, and the remains of a stale baguette sat on a crumb covered cutting board alongside a knife that showed many years of continual sharpening.

The full tour of the house took a speedy ten minutes and revealed three huge bedrooms, all beautifully decorated, a bathroom and separate toilet, and a lounge which led from the kitchen through an archway. In the lounge were two or three comfortable looking armchairs and a coffee table with a glass top that looked like it could have been donated by Robinson Crusoe; they were the only clues to the fact that it was a lounge as all the rest of the room was adorned with musical instruments.

One corner housed an upright piano, the other a wooden xylophone, while nestling in between was a set of impressive bongo drums. One wall was almost covered in stringed instruments; five or six guitars, two banjos, a Dobro, violins and a mandolin. He further produced a couple of penny whistles, a recorder and a Jews harp and according to Jean-Louis, he could play them all; but to what degree we are not sure as it seemed to us that when he was centre stage at the bar in Gavedun, his music was a variation of the same four tunes! But the crowds loved him.

Here at his house he was the perfect host, sweeping the table with an outstretched arm, he gestured for us to sit and play while he began expert preparations for our meal. Chris and I had been practicing a tune called Soldier's Joy, so when encouraged by Jean-Louis to play something while he worked, we tried it out together much to his delight.

As the bottle contents got lower, so the quality of music became higher. Unfortunately I was not at my best with the after effects of a stomach bug and happily let Jim and Chris take over the pre-dinner entertainment. Jim played a few blues and ragtime numbers, and Chris played whatever came into his head, both guitar and banjo which delighted Jean-Louis and somehow a communication developed between them without any comprehension of the others language. In a sober moment Chris played a beautiful version of Green sleeves which stopped our host's preparation while he watched and listened intently.

Instructing me to rake up the embers of the fire, he then put a grill over the top and placed two huge rings of Toulouse sausages on the grill, and while they cooked in the heat and oak-smoke we sat to our first course; some *saucisson* and a bowl of grated red cabbage dressed with a vinaigrette.

Just before he sat with us, he delved under the heaped pile swept to the end of the table and produced a fresh loaf and the knife. Of all the plates and knives and forks, not one of them matched but it didn't matter as we were all happy to be there together sharing this simple meal, good spontaneous music and the company of each other.

The sausage was cooked and placed upon a breadboard, where we cut and ate the sausage as required, helping ourselves also to a bowl of pasta in sauce bolognaise and thick slices of the bread. He apologised for his lack of dessert and opened a fresh *fromage camembert*. He explained to Chris in gestures how he should peel a garlic clove, slice pieces off and eat it with a slice of the cheese on the bread.

Keen to try this new experience Chris misunderstood and used the whole clove of garlic. As his face grew redder and his eyes watered, Jean-Louis collapsed in convulsions of laughter. Never one for using expletives, Chris later said when he had recovered, "Bloody hell, that was strong." But it didn't stop him from trying it again, this time with a smaller slice of garlic instead of the whole clove.

After the meal Jenny cleared away for him while we all returned to the music. Not to be out done by Chris and Jim, Jean-Louis produced his Dobro and showed us all what he was capable of. Blues, pop, ragtime, classics and hillbilly banjo, we played it all for the next few hours, and only when Jenny was showing signs of sleep did we decide to wrap it up and wind our way back home. We were all tired and the journey back for we three was almost silent of conversation except one comment from Chris who said, "Wow, what an evening."

A few days later we once again deposited Chris in the airport departure lounge with what we hoped were some nice memories.

With just about four weeks until Jenny's son Richard and his girlfriend arrived we had to pull out all the stops to get their room finished. During the journey back from the airport with Chris we considered how youngsters normally treat a bedroom, and decided they were definitely not going to sleep in the lounge.

We had actually completed all the building work on our first bedroom before Chris's arrival but it hadn't quite dried and the room was still very damp, and we didn't want to risk sending Chris back home ill. The new block work wall was cement rendered, leaving the original stone walls pointed to reveal the stones, a process called *pierre apparente*, which means stones apparent.

Taught by an experienced builder friend, Jenny feels she is the queen of *pierre apparente*, a title I am very reluctant to dislodge from her. Re-pointing brick work is bad enough, but pointing uneven stone to achieve the required quality is a skill.

Firstly the old clay mortar must be raked out to a reasonable depth, then using a new lime mortar, it has to be pressed, or more skilfully flicked off the trowel, deep into the cavity. Later just before the mortar has set, it has to be brushed from the surface edges of the stones and across the mortar to reveal as much or as little of the stones, as suits your required tastes, at the same time leaving the mortar as a whole, looking flat and true.

This is one of the most laborious jobs I have ever done, and while very capable of doing it, I will always concede to Jenny. The patience it requires as a time consuming task eludes me, but when finished her walls are stunning and she rightly takes pride in the achievement. When fully dry, the rendered walls had been painted cream and the exposed wooden beams were treated against insects and then painted dark brown. I fitted the sockets and light switches and we were ready for furnishings.

We had been to a local second hand furniture warehouse and virtually stolen a beautiful bed, paying an absolute song for it. Made in France during the reign of Henry ll, the wood was walnut, and curved in the most interesting designs. The shop owner explained the history of the carvings saying how they were for the growth of love and life within a family. The significance of the vine patterns showed the growth of the family, with relevance also to the many children the bed would hopefully produce. Perhaps this was not the best idea to place this bed in the room Jenny's twenty-year-old son would be using with his girlfriend!

We laid the carpet and assembled the bed before dusting and polishing all the other furniture retrieved from the barn, and the room was now ready for the drapes, bed covers and all that make it look like home.

The finished room was an utter joy to behold, and we were very proud of our achievement.

Richard last saw the room when it was a *Chai*, and likewise was stunned by the transformation. For Jenny the countdown to their arrival was like a child waiting for Christmas morning. It had been over a year since she last saw him and I could sense the emotion building within her. Fidgeting anxiously throughout the thirty minute journey to the airport, she was surprised to find the plane had arrived early and whilst I searched for a place to park, Jenny's eyes sorted through the dispersing passengers. One rucksack and a small case sitting on the ground guarded by a long haired hippy and a girl seemed to fit the bill.

"My god…" she exclaimed, "…look at the length of his hair!"

Then as Jenny put on a brave face and fought back the tears of emotion we bundled them into the car and headed home.

For Richard's girlfriend Vicky, an awkward time as she had not previously met us, so I chatted with her to break the ice. Difficult as it was, with Jenny firing a barrage of questions to Richard, directed mostly to the length of his hair and his obvious lack of personal hygiene, a phase that many teenagers do pass through unscathed!

As a boy, Richard's time here on holidays was spent mostly in the garden. His love of wildlife was apparent at a very early age, and it kept him absorbed for hours searching the garden for some new animal or insect. He would keep a muslin cage for his latest collection of Praying mantis and Stick insects; those that survived would be later released back into the wild at his departure, but his special interest was always the pond. Taking a chair he would sit for hours to study any visible movement and investigate the perpetrator. On this latest arrival, after dumping the baggage in their room he took Vicky for a tour of the garden; and his prime target as usual was the pond.

Over the months, we had eventually told him that his fish had not fared very well during the move, and he knew about the actions of the Heron, but still he was anxious to see for himself what the situation was. Back in the house he was giving his girlfriend a brief résumé of his childhood experiences here while at the same time marvelling at all the changes we had made to the house.

Most mornings we never saw them before eleven, and most evenings we left them watching TV as we retired to bed. He brought with him a huge halogen torch and most evenings after dark, he would again search the grounds looking for any nocturnal wildlife. One such evening he returned to the house very excited and opening his hand produced a strange looking reptile. About twenty centimetres long with a large head, it was jet black with bright yellow spots. He identified it as a Fire salamander, a secretive reptile that lives in upland woods. Pairing during the summer, the female keeps her eggs in her body until springtime when they will have hatched and only then will she go to water to allow the young to swim away. As they are not resident in England we all shared his excitement at this new discovery, within our garden.

They both enjoyed a happy week here, leaving the room like a bomb had hit it, and as luck would have it, we are not yet Grandparents.

Jenny hates airport goodbyes and this one particularly was an emotional strain upon her, especially not knowing when she would see her son again, and the tears began to quietly flow.

Back home the dog gave us a look that said, "Have you forgotten something?"

21

The house always seems empty when guests have departed, but we are always glad to fall back into our normal routine, which is usually on hold for the duration. Jim and I had continued to work together for seven months and developed a good working relationship. Most of our work came from my contacts and recommendations and for me it was good to have somebody of like-minded thinking to share my ideas with. Most partnerships develop and succeed when one takes responsibility as the pilot, and one provides the essential back up of the co-pilot, and both parties accept that, as it works for the overall good and success. Such was the case with us, some skills we shared and others one of us specialised in.

Now with Christmas approaching we could see the workload trailing off. One of Jim's new contacts was a chap whose business was aiding English folk to locate and purchase property here in France, and in addition he extended his assistance to finding trustworthy workmen. One of his clients had extended a kitchen by knocking down two walls and was now looking for someone to make good the electrics and plumbing which were left hanging in mid-air.

The property was further away than our preferred area of working, but we agreed to meet the client to discuss how we could help; they were charming and seemed relieved when we agreed to undertake what appeared to be few days' work. Probing a little further, it soon became apparent that there was a lot of work there and so we enlightened our new client to our capabilities. We must have made a good impression for they kept us busy for the following three and a half months. Jim and I were relieved that we had work to carry us over into the following year and our thoughts could turn to the approach of Christmas.

Jenny especially loves Christmas and her preparations were well advanced. For me, I was already planning how I could advance our work here during the break. Thoughts of sand and cement, building blocks and plasterboard, were in my mind. So we sacrificed cost on Christmas to stock up on materials.

"Mince pies" she exclaimed, startling me from my thoughts.

"What?" I said

"Mince pies, I'm going to make mince pies."

Bewildered by this sudden proclamation, I enquired. "Where on earth did that idea come from?"

Taking a deep breath she replied. "Well, what's missing is the smell of Christmas cooking, so I want to make a load of mince pies, and I want to pack them into nice boxes of six, tie them with Christmas ribbon and give them to friends as presents." Taking another deep breath she expanded further. "We have made many close friendships here, French and English, and I thought it was a lovely idea. The brits would love this little touch of home Christmas, and our new French pals here would enjoy the experience of tasting of this British tradition".

Gerard and Marie at the Pizzeria St. Pierre had always extended a special welcome to us and it was a pleasure for us to show our appreciation with this little gift. They were truly grateful for our touch of friendship as like two excited children they peered into the box and inspected the contents. In addition, we also would have mince pies for those little snacks when you fancy something tasty, and save a few Euros into the bargain.

Christmas day was a quiet time, a time for reflection on our achievements, and time together, time also to talk through and plan our future projects. So firing our enthusiasm between us, boxing afternoon we dragged out the mixer and started laying block work for the second and third bedroom walls. By the time I returned to work we had again made a valuable advancement towards the other two completed bedrooms, and found the time to relax, recharge our batteries, and have some well-earned fun. Neither of us can recall now where we went for New Year, but it must have been good because our diary records January the first as being – 'a lazy day zonked out with hangovers.'

The hour long journey to work each day brought me firmly back to the reality that to fund it all I need to spend more time working on other people's houses, than that which I could devote to working on ours. In consequence, any small progress towards our goal became a major source of achievement, and we took great pleasure in it. But our pot was nearing the bottom and had to be replenished.

Laden with tools and material and our lunch boxes full of food, we again made the two-hour return journey for a further three months. We gutted and refitted the said extended kitchen, renewed the ceiling above, repainting all the beams and ceilings in the kitchen and day room, and fitted double doors to close an open plan area. When we thought we were nearing the end, they would ask if we could quote for something else. We changed a downstairs bathroom to a utility room. Replaced old sink fittings for new, added lights and sockets and repaired faulty circuits, created cupboards, then to meet a time schedule, Jenny came with us and decorated a bathroom.

During the installation of an underground gas holding tank, the driver of the contractor's digger had lifted and fractured a forty millimetre water main which supplied the house and the adjacent out buildings. A large hole, three metres deep was quickly filling with water until I located the stop cock which was two hundred metres uphill where their drive met the road.

It was obviously unsatisfactory where it was, so I suggested that I could not only repair the water-main but also provide a manhole and stopcock adjacent to the house, and prevent a similar problem from becoming a major catastrophe in the future, when two hundred metres of water filled pipe at forty millimetres diameter, would have to be drained before a repair could be affected. The shocked look on our clients face as he visualised the bill from the water company, evaporated as he readily agreed to my suggestion.

During a later conversation between us they complimented us by saying,

"Do you know what we like about you guys? When you come across a problem, you just find a solution and overcome it." They had obviously had previous frustration with the lack of cross-over between French tradesmen.

The culmination of our efforts on site was the cement rendering of the outside of the house. Unhappy with the look of it, our client's wife admitted that in its day it was probably very contemporary, but now she wanted something different. To a small area at the rear, we applied our suggested alternative for her approval. She did approve and following confirmation with her husband we gained another few weeks work. It was three hundred square metres plus, and some of it over four metres high, so we knew we needed someone to mix for us.

Jim's son Oliver had been working with us on and off over the months and so we brought him in on the job. He proved invaluable to Jim and me as we teetered on top of the scaffolding, feeding us with bucket after bucket of wet cement, for three weeks. Some mornings, when the sunrise allowed, we started early to finish a section before the heat dried it too quickly. Some days, we stayed late to finish a wall, and still the hour's drive back home. When finished, and the debris was all cleaned away, we did a tour of approval with the client.

Admitting that anything would look better than it did, she expressed that the finished house looked far better than she thought it would. For Jim and me it was a good feeling; but tainted. This was the last job I would be working on with Jim.

I had decided to split and return to working on my own. I had felt the tension growing within me over the previous weeks and when I discussed it with Jenny, I realised what was causing it. The close working relationship I had with Jim had changed and I felt a barrier forming between us. The Jim I knew had gone and been replaced by a different man. Two's company, three's a crowd; especially if the third is family. The flexibility I enjoyed on my own and to a certain extent with Jim, was being overtaken with organising three people and the necessary thought and planning for what had now become a small business.

Two guys working together, earning a reasonable living was one thing, but this was something else, and I didn't want it. Jim took it hard, like a personal insult, and became more and more distant. I was feeling like an outsider. The fun together disappeared and during those last weeks we rarely spoke, feeling sad when for a brief instant I would see a return of the pal I once knew. We kept in touch but conversations were cool and Jim continued with the client for many weeks afterwards. For myself, I knew it was a good decision as I felt a great weight lift afterward.

Back in January, the New Year winter had deepened. Our stock of wood from the roof was disappearing fast and for the first time we found ourselves looking for logs to buy.

A friend introduced us to a farmer with logs for sale and we met on the edge of his woodland. We agreed his price and he used a spray can to mark off the two cubic metres we wanted, money changed hands and he left us to return on our own and collect it the next day with the trailer.

It was cut, split and stacked in one-metre lengths on ground that didn't look firm enough for a car and a loaded trailer, so we had to carry it a few logs at a time across the twenty metres to the car and trailer which was parked on the firmer ground of the access track.

Two trips and we now had enough seasoned oak split logs to see us through the winter, weather permitting. All we had to do was cut it into lengths more conducive to the stove.

Our eleven ducklings were not ducklings anymore and feeding them all had become costly. With so many birds in the pen we had been allowing them the freedom of the grounds but they always seemed to prefer the flower beds and garden. In short they were becoming a nuisance and we had to remind ourselves of the primary objective of keeping ducks and chickens; so we decided to reduce the numbers.

The Restaurant de Grande Bois was one of our favourite venues after a busy day when we just didn't feel like cooking. We always chose the *Plat de Jour* at ten Euros and received a five course blow out with wine included and the second course was usually the delicious home-made pâté.

Lunch times the restaurant was always busy with commercial regulars, but evenings were a quiet affair, and so we had a chance to socialise with our hosts during coffee, as we were usually the last to leave.

We have never managed to work out if there is a relationship between Yves the chef and Chantelle who serves us, or whether they are just business partners? She is a large bubbly woman with a ready infectious laugh, while Yves is shy and retiring, before that is, he has had a few cognacs behind the bar when all the evening's cooking is done. Full and contented we met them at the bar to pay our bill. The tin box under the counter rattled for my change, which as usual I will probably not pick up, and I prepared to ask my question as two extra cognacs mysteriously appeared.

"If I provided him with four ducks, plucked and cleaned..." I asked, "...would he make me his pâté and share the proceeds with us?"

My timing after his cognacs proved correct as he readily agreed, "*Mae Oui*", so we shook hands on the deal and I agreed to return with the birds in two weeks' time. Sometime later, fourteen small Kilner jars adorned a shelf in our food cupboard, but unfortunately they didn't last very long because we couldn't stop eating it.

Sadly while dining there one later evening we noticed the absence of Chantelle, and when prudent we asked Yves if she was ill.

"No" he replied, "She's gone."

We were stunned by this sudden departure but said no more to him on the matter, as he was obviously embarrassed about it. They were a good team together and we remembered a previous conversation when we had been complimenting their cuisine.

Chantelle told us that their idea was to open a restaurant which provided the sort of food that grandma would create. They certainly succeeded in that. Yves struggled on for a while but it was obvious he couldn't manage on his own doing everything. A few new faces came and went, but in the end he gave it up. Now when we pass, we look at the four apartments it was converted to, and remember with fondness the happy times we spent there.

22

My mobile phone rang...it was Jenny.

"I think you had better come home, there is an awful smell of burning plastic coming from the *grenier* I think."

An hour away from home and it sounded like the house was about to catch fire, great! When weighing up all the possibilities of a fire in the loft space, an hour-long drive was a long time. Fortunately mid-morning tended to be quieter on the roads, other motorists and Gendarmes included, just as well as I do believe I might have broken the speed limit once or twice; must have done as I have never been able to duplicate the same short time for the journey!

Exiting the car before the engine had stopped its revolutions, I was met by Jenny.

"It's OK, don't panic I've found the problem."

A quick wiring job seven years ago to speed up the use of a holiday home had never been attended to for a more permanent and safe fixture. Time and the constant passing of electrical current had heated a connection box to melting point.

A prompt repair had us back up and running again but now the proposed re-wiring of everything, except our new rooms, had taken a sudden leap to the top of the list. A priority was the installation of a new fuse box/consumer unit to balance the load and separate different circuits and at the same time making provisions for additions at a later date as our work progressed.

Then on a day when it poured with rain non-stop, the second bedroom took a leap towards completion. Under the barn canopy in the dry and next to our pile of sand, we set about mixing the mortar for the walls.

Applying it was a hazardous job because the only part of the floor that was concreted was the part that the walls were built on. It was a case of step down to load my hawk from the barrow, and then step up to apply it to the walls. When I came home from work and few days later, I was amazed to find that Jenny had concreted the middle section on her own.

Finally eleven days later we closed the door on the room, decorated, carpeted and all its furniture in place, ready for the next visitor, Rodney.

He has a degree in mathematics and he taught for many years, but a later career change took him into the world of computers. Now he lectures in computer language at the seminars of multinational companies. In constant demand, he rarely takes a break or holiday, so for him a few days off without wearing a suit were to be relished.

On arrival we gave him the tour and progress report and then, following a comment by Jenny about her need to prepare the veggie plot for the coming season, she gratefully accepted his offer to spend some of his week here relaxing while weeding for her.

We spent a happy evening catching up and exchanging news over dinner, and with a promise of a few good days ahead, we all looked forward to helping move winter on its way from the garden. Of course, late February does not provide weather you can rely on, but the following morning's offering greeted us with a little surprise.

A warm southerly breeze had lifted the temperature considerably, but with no relent it continued to get stronger as the morning moved towards midday, no gusts, just a constant strong wind.

After lunch Jenny retired for her siesta while Rodney and I sat to read. The book rested on his lap, open like his mouth, not closed like his eyes, and his snoring almost drowned the howling wind whistling through the ill-fitting door!

For three days and three nights the wind kept up the onslaught without ceasing. Venturing outside for anything was not pleasant at all; then as sudden as it had arrived, it just stopped. My thoughts over those few days turned briefly to the folk who live in the path of the Mistral winds. You can understand why the divorce rate rises dramatically, and crimes are blamed on the Mistral. They say it can blow the ears off a donkey.

We are always sad when friends go back home, if only because the veggie plot didn't receive the promised weeding after all. We forgave him though because to show us his gratitude for looking after him, he had taken Jenny to a garden centre and bought her two sapling fruit trees for our meagre orchard.

She was delighted and both trees quickly established themselves and started to show promise. She was definitely not delighted when a month later she stood on the drive with the remnants of one tree in her arms and tears flowing freely down her cheeks.

On one of his visits before we split, Jim had excelled himself. On leaving, he had reversed his car over the tree flattening it to the ground. Then as he moved off it caught under his car and was dragged halfway along the drive until it freed itself.

Completely unaware of this major transgression, he gave a cheery wave and disappeared from our sight, leaving Jenny standing distraught on the drive. Replanted and tended lovingly it survived for a while but in the end it gave up the fight. We never told Jim, preferring to forget the sad event.

I always love the changing seasons.

Summer with its heat and warm lazy evenings outside with friends, finishing a bottle of wine as the sun descends and gives way to the chorus of frogs and crickets. Sleepless nights spent under a thin sheet with a fan attempting to circulate the airless heat.

The cooler days of autumn that bring the first fall of leaves, and swallows lining the overhead cables ready to depart for warmer climes.

In winter we await the crispness of the first frosts, and I can see nature's secret places revealed to us once more through the silent bleakness. But spring time always brings new surprises. The first warm days that awaken the garden from its slumber remind me of all the effort required in the coming weeks. I look for, and I am rewarded by the arrival of each migrating visitor that flies within sight or sound.

This spring I rebuilt the pantry to great improvement, while outside a Wren had similar building ideas. Industrially flitting to and fro across the garden he had discovered a cavity in the block work of the bar-be-cue and was busily lining it with moss from the adjacent lawn edges.

After a week's absence he returned and continued. He hadn't been very far away because we could hear his song which is apparently the longest and strongest of all British bird song. Strange we thought that he should stop and start like that but my research has told me that a male Wren will build two or three nests, then when he has successfully found a mate, he will show her each one, and allow her to choose. Sounds about right!

Frequently heard, but rarely seen, the Golden Oriole is a very secretive bird. In springtime and throughout the summer months we hear them in the woodland next to the house and in the trees by the river in the valley, never quite close enough to warrant investigation, even with binoculars.

On a rare occasion while I was converting an upper room without a window fitted, I heard the familiar call, a short melodious piping whistle, and cautiously peeped around the opening. Oh what an utter joy to behold a pair of them flitting amongst the branches so close to the house, a sight I hope to be repeated.

Likewise we had heard the Hoopoe and seen fleeting glimpses as it moved from tree to tree, but not what you would call a good look. At the same pal's house I heard one outside and when I arrived home later I excitedly related to Jenny how close my bird had been, sitting on an electricity pylon for me to clearly see.

"I know what you mean", she said, "There have been a pair of them feeding on the top lawn here." Her revelation did deflate me slightly but she then went on to say. "But I did video them."

We soon had the camera hooked up to the television and shared her triumph at this excellent footage. A rare summer visitor to England, here during the summer they are in good numbers, even if you can't always see them, you can hear them. Cinnamon neck, chest and shoulders give way to black and white striped body and wings. They have an erectile crest which I have yet to see, and a long curved beak for probing the ground for food. When the crest is lowered they look like they have a pencil stuck across the top of their head.

Musing one day, Jenny announced, "Here we are with summer just around the corner and we still can't use the pool. Are we ever going to get it finished?"

The dictionary definition of nagging is, "Constant repetition of unpleasant truth." Well, who believes in dictionaries anyway? But she was right, what we needed was a shot in the arm to spur us on. So we ordered the edging *margelles* tiles and the special carpeting for under the liner.

It worked and on a fine day we fired up the mixer and began concreting the dive well. We had cut and laid steel reinforcement over the entire base, and with the shaping difficulties present for the dive well, I decided to rough concrete the shape first. This proved a good solution as we were able to do it a few mixes at a time, getting the shape and slope right in readiness for the final over screed later.

Jenny didn't have the strength to mix, barrow and tip the final mix for the screed, so she elected to lay and trowel instead. Spraying a latex bonding on first she achieved an excellent finish under my visual direction for the shaping from above. In a few hours half of the area was done when Jacques arrived and took over from her, relieving her aching arms and knees. In a short time we were soon standing poolside admiring the finished floor.

The next morning I looked with satisfaction to the finished bottom - at last, and discovered that a pigeon had walked over the unhardened screed of the dive well looking for a drink; thanks Beryl!

Where the walls met the bottom I later cemented a 10 centimetre fillet to soften the angle and we were now ready to fit the liner. We paid great attention to sweeping and vacuuming the base first to remove any tiny stones, and then carefully laid the under-carpet, a synthetic material designed to absorb any imperfections in the screed from damaging the liner. Smoothing and flattening in stocking feet and with dusk approaching, we were reluctant to leave it unprotected overnight in case of rain or a damp night, and so ventured to fit the liner.

Manufactured in the United States, the quality liner weighed a tonne. In its box it took great effort by both of us to heave it into the centre of the pool without disturbing the under-carpet.

Unboxed and laid in position we unrolled it to find a ninety degree turn was in order. Unrolled again we excitedly began to insert the edges into place at the rim, working toward the deeper end. Clipping the final edge into place I hooked one leg over the rim and climbed out.

"How am I supposed to get out?" exclaimed Jenny.

I said, "Just like I did!"

Frustrated she replied, "I can't get my leg up there."

So with the aid of the step ladder, I pulled her out. We stood in the moonlight on the side excited that we had pushed on and pleased that we were now ready to vacuum the air from under the liner to achieve a creaseless fit and commence filling with water the next day.

The following day, when I arrived home for lunch Jenny excitedly directed me to the pool. Eager to continue, she explained how during the morning she had removed a small section of the liner from the rim and inserted the vacuum cleaner pipe two thirds of the way towards the bottom, as directed by the instructions, and taped it in place to seal off the air.

On starting the motor the liner had been sucked into place, removing all the creases, and she had begun to fill our pool with water.

Suddenly all our hard work and frustration was becoming a swimming pool as fresh clear water - a quarter of the total required, lay invitingly on the bottom. Unsure how long it would take to fill completely, we turned the hose off overnight and resuming the next morning it was full by early afternoon. Twenty two and a half hours. We always knew we would be pleased when it was usable, but we were absolutely stunned by how fantastic the liner looked, priding ourselves on the choice of pattern.

Mains water temperature did not allow even the bravest souls to take the first plunge and so we continued to wait while the sun warmed the water. I knew that as soon as the pool was full I would want to test the pump and filtration, so I was glad at this stage that I had spent the time and installed it previously.

The filtration system is a little different from those normally installed as it all sits neatly under the pool steps. A manifold runs left to right between the bottoms of the hand rails of the steps and supports two fifteen centimetre tubes which house the filters. The tops of the tubes lie just under the water surface. On one tube a floating skimmer draws in surface debris, while the other draws from under the surface; and from here, via the manifold it passes up one arm of the pool steps, through the above ground pump to return down the other hand rail. Re-entering the pool just above the base it causes a circularized current around the pool.

We had never seen the system in operation but something appeared to be causing a restriction in the water flow because the skimmer wasn't working. After a couple of hours testing all my pipe work we decided it must be something to do with the flow though the step pipes. Sure enough and after the removal of a good quantity of industrial paper towelling from inside the pipes we soon had the flow as we thought it should be and the skimmer working perfectly.

Brave naturists we might be, but we both agreed it would still have to absorb a good quantity of the sun's heat before we ventured to test the water and we left it to its own devices to do just that.

They all seem to have busy lives, so when our Sons and Daughters descend on us with their partners they all prefer to spend most of their time here just chilling out in the sun, or in winter months they take advantage of our huge video and DVD collections and relax in front of the fire after we have waited on them hand and foot.

This for Lynsey and Nick was a third visit, and the first with a proper bedroom. This time and against the norm, they left us in peace for a few days to venture south and discover the delights of the Pyrenees. The evening of their return, we decided that Gerard and Marie's pizzeria was a good place to hear all about the trip.

Lynsey rarely drinks, and in relaxed holiday mode she was soon the life and soul of the evening after a couple of glasses of wine. Nick as usual was trying to empty the lager barrel. The silly singsong on the way home had us all in fits of giggles, and was a nice finish to the event. But Lynsey had her own ideas how to round off the day.

Ambling toward the door hand in hand with Nick, she released his hand and turned away. Baffled, Nick watched as she walked away removing her clothes, as Jenny and I looked quickly to each other and quietly spoke the words, "She's gonna christen the pool."

Reaching the edge she tossed her knickers on the grass behind her and bravely jumped straight in and began swimming up and down berating Nick for being a wimp and not joining her.

"I'm going to have to go in," said Nick, "…or I'm never going to hear the last of it."

Arm in arm with Lynsey he reassuringly stated that it wasn't as cold as he expected. We left them to it after that, and although it was some time later that they both appeared back indoors we decided that they had not been up to any hanky-panky. But that's their secret!

23

When Keith and Margaret let us know that they will be arriving for a few weeks, we usually spend a few hours at their barn before they arrive, so that they can set-up their caravan without having to first cut grass and strim back weeds. To show their appreciation Keith readily pitched in to help us with the back filling of the pool dig.

A weak dry mix of sand and cement fills the gap between the walls of galvanised steel and the dig hole, which was then to be hosed with water to consolidate and harden. For us a little more involved as the dig sides had collapsed from their original straight shape and we had to correctly lay the drainage piping to assist the offending source to by-pass the pool and continue at a correct fall back to its original route to the pond.

To do this and collect any other underground water Keith helped me lay perforated plastic underground tubing, wrapped in a porous material to keep plant roots out but allowing water to enter. Marking the outer side of the pool at both ends for high and low level soon showed that the fall was not great and so we needed to pay attention to our decreasing marks every half a metre to achieve a decline with no flat spots which would allow water to lie.

Not as easy as it sounds as the tubing has a mind of its own and refuses to lie unrolled and flat, preferring to recoil at will and cuff anybody in close proximity. We soon learned that a few well-placed stones helped to hold it in place until sufficient mix was covering.

Fully back filled and hardened a few days later we were encouraged to see once again a constant trickle of water entering the pond.

Eymet is a strange place; but for me it offered two good things. Firstly my chiropractor resided there, and secondly there was an excellent computer engineer there also, both of whom have successfully got me back up and running. South west France is an area of outstanding summer weather but it is also very susceptible to violent electric storms. Without protection, a surge through the power or telephone line can knock out a PC immediately.

Fortunately I was very new to computing and had very little data of importance stored, when one such storm wiped out the mother board and processor within my PC, but my engineer managed to retrieve all the data from the hard disk. Phew! The cost set us back by a few tonnes of sand and a good few bags of cement.

Eymet, pronounced aymay, is a *Bastide* town, which roughly translated means walled town. The history of this region during the middle ages has shaped many features of the area, including the town planning. The necessity of defending a settlement and the civic functional ability of it has proven well as most of these towns' buildings date back to that time.

Today around the towns' central squares, the shops and offices have been sympathetically repaired and maintained, and local authorities have repaved and upgraded the public areas without detracting from the medieval essence.

As these towns grew the streets and alleys that radiate out at right angles show many different faces as the financial ability decreases the further out from the centre one ventures.

Like so many French towns Eymet is a mixture and often a rusting pair of gates will hide a beautiful courtyard and superbly renovated mansion while next door might be a building in serious neglect.

Closed shops that were once thriving businesses show little remaining paint upon the old wooden facades which are slowly rotting and falling away; windows festooned with cobwebs and dust.

A discreet closer look through one window revealed a scene behind of a carpenter's workshop. It told a story of a man who simply became too old to continue and one day laid down his tools at the end of a day's work, retired to his living quarters above and never went back.

It is an area which attracts many second home owners; Parisians, Dutch, Belgians and English have all bought properties and brought them back to the splendour they once displayed and Eymet is an area that has particularly attracted the English for permanent residency.

The percentage of English to French is I am told quite high and some resentment has crept in.

The local supermarket has sections which sell a variety of products from Heinz beans to Ambrosia creamed rice pudding and Bisto gravy.

One of the bars is like a trip to any English local pub. The same customers sit every night on the same chairs and tables, having the same conversations with the same people about the same topics. I personally find all this a little sad.

I ponder on the question as to why people are attracted to live in a beautiful and historic area of France, an area which has developed a culture and social structure so rich and warm; and then re-adopt all the habits and behaviour they came here to avoid?

Fortunately a vast number of English people have integrated well, make a firm effort to speak the language and have formed close friendships with French families who accept that there are always the exceptions that prove the rule.

July sunshine was bathing the garden in glorious heat. Across the meadow in front of the house the rising heat shimmered, stirring a faint movement in the blades of grass. The only sound I could hear was coming from a speck in the sky as a mewing buzzard circled higher and higher to glide on open wings to newer hunting grounds.

A gentle sleepiness came over me as I lay there naked absorbing the heat, and while awaiting the time to take my next cool-off in the pool, I fell into a gentle doze. Suddenly I became aware of voices on the drive; unusual as most visitors would arrive by car and knowing our habits in the sunshine they would sound their arrival with a sharp toot on the horn. Sleepily I grabbed for the sarong and stood to greet whoever would be coming into view any second.

Pleasantly surprised, I greeted our neighbours Jacques and Veronique with their daughter Marie-Ann. Although we had regularly swapped *bonjour* if we passed them, shamefully we had never actually introduced ourselves during the two years since they had become neighbours when building a new house along the lane.

They had come to invite us to their '*crémaillère*', their house warming party. It took us a while to cotton on, but they were saying that after two years they thought it was about time. Marie-Ann proudly produced the invitation she had carefully printed on her PC, and drew our attention to the wording inside. They had thoughtfully written the inner details for us in English. Jenny was pleased to discover that Veronique, or as she prefers Vero, did speak a little of our language, and with Marie-Ann who was learning English at school and keen to put it to use, the three of them managed to have a good chat.

During the winter months without the foliage cover, Jacques had been watching the progress of our pool from the road as he passed by, and he was interested in having a good look up close, so we did the man thing and talked pumps and *piscines*. They were so warm that we felt as if we had known them for years, and as they left a while later we both agreed how much we looked forward to their house-warming.

To the north and east their house nestled against a corner of oak woodland and has views across open fields to the south and west. The small south facing garden sloped steeply down from the terrace towards their swimming pool, and was planted with many young shrubs and borders.

A few weeks later we arrived for the occasion at midday and were surprised to see that to the side of the house there was sufficient space to erect a marquee set with tables and chairs for a hundred people and room still for the drinks bar. We greeted our hosts who directed us to the bar for an aperitif, and we received more greetings from folk interested in whom we were and where we came from.

It always comes as a pleasant surprise when the French people we meet use some English words. Not so much for the communication assistance, but because it always breaks the ice on the on-going conversation when I ask in French, "Ah, you speak a little English?"

Invariably they will deny it or say, "Just a leetle, but English is very difficult."

I add my further comments about the difficulty for us of verb conjugation and all the different tenses the French have. It seems to bring us closer together and foster a friendliness that would otherwise not be there if we made no attempt.

For me, plunging into conversation dispels the English inherent fear of making a fool of one's self and being seen to do and say the correct thing. Our pronunciation attempts evoke rapturous laughter which we have learned to share, but someone is always ready to patiently correct us until we have it right. We don't always remember later but that's another story.

Jenny was pleased to find François and Rene, sitting chatting with the mother of another French friend we knew, and went over to say hello. I started a conversation with a chap who was a bit of a local historian and I learned another little gem.

Our house was to the south of Jacques and Vero's, out of sight from their garden behind the brow of the hill. Between us was a small cottage owned by the widow of a Bordeaux carpenter. This small cottage had been used as a holiday home for her and her mentally handicapped son, but now it was on the market to be sold. I corrected my storyteller when he mistakenly thought that this little cottage was where we lived but he told me this story relating to it anyway.

In past years it was owned and farmed on a very small scale by a rotund Frenchman and his wife and they took great pride in their wine cellar under the house.

Access to this cellar from a small door outside and to the rear of the house was no secret, but somebody was depleting his wine stocks during the night on a regular basis. Unable to catch the perpetrator red handed he had resorted to basic science and rigged up a tripwire from the door to raise the alarm.

Sure enough it worked and in darkness he pursued the culprit over the fields armed with his shotgun. Firing what was probably a warning blast, he was later mortified to learn that he had shot the man dead and unable to cope with the shame he later committed suicide. His wife disappeared and was never to be seen again. I mentioned this at a later date to François and Michele, Jacques father and they both confirmed the story.

By now the number of guests had swollen to full proportions and the endless supply of aperitifs had every one in good humour, and hungry. Instinct tells a Frenchman when food is imminent and the tables and chairs began to fill with people. We had the same idea and joined them as platters of lovingly prepared food began to arrive and soon covered the tables.

A prune tray could be teardrop shaped or rectangular and about ninety centimetres long, has open slats across the bottom and was designed for drying plums into prunes. South west France is world famous for the '*Pruneau d'Agen*' which is now a much commercialised business. But in days gone by growers could have many hectares of trees, or just a few in a garden and many growers would have had a prune oven somewhere on the property.

The older wooden trays are much sought after as decorative memorabilia, but in this instance covered in aluminium foil they made excellent serving trays for our food. Trying to recall now the full menu is rather difficult, but I do remember that there was a constant flow of many courses throughout the whole afternoon, and into the evening.

Teenagers and children had been taking full advantage of the pool most of the afternoon, and now after many glasses of wine, some of the adults were having similar ideas.

Some party-goers were looking for something a little more entertaining than a good conversation with long lost family members and friends. The protestations of one lady, suitably dressed for the occasion in a nice dress, high heels and a posh hair do, went ignored as she flew through the air and landed with a great splash in the pool.

It later transpired that with good humour she had been pushing her luck and winding up this chap all afternoon and accepted her just reward graciously in the joviality of the event. She must have expected this retribution as she later appeared just as polished in a new outfit.

By late afternoon the summer heat was beginning to get to everybody. The pool was in constant use while the oldies were content inside the cooler space of the *sous sol*, an under floor space below entrance level, which serves as garage, utility room, winter drying area for the washing, boiler room, etc.

Hot and sticky, I also could not resist the inviting waters of the pool, even though it had turned a bit milky with the more than usual usage. Unprepared for a swim and not able to swim as I normally would, I had to empty my pockets and swim in my shorts. It was glorious to cool off and I can well understand why the fully dressed lady bore no ill feeling towards the person who jettisoned her.

I was however not prepared to spend the rest of the evening in wet shorts, so I quickly walked back down the road to change my shorts and feed the dogs, and I thought it would be a good idea to return with my banjo. A few people were sitting on the patio playing guitars and singing and as I joined them the unusual shape of the case received great interest. They were obviously keen to hear me play and I set the tempo with something a bit lively. I soon had the guitarists jamming along, and later relinquished the instrument to one of them who was keen to try something new.

Soon as darkness approached the *sous sol* took on a new identity as the disco began and we musicians gave over the responsibility of entertainment.

It was entertaining to watch people after a day's soporific intake of food and drink, and how they suddenly became revitalised when the disco music beckoned. Before long they were all on the floor with smiles on their faces showing either their age or their skill as the music throbbed from the speakers.

Dancing always makes people hungry, how after what we had all eaten I cannot say but it does. Our hosts also must have known because after an hour of intense dancing and bodily gyration a rich aroma of bar-be-cued food began to arrive. I did earlier wonder what was to become of all the left over salads. They had all been re-dressed and re-stored in the refrigerated container behind the house, and there they sat awaiting the serving of huge platters of sausages and belly pork, with yet more salads and accompaniments.

Jenny has what we both call her 'switch'. After her cancer treatment in England her consultant said that sometimes she could expect bouts of unexpected tiredness to overtake her for no apparent reason. Normally I can recognise these happenings and discreetly ask. We had filled ourselves with food and drink, learned something about our local history, swam and skylarked, musically entertained, shared precious moments with dear friends and neighbours, danced our socks off and filled our stomachs yet again; and now all the signs were there, Jenny's switch had gone, she was ready for bed and so in fact was I. We left our hosts with our grateful thanks for a wonderful day and firm in the assumption that their house was now truly warmed. The temporary diversion of the party was a welcome diversion, because in two days I was due to leave for a week in England.

24

Jenny always misses me terribly on the rare occasions when I'm away. She is perfectly capable of looking after herself and always surprises me on her achievements while I'm not at home. It's just that she doesn't like to be alone, and I worry because she will often attempt something that would be better left for the two of us, and then she ends up having some sort of minor accident.

But this excursion was special. It was the eightieth birthday of my dear Father, and he didn't know I was coming. Greg collected me from Stansted airport and together we arrived midmorning unannounced at his front door.

Never one to show excessive emotion he was visibly impressed as I hugged him at this great achievement in age. After a lengthy explanation of all the conniving between my step mother and Greg, he dragged me into the garden to view his latest construction.

Unimpressed with the size and available space for all his tools and material stocks inside the garage, he had constructed a new shed/workshop at the bottom of his garden across nearly the full width of it and as big as a large caravan. Ably assisted by his wife Minnie, he had made it double skinned and insulated it and installed an electrical supply and heating.

Rightly proud of their achievement, he now had room back inside the garage for his large BMW motorcycle which, weather permitting, gets regular usage at their combined age of one hundred and sixty plus. He has said though that now when he drops it he finds it hard to lift it back up again. This all gives me fresh hope for what Jenny and I have to achieve, thirty years younger!

Time spent with Dad is very precious as the older I become the more I realise that these times are limited. Fortunately they are both in excellent health for their age and are able to visit here and take pride in our achievements.

He knew he was going to celebrate by lunching at an Italian lakeside restaurant with my brother and his wife, and although my daughter Emily couldn't make it because of work commitments he still had his two sons and a grandson to share his day, three generations of us.

Back at his house later we all shared the pleasure while he opened his presents. Jenny had hand made him a special birthday card and right on cue she had telephoned to offer her personalised wishes for him just after he had read it. At that age it is always difficult to choose a gift; we all hoped that he found many hours of pleasure from his new DVD player.

Since residing in France one of the very few things I miss is the Old English pub; the smell of beer and wood smoke absorbed into the fabric of the building, ancient oaken beams and faded wallpaper, and ceilings turned brown with years of dedicated tobacco smokers and a landlord with a ready smile to pull a pint of proper English real ale, the sort of local that always finds an old friend who has also popped in for a quick pint and a chat. It's an institution unique to English pubs that the European bar doesn't quite fulfil in the same way.

I had a few spare days so I spent a happy couple of hours in one such tavern with two pals catching up on the years. I learned to my interest that a friend from before my children were born had located his business close to my Dad's house.

Standing unannounced in the entrance of his workshop, he registered my presence and looked up.

“My god!” He exclaimed as a big smile grew bigger across his face. “I was thinking only the other day about whatever had happened to you.”

I hadn’t seen Chas for years and together we worked out when we last saw each other by recalling the ages of our children, and we were both amazed that over twenty five years had passed since.

A little grey at the temples and the crow’s feet to the side of his smiley eyes a little more pronounced, but he was exactly the same Chas I knew all those years before. I stopped him working for nearly an hour as we swapped recent history, before leaving with a promise that we would keep in touch and with my ego boosted insofar as he said I hadn’t changed a bit.

It is a strange feeling to see again the familiar places of my home town, to realise that here are my roots and many old friends; but it has changed. Once thriving local shops have closed and re-opened as estate agents, tattoo parlours or fast food outlets. Gone are the corner shop butchers, bakers and ironmongers, victim to the supermarket giants.

In my school days, to earn extra pocket money I used to leave my house at five am on a Saturday and walk two streets away to rouse our local baker at his home. Opening the front door in his pyjamas, he would return upstairs to dress while I made the tea. Then together we drove back to open the bakery opposite my house, to fire up the wood burning oven for the day’s bread.

While he monitored my fire up to baking temperature I swept and cleaned the floor of the little shop. Above the sloping bread and cake wire racks, the upper walls were covered in his certificates of merit for baking.

Using a worn and squeaky sack barrow I ferried the flour from the store room along the yard of cobbled stone. I watched as he measured the flour into the huge dough mixer, by guesswork attained from years of experience.

It amazed me how the dough doubled in size, then cut and rolled into loaf shapes it was placed on baking trays to rise again in the proving cupboards under the smooth wooden benches.

As the first batches of bread began to give off that wonderful aroma from the oven, his semi-retired father would join us from the integral house and start working with the second mix of the day.

Both bakers were perfectly groomed gentlemen, outfitted in white collar and ties, sleeves rolled up above the elbow and a crisp white apron from waist to ankle, just above polished shoes.

While we waited for the first batch of bread to cook, Harry the old baker lit a gas ring next to the oven and set a frying pan of sausages to cook. If he was in a good mood he'd give me one of the sausages that were sizzling in the pan, wrapped in one of their bread rolls. For a starving teenager this was a rare treat that I relished, and I ate it with the butter dripping through my fingers.

This sustenance for a hungry boy would keep me going as I carried tray after tray of hot bread to the cooling racks in the yard, trying to avoid burning my inner arms.

After my speedy lunch break I had the unenviable task of the week's clean down. On hands and knees I groped under the mixers scraping hardened dough from the tiled floor before mopping and drying. Every machine had to be thoroughly cleaned whether used or not, and all the ingredients replaced to the places of storage at the far end of the yard in the cool room.

Lastly I cleaned the cobbled yard with a stiff broom and hose pipe before finally after a stringent inspection of every inch I was paid my small recompense and allowed to leave.

I must have enjoyed the occupation because during one summer of school holidays I worked six days a week for the entire six weeks.

Once in the area many years later, I took Jenny into the shop one quiet afternoon and received a warm welcome. Of course the old baker had passed away and all the machines had a sign of redundancy and the oven was cold. When I questioned him about it he said that he no longer baked, the demand wasn't there anymore. No more daily bread, no selection of cakes and pastries, no more sausage rolls that I minced the fillings for with onion tears streaming down my face, no more special orders for his prize winning wedding cakes, but just enough rolls to fill the demand for his daily sandwich fillings.

This is what two generations of master bakers were now reduced to for survival; no more than another sandwich bar, such is the price of progress in our busy lives. His face showed the sadness behind the smile but the crisp apron and polished shoes remained the same.

The experience made me reflect on the French Boulanger; his shop full with daily customers for his different variety of breads and patisserie, seven days a week he bakes and his shop is thriving. The French boulangerie is an institution like the old English Tavern; I for one hope they both stay that way.

Progress towards finishing the third bedroom was a slow affair. My temporary tool bench - the old door straddling across two piles of building blocks - had gone, and now that the room was empty and swept clean ready for the next stage of progress, we began to see the potential of this large room for our bedroom.

With the fully glazed end wall, we could imagine sitting up in bed with cup in hand, watching the rising sun as it appeared over the hill on the far side of the valley. Then looking upwards at the underside of the roof tiles we came back to reality.

The ceiling had to be insulated and plaster boarded, and three walls - one of block work and two of stone, both needed a finish applied. The insulating of the ceiling was a job we both didn't relish. Cutting and fitting sheets of insulation board - double thickness, between irregular oak beams to achieve a reasonable fit capable of keeping the winter heating in, was a tedious and time consuming process that took us more time than expected.

Events though had taken a turn to make us speed things up considerably. Greg and Emily, along with Eugene, an ex-partner of their mother, had taken advantage of some very cheap flights for a quick two day visit, and to accommodate them we urgently needed to use our new room. The boys would happily double up in the same room; Emily of course needed one of her own which left us to make some sort of temporary sleeping quarters in a building site. We would be looking at the early morning rising sun a bit earlier than anticipated.

Jenny panicked as she always wants everything perfect, while I reasoned the situation to make the best of what we had. It didn't take us long to staple plastic sheeting over the whole ceiling which covered the insulation and at least made it draught and insect proof, and it was after all July. We moved in the essentials - our bed and a couple of rugs to cover the rough concrete and *voila*, we had a temporary bedroom.

This was a time of excited anticipation for Jenny as it had been over two years since she had seen Greg and Emily.

We always enjoyed quality time with family just doing normal family things together. It did infuriate us that our young adults refused to start their day before eleven o'clock in the morning, but eventually we do the tour guide thing to share the pleasures of why we live here.

As their departure loomed it felt like we had spent only hours with them before they were leaving and it was a sad time for us as we watched them disappear through security check in at the airport. Returning from the airport we took a small detour and were soon enjoying a glass of wine together with Keith and Margaret, a valuable aid to lifting our spirits.

Our income had stabilised and in its continuation I enthusiastically met a retired English Lady on site to discuss her requirements. The property was a terraced town house over four floors, and as we moved upwards through each floor discussing the work, a pattern began to develop; most of her needs were to finish where some other worker had left off. There was also some exterior building work.

Something about this was sending alarm bells ringing, especially as some of the exterior work was over four metres above ground and access for the materials was difficult to say the least.

I decided to go with my gut feeling and declined the work, saying that I wouldn't be able to meet her timing requirements. A good decision as I later discovered, because the reason there were so many unfinished jobs was because past workers had refused to commit to any more unpaid hours. Her unusual name was Robin; an onomatopoeia perhaps but take heed of your gut feelings, in my experience they often prove the best judgement.

25

At ninety one, Uncle Ralph is incredible. He retired and moved to France with his third wife Celia thirty five years ago, to live in a small commune some thirty five minutes' drive from us. But how Ralph came to own an old stone farmhouse similar to ours is an interesting story.

He came for a holiday, staying with friends who owned a cottage here and fell in love with the area. Towards the end of that stay, he expressed how nice it would be to own a small holiday home and learned that there was a house - that might in the right circumstances - become available.

The owner of the house was a gambling man who had run up a few debts he was unable to discharge as quickly as was necessary. It was thought that should the right approach be made, a deal might be struck where the property could be purchased for a thousand pounds. And so it was that an old stone farmhouse with an adjacent stone barn, outbuildings and a sprawling garden came to pass into Ralph's ownership for a very reasonable price. Apart from a new roof it has changed little since those days.

In his working life Uncle Ralph was a physics lecturer, with a keen practical aptitude to engineering. In retirement he fosters his love of anything electrical or mechanical, and especially clocks which he can skilfully dismantle and repair.

His workshop is sited underneath the barn mezzanine. Above warped beams and worm eaten planking, the previous owner's stock of straw for the cattle remains exactly as it was, except for some slight disturbance by Ralph and Celia's investigative cats.

The workshop is an Aladdin's cave of tools and equipment, with a lathe, drilling machine, motorised polishing wheel and workbenches. At one end is his general work area with regimented rows of tools neatly hung in ever decreasing sizes, the other is his electrical laboratory with oscillator, voltage verifier and transformers, and many items in various stages of repair and test.

Famous for his knowledge and skill he has written papers on sound reproduction, specialising in loudspeakers. Underneath, the benches are full of other useful equipment, all systematically stored in case he needs it. An absolute magpie, he throws nothing away stating, "Oh it will come in handy sometime."

Tea chests – a rarity today, lay stacked on their sides in double rows three high to form a centre isle giving access to both sides. Every space is packed with an assortment of tins and boxes, bottles and bits collected over his vast years, most of which came with him from England.

One solitary small window sheds light upon his work table where he repairs clocks. From necessity his table straddles a narrow concrete step, and so Ralph boxed in the lower level, creating a floor to accommodate his stool and feet.

Sitting at his work bench he faces three of his restored clocks. They are mounted high against the low ceiling to give the weights sufficient working distance; the cases are made from clear Perspex so he can enjoy his love of simple mechanical working parts.

A man of small stature and thin greying hair, he is in his element in this environment. He always welcomes my questions about what his latest project involves and how he will achieve it, often going into minute details of explanation that sometimes make me wish I hadn't asked!

He can dismantle an old clock down to every single part, nut and bolt, which he carefully places in one old tin tray ready for restoration. Cleaning every part to assess its condition he uses an electro-chemical process to remove any corrosion. Then remaking or repairing any broken or excessively worn parts on his lathe, each disassembled part is placed lovingly into another old tin tray ready for re-assembly.

He has an old wooden cabinet between his electrical bench and the lathe, which is nearly a metre wide and my head height. It has at a good guess sixty draws that are home to his selection of set screws, washers and nuts, and many draws of miscellaneous items cannibalised from useless things over many years. The cabinet itself is a work of art!

If he hasn't got something or a part he needs for a repair, he'll make it somehow. If it needs welding or brazing he has equipment for that too. In a corner stands an old concrete drainage pipe, crammed full of metal stocks for the many different requirements.

Once during past years, he was suspicious about the continuity of voltage arriving at the house; in consequence he set up a voltage meter and over a few weeks recorded the variations in voltage to verify his suspicions. He later contacted "*Electricité de France*" to voice his complaint strongly.

He readily adopted the French style of driving; only move your foot from the accelerator when absolutely necessary for breaking, and never indicate your travel direction. His frequent requests to local farmers for assistance in dragging his battered Peugeot from yet another ditch never seemed to register with him that his reflexes had slowed with his age. Celia says she would prefer one of the gravity defying rides at a funfair, but she has learned through bitter experience to say nothing and grit her teeth.

The nearest town of any significance to them is Villeréal - a busy *Bastide* town bustling with tourists in the summer months, and over their years of residency in France they have established themselves within its thriving community.

Knowledge of Ralph's ability with clocks soon reached church wardens and he was asked to give an opinion on the defunct and silent church clock. It was sited high in the right hand tower of this magnificent church and the metre-diameter face of the clock overlooked the main square and it was driven on its circular motion by the workings set within the tower behind thick stone walls.

Inside the church at the base of the left hand tower was a stout oaken and studded door. A huge and aged key hanging from a worn piece of string in Ralph's hand gained entry to the foot of a flight of spiral stone stairs which were worn and rounded for two thirds of the climb. Here the steps changed to wood and it was a nerve-racking experience as they creaked and moved underfoot during the ascent and I expect to fall to the church floor at any moment.

When I question Ralph about the change to wood he explained that many old churches developed a shortage of cash during construction and the change from stone to wood was an all too frequent economy.

Relieved to reach the top, we exited another door and Ralph lead me across the open-air bell gallery to reach the clock house on the other side. It was a hazardous journey; the low parapet wall to my right seemed to have shrunk because in this open area the pigeon shit was ankle deep and after the early morning rain it had become like impact adhesive to walk on; but the high view over the town square on market day was splendid.

While I waited for Ralph to select the second old key to open the clock house door, I looked left at the huge main bells. From the ground they were just three bells, but standing glued to the parapet alongside them was awesome. The decorative detail close up showed the true craft and splendour of the foundry that cast them many years ago. I shuddered to think how they were lifted into position.

Years ago, Ralph's initial inspection of the motionless and silent clock revealed that the grand mechanism was barely visible through its encasement of rotted and collapsed wood, all blanketed in many years of stinking pigeon poo, feathers and nests.

Access through the chest-high oaken door required great force to sweep the latest layers from behind it and gain entry into the space surrounding the workings. The gap between the mechanism and the walls did not allow the passing of two people and was broken only by the huge rod which passed through the wall to turn the hands.

The failure of the clock seemed to be obvious to Ralph; it was on first inspection seized solid in a mixture of ornithological glue, feathers and nesting material. Miraculously the support frame of oak timbers was still in a good condition but his first efforts were devoted entirely to removing the offending birds and blocking their re-entry.

He spent painstaking months of work in a cramped space, scraping and cleaning years of hardened bird lime from the aged metal, then loaded it into suitable containers for the journey back to ground level before any consideration to dismantling and repair was possible.

Two great side plates nearly a metre long and half a metre high were set apart at a distance of another half a metre supporting the silent cogs and spindles alongside the huge cabled drum for winding.

Eventually when it was all sufficiently cleaned, Ralph was able to begin his dismantling for removal piece by piece to his workshop where he lovingly began the task ahead. Separated to individual items he could now attend to each part to bring it back to the splendour it was when it left the original maker. Many months later each piece began the return journey, to be assembled lubricated and connected to the drive rod for the hands outside on the face.

The clock still turns and keeps good time today because for all his efforts he returns each Saturday with Celia, and while she shops at the market and chats with friends he again climbs the stairs to recoil the spring for another week's accurate time.

Many holiday makers and family friends were spellbound by Ralph's explanations of the clock's history and like my first time, they readily took the trip to the towers to see the inner working of the clock. Only when back in the cafe did they realise that they had been conned.

"Would you like to wind the clock?" He asks, and of course they reply, "Oh yes!"

It's an energetic task turning the stiff handle numerous times to wind it, thereby saving him the trouble!

Above the clock on another level, the single bell that chimes the hour hangs, and the monthly maintenance it requires is not for the faint-hearted. One has to duck under the main bells to get to the rear of the tower, where a life-threatening ladder stands leaning into a small opening in the stone wall, on the same level as the nave roof.

Horrified that at ninety one, Uncle Ralph would climb to this height in such a dangerous situation and on such a fragile looking ladder each month, I asked if he actually did this.

"Well I used to." He confirmed as a matter of fact, and taking another shallow breath he further added… "But now someone else does it for me."

Later, back on terra-firma in the café where the air was foggy with tobacco smoke and guttural French conversation, he was happy to reveal to any sympathetic ears, further history of his lifetime's achievements while we all sipped steaming fresh coffee and Aunt Celia groaned quietly to Jenny, "Not this story again!" and Ralph's eyes flicker in her direction to register his momentary disapproval.

I have always found that listening to older people, rather than just absorbing their conversation can be most revealing. By planting the right seeds it amazes me that so much history is locked inside people's heads and for the most part lost forever. I consider my Father and how much I actually know about him as a person before he became my friend; only then do I realise how little time I have to know him better.

I have nick-named Aunt Celia 'The Oracle' because she was so knowledgeable. She was an insatiable reader with a keen interest in politics and current affairs. Her acute mind could recall events in modern history with text book accuracy and I loved to tease out her stories.

At over eighty she was still razor sharp, honed by years of experience being an indispensable secretary, sometimes to the rich and famous. Her cakes are legendary, and still now on rare occasions she will produce *haut cuisine* moving around the kitchen and her chosen produce with all the dexterity of a celebrity Chef. Ralph though prefers simple nourishing food with natural ingredients. He made and ate his own muesli supplemented with fallen fruit from his garden, cutting the bruised and rotten areas off he wasted nothing.

Unless it was for a special clock or some other well engineered moving item, Ralph was reluctant to part with any of his money. If it works Ralph won't replace it however old. Consequently - and I shall never know how - Celia copes with working in a kitchen that would have been modern fifty years ago.

Ralph's only concession to modernisation has been a miniscule second-hand stainless steel sink and drainer which he cut down in size so that it fitted over the original stone sink within the confines of the bay window. It had long since given up the art of reflection.

Celia's work surfaces were the top of the fridge and the laminated board fitted next to the cooker for the kettle to sit upon, and a dining table. She did have a sideboard but said that it was too low to be of any use and anyway it housed her only electrical conveniences the microwave and food mixer. She did add a small base unit for storage but had to buy it herself.

Their bathroom was a major bone of contention between them. The hideous green Formica shower cubicle was bought second hand by Ralph and installed over thirty five years ago. Likewise was the history of the wash hand basin and the ceiling mounted light and heater. It was a dingy wood-lined coffin of a room and Celia detested it.

But the millennium brought a ray of hope for Celia and a chance at last to acquire the bathroom she always wanted. Ralph had been tentatively broaching the subject of a special limited edition commemorative clock he was very keen to buy. Priced at nearly two thousand pounds, Ralph knew he was going to have to make some serious capitulation to get it. Celia of course seized the opportunity to reawaken the question of modernising and extending the awful bathroom she had been using for the last thirty five years.

Ralph did capitulate and a builder friend was engaged to do the work including the technicalities of the necessary extension within the adjacent barn area. Celia was overjoyed and although she didn't show it to Ralph she was delighted with this major psychological triumph.

The clock was placed in pride of place on the dresser in the lounge and received constant admiration by Ralph on a daily basis. Every caller was expected to admire it and receive a mini lecture about its provenance.

Eventually after months had passed, the builder began to wonder when he should start the bathroom project and so visited Ralph to verify the situation. The answer he received was not what he expected as Ralph replied, "Oh I don't think we need to bother about that now."

Celia was devastated. It took her months to come to terms with this betrayal and she has never forgiven him.

Such was the pattern of their lives together until in recent years his age overcame him and the cancer in his stomach took him away from her. He knew there was no getting out of this one and he gracefully gave up, in the knowledge that his age at over ninety had been a good run.

The tiny church in their commune was packed to standing room only for the requiem. A haze of exhaled breath clouded the air as the thick stone walls and flag stoned floor stole any heating. A local choral society sang an emotional goodbye to their friend and member of the past twenty five years.

When the dust had settled after the funeral, Celia gave the clock away to someone she knew would appreciate it; she never did!

For all their trials and tribulations together I believe Celia misses him dearly in her life. She struggles on with failing eyes that have forced her to abandon her little car, her independence, and now she cannot read without the aid of a huge magnifying glass. I wish I could find more time to be with her and chat about nothing specific.

26

I had been commissioned to re-lay a kitchen floor with large quarry tiles in an interesting medieval property in *Monpazier* which spanned one of the entry arches to the historic *Bastide* square.

At ground level and to one side of the arch was a sizeable entrance hall incorporating a cloakroom and staircase - entry to a further three levels. The kitchen was directly above the entrance, recently refitted and very contemporary. The owners thought that the original cracked and worn floor was not in keeping with their new kitchen.

The staircase continued up from the kitchen into a large lounge and dining area which was above a separate apartment on the other side of the arch - and then there was a bathroom and bedrooms at the top via the continuing stairs. Unable to undertake the impracticality of lifting the old kitchen floor, we agreed that I would source the products to effectively re-lay over the old.

This would necessitate roughing the old floor with a diamond disc grinder and using a special adhesive. I brought it to the client's attention that it would produce a considerable amount of dust and suggested how I would contain it, but they decided that no precautions would be necessary because they would need to clean everything after the completion of work anyway.

So I wrapped myself in protective clothing, and with goggles and a face mask I started with the disc. It didn't take long before I heard frantic cries of "STOP! STOP!"

It was during the height of summer and to alleviate the stagnant heat within the house they had opened all the upstairs windows to bring some circulation of air from the ground level via the front door. The whole house was reacting like a huge chimney and my disc cutter grinding away industriously below was behaving like the fire in the grate.

Huge columns of choking white dust were being sucked up through the whole house and they suddenly found they couldn't see each other across the room. They conceded to my previous advice and fortunately saw the funny side of it, later agreeing that the client isn't always right.

A pal, who for a day had helped me with the tiling of the kitchen floor, had called at our house to see how it had all worked out in the end. Finding I was expected home soon he stayed and chatted with Jenny. On arrival I walked down the path towards the front door and couldn't quite take in the unusual scene before me. It was their expressions that were strange as if waiting for some answer to a hidden question.

Then I saw it, a fleeting movement at their feet, a black and white brush sweeping furiously from side to side which suddenly launched into the air and followed the owner down the path towards me.

Two small front legs stopped inches before my feet as the rear end and two additional feet slid in neatly behind to the sit with the brush still sweeping and the whole black and white tiny puppy quivering for approval. Automatically I reached down to greet this new being and my hand received a rich coating of saliva, while my mind raced through the whys and wherefores'.

He knew he had received my approval and darted back to the security of his new mum with a quick look up as if to say, 'I told you it would be OK'; and so it was on that our family increased by one more and Jenny explained how a shopping trip to *Monsempron-Libos* market during the morning had inspired another of her impulse buys.

At the market, a young man was sitting behind a box of fluffy puppies, with a sign that said, "Free to good homes!"

Free was indeed a bargain and as she stopped to look, one placed his front paws on the top of the box. He had obviously had enough and thought that Jenny was a likely candidate.

We spent the evening watching and playing with him as he slipped between bouts of electric energy and exhausted sleep. At bedtime we penned him into a corner with a bowl of water and a dirt tray, then went to bed certain we wouldn't get much sleep. He howled for an hour then crashed, and in the morning he licked us to death as we renewed the bond.

Choosing a name for a pet is never easy. The animals don't care much to my knowledge but it should be the sort of name that you would happily use on a crowded street. When Jenny asked what I was going to call him my thoughts went back to another dog which I suppose was half mine.

I once became step-dad to a hyper-active Spaniel called Gemma and a Border terrier called Henry. Henry was a middle aged dog of strong character who if unhappy with any discipline administered would turn his back on you and refuse point blank to make any acknowledgement what-so-ever of your existence.

On occasions I would take a turn to walk the dogs on my own, up into the fields and woodland adjacent to our home, but unlike Gemma, Henry's reputation determined that he was always retained on a long leash because of his ability to disappear for two or three days.

Unfamiliar with his true character, I felt sorry for him watching Gemma freely coursing the fields and hedgerows, so I decided to give him the benefit of the doubt for a while. He soon had me lulled into a sense of false security trotting obediently close by and returning to my call if he strayed a little far. Then suddenly he disappeared into the long grass and that was the last I saw of him for three days.

I trekked the wooded hills for an hour calling his name in vain with a muddy Spaniel at my side, before I returned home unsure even as to which direction he had gone. Three days later he appeared outside the garden gate, exhausted and stripped of fur on his front lower legs, stinking and covered in dried mud!

We had a dog-flap giving the dogs access to the garden, and arriving home from work one day, I discovered just how much Henry liked to dig. All one side of the fencing had been undermined and the flowerbeds desecrated in his successful attempt to terrorise next door's cats.

I had to dig down a foot and install steel mesh to thwart his future escapades.

He did however have his good points and was a joy to have around even if he was randy. After a walk, a bath or just for the hell of it he would frequently try to shag the Spaniel. He never actually managed it because she was either too tall for him or too plain daft to know what he was up to. So we thought it would be a good idea to buy a Border terrier bitch to keep him company, satisfy his obvious need and further his line as he wouldn't last for ever.

We registered her as "Henry's Hanna" but for us she was plain Hanna and was adorable. Poor old Henry had to stay on the leash of course which really pissed him off, but Hanna soon latched on to Gemma. As a young immature dog she didn't have the energy to keep up with her roaming buddy and soon returned to Henry and us.

But later as her stamina and muscles developed she would freely clutter off in hot pursuit and we would watch their progress through the motion of the long grass as she powered along behind Gemma the spaniel like a little steam engine. She was special; special because I had saved her life.

Sparring together as they often did Gemma had caught her canine teeth under Hanna's collar and was slowly throttling her to death. A frantic phone call had me rushing home from work, five minutes away. Demanding a sharp kitchen knife I quickly removed the collar as Hanna lay limply unconscious on the floor, and Gemma retreated to her bed fearing she had made some serious transgression. Quick thinking about how I could revive her brought into fruition all my training for first aid during my youth in the Boy's Brigade, but how do you give mouth to mouth to a dog?

Gripping her muzzle in one hand to keep her mouth closed I put her nose in my mouth and gently inflated her little body. My own heart was pounding as I repeated this, each time watching carefully the inflation then waiting the few seconds while it deflated.

After three or four times I felt some small movement then suddenly she rallied and breathed on her own. Bewildered as to her own demise she lay there recovering while we worried as to the long term effects of this long time without breathing.

She was still very subdued during the consultation at the vets so we agreed that he should keep her overnight just in case. The next day when we returned home with her she jumped and bounced around the other two and Henry tried to shag her.

Jenny pondered on this lengthy explanation and said, "Well you can't call him Hanna, but you could always call him Spanner". And so it was that we found his name and it suits him well. He's my Friesian dog, black and white all over, but why is it that the white bits are the bits that are always susceptible to getting dirty?

Arran, our collie is so laid back we have a job to get him to perform bodily functions; except the odd emergency during the night on the kitchen floor. He took Spanner in his every day stride, literally.

Full of energy and darting around the garden Spanner's brakes had yet to be operationally perfected and frequently he overshot, or more to the point undershot as he passed between Arran's legs continuing through and out the other side, and Arran with his one good eye swinging his head from side to side in search of this atomic puppy.

As Spanner's brakes and steering gained confidence you could imagine him thinking

'Fooled again', as he administered another needle sharp nip to Arran's nearest leg before darting off again. Arran was very tolerant and although he is quite happy with his own company, he was obviously enjoying this new attention and four legged company.

The Siamese cats Minka and Sulin were disgusted; Minka at three years old wouldn't come near the house and would only warily enter when starving and encouraged by Jenny with a bowl of food: he always was a neurotic cat. Sulin at over twenty just glared at him, and if he came a bit close for an ascertaining sniff he received a half-hearted pat on the nose from an arthritic paw and a warning hiss.

Bit by bit they all learned to tolerate him and we did our bit on their behalf by training him to 'LEAVE' when he became boisterous. Animals seem to have a built in mutual respect for each other and they all soon fell into the pecking order. He had quickly become an integral member of the family.

As a Border Collie/Spaniel cross, we expected him to grow nearly as big as Arran, so Jenny had bought the same size dog- bed for him and they did look strange side by side; one filled with a great furry collie and the other housing what looked like a deflated football huddled to one side. He must have felt the same, because before he grew too big we would often find him squashed in beside Arran.

After a couple of minor accidents he was house trained, well the rear end was. The front end thought that anything was fair game. One such investigative adventure robbed us of quite a quantity of a precious commodity during the night.

Unable to buy it here in France, our preferred tea bags are shipped out to us via any friends arriving, and under strict instructions to reduce baggage, they decanted them into a plastic carrier bag for ease of insertion into a suitcase.

After a jolly evening re-uniting with the recent couriers and the necessary lubricant, we had waved farewell and gone to bed, forgetting to lift from the floor, anything of remote interest to a puppy!

"Oh what's this?" Spanner must have thought. "Looks jolly interesting, is it edible, strange place to leave a carrier bag, I better tear just a little hole and have a sniff."

The little hole grew to a big rip, and then having thoroughly investigated half of the whole tea bags he had strewn across the floor, he had then proceeded to investigate the delicate taste of the contents of most of them. It must have quietly kept him amused for a very long time as I know it took us probably the same amount of time to clear it all up and salvage what we could. We left him in no doubt as to the result of his first testing of where his goal posts were but we kept our amusement secret from him.

We treasured and watched him daily as he grew into a real character; even Minka capitulated but only as far as swapping sniffs of each other, which when achieved reverted to quickly concealing himself out of the way to observe this lunatic. Sulin continued to treat him like a low life, rarely acknowledging his existence.

We learned to recognise his little messages from the pleading look on his face as he sat so close to his known exit blending almost into the fabric of the door, that this was his way of telling us that it was time for extra curriculum toilet duties. He demanded attention at our every movement and would sit at our feet beating a paradiddle with his front paws and vibrating with excitement, then the second we made to move off he could pre-empt the direction and spring to the side.

The play value for a puppy of any inanimate object is endless. Small logs can be dragged from the wood basket beside the stove and along with all the junk mail left discarded within reach they can be shredded and distributed across the open floor area in the dining room where both dogs slept.

In the mornings when we appeared from the bedroom sleepy eyed and in desperate need of our preferred source of caffeine there he would be, whatever transgression he had perpetrated during the night, bouncing excitedly at the potential of another days play.

Arran might appear to be a bit thick sometimes but he was acute enough to know when a bollocking was due and stayed in his bed innocently watching the proceedings with a look which said, "I told you so!"

Their bedding is made from cut-up old duvets which are folded double and placed to give a comfy and warm base to the plastic moulded dormitory. Arran's bed when left to its own devises will stay in place for weeks - airing and washing aside.

Spanner nests! We haven't seen quite how he does it but he nests. His duvet looks like it has been soaked in water and then moulded intricately to his curled body shape and allowed to set firmly in this position. He must feel that this work of art is a cherished attainment as his obliging nature often donates the same boudoir for his new found pal Arran.

On some occasions when we need them settled and out of the way for some domestic chore we send them to the sanctuary of the dog bed. Thinking that perhaps Arran is being a little stubborn when we have to tell him again, he will give us 'The look!'

The look which says, "Hey, how am I supposed to get in that?"

Only then do we realise that Spanner has done it again and there is another nest waiting for Arran, about five sizes too small. Into the garden with it for a firm shake and laid flat once again Arran is at last happy to install his copious furry body on his duvet with a lung collapsing groan.

Arran's groans are famous. Like people who will relax in a chair and perhaps exhale a deep sigh, Arran's deep relaxing sighs go on for a full thirty seconds sometimes and are quite vocal.

In the past we have heard a motor cycle as it came down the drive, decelerating to a stop outside the front of the house. Rising to look and see who our two wheeled visitor is we have realised that Arran has voiced one of his particularly long and audible sighs. Another version is a kind of dog purring; we think perhaps this is a habit he learned from Sulin as she was a good purrer.

At the height of one particular good session during an evening's television it became so irritating we had to abandon the film and take him for a distracting walk around the garden to shut him up. As he got older, so did his hours of inactivity, preferring to engage in his highly perfected occupation of sleeping, usually right across the many well used routes in and around the house. When he sleeps he dreams, and in his dreams he is often chasing some unseen, unrecognised phantom and barks a stifled warning to his family.

"Arran, dreaming!!" usually wakes him from this latest doze and another motorcycle arrives. That's dogs for you!

27

The developing situation between my sister and I had sadly deteriorated. We were both guilty of a lack of communication. She had relied on me and probably felt that I had let her down: I had devoted four months of intense work to her building project which had become all consuming; I ate, drank, and slept it and now it had all gone sour and I'd walked away. It took me nearly a year before I really came to terms with it all, trying to find answers to unanswerable questions of human nature.

In fact she wasn't my sister at all, but I called her that because of the way things were. Years ago, a brief affair had taught us both that we were searching for different things and with romance not an option we developed a deep supportive friendship.

Infrequent contact always seemed to be spot on cue, like we each knew the other needed a friend. We'd drink whiskey together and then laugh until the tears came; that was our way.

Jenny met her before we moved, and an instant friendship carried on when she came to France to stay with us for a week. She fell in love with our dream and wanted one of her own and subsequently bought an old stone house along our road.

The roof and walls were good and the front door led into a large *salle de jour*, a day room with a huge open fireplace and a shallow stone sink with no running water. From the entrance room a further door led into a bedroom, and from there down four steps, was the second bedroom which housed a wash hand basin and the only water supply in the house which was straight from the cold mains.

A flushable toilet had been installed behind a meagre wooden partition to the outside of the house and under the roof overhang; the only protection it offered was from prying eyes, and it was filthy. To the rear was a semi-detached barn with cattle byres for five cows; its doors were hanging off and it was filled with broken and redundant farm machinery which had a covering of worm eaten and rotting beams and planks discarded there when the roof was renewed twelve years previously.

Under the house a wine cellar had been gouged from the bedrock. Standing was only possible just inside the shallow door as it diminished in height towards the rear through a curtain of spiders' webs where I found two bicycles that were about to disintegrate into a pile of powdery rust and five fragile wine barrels. Brittle kindling wood lay stacked everywhere and in one corner where the bedrock was still soft there were quite a few little tunnels about rabbit size.

I spent two hours in and around the house taking measurements and conceived a refurbishment plan which took another three days to appear as a drawing. The house was capable of incorporating three bedrooms - one en-suite, a bathroom, utility room, kitchen diner, and a lounge. It would also be possible for the conversion of the barn into a two bedroom *Gite* for holiday-makers, but that was to come later.

I teamed up again with Jim for the duration of the project; it worked very well and we had a lot of fun re-kindling our previous camaraderie. Jenny and I knew what Jim was like but decided nevertheless to offer him the facility of lodging with us and we greatly enjoyed his company. In the evenings sometimes we played music together or engaged in some philosophical conversation. It was restrictive with a third person permanently around, but we had adopted the attitude that it was only temporary and therefore had an end.

Back in England, Sis was assured by her estate agent that her home was very desirable and would quickly sell at top price. She took the agent at his word - 'within six weeks,' and so decided to retire early and move out to France as soon as the house had the basic amenities available for her to live in.

After a traumatic divorce she'd spent the last twenty years as a single parent with two young daughters and now they were grown and settled, she felt it was time to re-start her own life. She didn't however relish telling the family of her plans to move to France and she received a mixed reception.

One daughter gave her firm support, while the other selfishly increased the emotional pressure against it. But she booked her flight and gave up her job and came anyway, knowing that it would mean a brief stay with us while minimal accommodation was completed.

In six weeks Jim and I had gutted the place from cellar to loft. We dug out nearly half a metre of bedrock from the cellar floor and built new walls within the area for a bedroom en-suite. Then we constructed a new 'level' floor over the cellar rooms, correcting the original floor slope of twenty five centimetres and incorporated sound insulation, water pipes and electric cables. We changed the access to the cellar rooms with an internal staircase; then redesigned the layout of the internal walls above to create new rooms and give the access to other new areas.

Demolishing the old privy we enclosed the roof over-hang and created a new cloakroom and utility room accessible from the kitchen; we also knocked through into the barn and because the levels were slightly different we were able to incorporate a third bedroom and the main bathroom, sitting comfortably above the proposed holiday *Gite*.

Sis arrived and was eager to see the house once more. She was stunned by the transformation and found it difficult to take it all in. She gelled with Jim straight away and she couldn't wait to pitch in with us and help where possible.

Jenny and I organised what turned out to be a great evening when we invited the neighbours to our home to meet her. Jim entertained us on the guitar, Jacques and Vero took turns trying to play Jenny's didgeridoo which caused hoots of laughter, and while everyone nodded politely to Rene's guttural French, François fed nibbles under the table to Spanner, always the opportunist.

As the months passed, we introduced her to our circle of friends when opportunities arose and her bubbly fun loving nature was readily accepted although some couldn't get to grips with the "Sister, well not actually" explanations.

I was totally committed to the project and somehow didn't see the mounting pressure keg. Jenny was feeling the pressure of a full house and Jim's little ways were becoming an irritation.

Sis was counting the days to the arrival of both her daughter and five-year-old grand-daughter for a planned six weeks' stay, and getting worried about completion dates.

Jim was picking up the negative vibes from Jenny and had been discussing it with Sis and there I was stuck in the middle trying to keep the whole lot together at home and still run the project to schedule.

Eventually the keg blew; Jim decided to move out and camp in the garden of a building site and Sis decided to move into whatever space was available. On site we tried to maintain the same progress, which was difficult with a live-in client who liked to sleep late. Plus we were soon to have the added complication of Sis's daughter and grand-daughter for six weeks and I was concerned about safety precautions for a five year old.

Reeling from the trauma of the past weeks, Jenny found difficulty in maintaining the same relationship with either Jim or Sis and the same was evident in reverse. Jenny does have her faults but it seemed to me that as a closer friendship developed between Jim and Sis I was being excluded and to a much greater degree so was Jenny.

Conversations were abruptly terminated when I arrived on site and an excluding attitude developed from them towards me and I was defending verbal assaults about Jenny.

Finance too had become a serious issue, and a very important revelation by Sis, previously unmentioned was quickly depleting the budget in favour of her unsold property in England. The forecasted six weeks for the sale of her property was turning into six months with no end in sight, and I was surprised to learn that she was running out of money, despite that just over half of the forecast budget had been used.

The stress was mounting on site and at home; a balance had to be achieved between a project I really cared about, and people I cared for also, especially my wife who was taking the brunt of my misgivings in the evenings. I should have spoken to Sis weeks earlier and brought things back on track to suit the situation as it developed but it was too late now.

She put the Gite on hold but the house was all but finished so I offered the only solution to suit both my sanity and her situation and she agreed with relief and I backed away from the project. Jim stayed on for quite a while, completing some finishing jobs and eventually he moved away.

I saw Jim on his own on site one day, and stopped to say hello. The conversation was cordial but awkward. I asked him, "Jim, what happened here?" He considered my question thoughtfully, and then briefly replied.

"I don't know…but I think we were all at fault somehow."

I don't see him anymore but I hope he's happy.

Many people make the mistake of buying a dream before they have the money in their pocket, you can give or indeed take all the right advice but in the end the dream overrides. It can nearly break you; it nearly broke us and it nearly broke Sis.

In the end she put the house up for sale and went back to England and we're saddened to learn that she feels that we sold her a dream she couldn't achieve.

I find it sad that in an attempt to appease their lack of good judgement, people will always seek to dump the blame elsewhere, often eliciting support from any willing ears to justify the stance, and quite unaware of the future impact.

We lost what we thought were special friends because they believed what Sis told them and it took us a long time to realise that perhaps these people were not real friends in the first place!

28

The aftermath of the situation with Sis was having long-lasting effects. During the following weeks I was fortunate if I found some occupation which diverted my thoughts from constantly evaluating the affair. I questioned my practical ability and I looked hard at my business acumen.

Had I bitten off more than I could chew?

No I hadn't!

Were my practical skills up to it?

Yes they were, together with Jim we had done a good job.

Was I right leaving? Yes I was.

I mentally reviewed everything; round and round day and night looking for truthful explanations so I could close the door and move my life on.

One day Jenny was suffering with a bad case of the blues and just couldn't seem to bring herself out of it; surprising really because it was her birthday. Perhaps it was one of those women's age things, but try as I did she didn't seem to want to be cheered at all. It probably didn't help when I announced that I was going out for an hour during mid-evening. It helped even less when in answer to her questioning as to where I was going, all I said was…

"Secret squirrel!"

On my return an hour-and-a-half later at dusk, I found her in the rear garden un-pegging the washing from the line and little improved during my absence. My pleas for her to come to the car with me met strong resistance but she grudgingly came because I said it was something special for her.

"Open the door then," I encouraged.

"Oh Robert what have you bought," Hand on the door.

"Why don't you open the door and see before it's totally dark."

As she opened the door and peered into the inner gloom up popped her daughter Sarah who was crouching in the foot well saying, "Hi-ya! – Happy birthday."

"Oh… my… God," just about managed to be heard before all the doom and gloom of the day evaporated in a flood of tears.

During the loving embrace of mother and daughter re-united again after so many months one hand broke free to inflict me with a sharp wallop and accompanying the words...

"You swine I knew you were up to something!"

Her uncharacteristic morosity evaporated immediately as the three of us went inside. Sarah and I giggled like errant children during the barrage of questions from Jenny as she demanded an account of how between us we had managed to keep the secret. In fact it wasn't that difficult, but to Jenny it would have been quite an achievement because she can never keep a secret.

Sarah's all-too-brief visit was the tonic we both needed to jar our thoughts away from recent events and move on; we looked forward to furthering the medication in a couple of weeks' time when my son Greg was coming out with his girlfriend Leila. They are both good company and a pleasure to welcome here.

Family meal-times are special; it's a time for us all to be together and just relax and chat. Greg is a proficient cook and frequently telephones for my recipes to impress his guests. During dinner one evening Greg chose a *crème caramel* for dessert and announced he was going to eat it in one. He prepared the plastic pot and then tied a makeshift bib around his neck while we all laughed then finally he upended the pot. He did it to hoots of laughter from us all and Jenny and I later voiced that we couldn't remember the last time we had laughed like that.

Greg is always keen to pitch in and help us with any physical work on the house and Jenny was anxious to see some movement towards the conversion of the barn. Rainy weekends always frustrate me with so many outside jobs to do and during one previously rainy weekend I had appeased my boredom and worked inside the barn preparing a third of the earthen floor area ready for a concrete base. Greg's presence was a golden opportunity not to be missed. A pair of willing hands is always gratefully received and once again we surprised ourselves on completing thirty square metres of concrete ahead of schedule.

A week disappears quickly and all-to-soon we sadly watched them disappear through security at the airport and quietly drove home to pick up on reality.

The abrupt termination with Sis had left us with little income. I managed to find a few small jobs but my main source of work was the grapevine, and that had withered and died along with our friends. The only foreseeable action was to fall back on my metalwork profession, so I constructed a CV and a short explanatory letter in French and made a list of the local companies likely to use my skills.

I visited each in turn and walking in unannounced I introduced myself, offering my letter and CV which explained much more than my skills would allow linguistically. I received a warm reception at every location but accompanied by the phrase…

"*Désolée mais* c*'est très calmé a moment*".

Unfortunately local requirements for metal work skills are very much associated with agriculture and approaching Christmas was not a good time to be seeking employment. They were sorry but explained that at present things were very quiet.

We had a very meagre Christmas celebration but used it along with the following weeks, to great advantage finishing a lot of jobs not requiring any cash devoted to them.

One dismal day in the New Year as depression was becoming a major threat the phone rang. As I persevered with the conversation in French frantically trying to absorb the meaning from the few key words I did understand it dawned on me that I was being offered a job and only five minutes away. Face to face is far better than the telephone when trying to grasp the finer points of French and so I headed off in the car at once.

I met Laurent, a stocky man in his late thirties with a handshake like a gorilla. He showed me his full order book for the New Year and told me where he hoped I would figure in the fulfilment of it and so I came away with a firm contract for one month, but open ended for extension if necessary.

I soon settled back into workshop life using my thirty five years' experience and Laurent quickly began to rely on my skills and understanding of his requirements. Laurent split his day like most small business owners; in the workshop as much as possible and in the office as little as possible; Corinne his wife dealt with the administration.

I met Louis, a Fernando Alonso look-alike who worked all day like an excited spaniel provided he didn't have to do too much thinking about it; and Carlos who magically machined parts for broken and aged farm machinery, when he deigned to be there.

Louis and Carlos were both Portuguese with differing language skills. Louis spoke French with a strong accent rolling one word into the other and I rarely understood a word. Carlos on the other hand was much easier to understand. He spoke a little English and had a great sense of humour which established an instant friendship between us; and then there was Philippe - Laurent's older brother.

Philippe looked like one of those skilled tradesmen best avoided. He looked nothing like Laurent, he was slim and spoke little yet I could feel him watching me from under the rim of his beret. One day, having made his final assessment of me he sauntered over. From that day Philippe and I became immediate friends when he divulged his command of English and plundered my tobacco pouch. Now as a regular visitor to our home he just plunders my whisky.

I felt I had been accepted when I was asked to stay behind one Friday evening for *apéritifs.* In the small restroom I met Clarice, Laurent's jovial father-in-law, and one or two local farmers who came and went - they seem to have a nose for when the bottle is open.

I arrived home at seven thirty and swung in through the door and announcing, "I think I'm pissed!"

It was the beginning of nine months of stability for us, the money wasn't great but it was regular. My spoken French improved dramatically with the necessity of communication, ably assisted by Philippe and Carlos and Collins pocket dictionary in pride of place on top of my tool box.

My understanding of Laurent was still a struggle as he spoke very quickly, often cutting the last syllable to the bare minimum making it difficult for me to recognise. *Attente* meaning wait, came out as *Attang* with the 'T' being lost somewhere in the nose. He was however very encouraging and patient with me as my vocabulary and understanding increased. We each learned the others peculiarities and he frequently corrected my bizarre pronunciation - after he stopped laughing!

Throughout the day the *Agriculteurs* would arrive. Sometimes it might be a broken tractor with a missing bolt or a lost linkage that had fallen off somewhere within a field, or maybe a split flexible hydraulic pipe in need of immediate replacement from the huge stocks of differing sizes with their connectors, or maybe pinions for the three point lift on a tractor, drive belts, or lubricants. In fact any mechanical problem that stopped farm work arrived at the door.

Each one of them would always say a quick "Bonjour" to us all, accompanied by the obligatory handshake from gnarly fingers and leathery skin. Some knew that I was English and made a direct effort to converse with me, and sometimes they used their small knowledge of my language. I am constantly surprised how many French people unexpectedly speak a little English and are eager to use what phrases they know. It amazes Jenny also when we are out somewhere and what appears to be a total stranger recognises me from the workshop and a brief conversation ensues.

Most of my work was centred upon the manufacture of new items for a company that produced and sold agricultural equipment, while Louis seemed to be always lying under a tractor or a trailer of some sort. Piles of rust, dried mud and straw would fall around him as he hammered and banged an essential broken and rusty bracket back into place for re-welding.

On one occasion I watched him and a welding torch disappear up inside the bowels of a very aged combined harvester. The giant machine was fresh from the harvest fields and full of grain and straw. He banged and crashed about inside while sparks flew out everywhere and I visually located the nearest fire extinguishers for the possible inferno which fortunately didn't happen.

Later a smiling farmer returned for the machine and climbed high into the cab to continue harvesting; but the smile wasn't there for long. As the engine of this huge machine fired into life and it slowly exited the workshop towards the gates and the road, suddenly there was a chilling loud bang and clatter as gusts of thick black smoke erupted from the exhaust and the engine died.

Berets were removed and heads scratched as their faces showed a picture of doom and gloom. A tractor arrived and towed it across the road and into a field where within a few minutes the assembled onlookers had risen to eight. Then after the further removal of berets and more scratching of heads they all departed and abandoned the giant machine to silence.

Two weeks later a smart van appeared with the sign 'New Holland' on the side. Very soon afterwards two or three familiar faces re-appeared with a hoist. Dressed in smart clean overalls the manufacturer's engineer climbed upon the silent giant to supervise the removal of the defunct engine and the replacement of the new one which was patiently waiting in the rear of his van. It quite surprised me that such a monstrously huge piece of equipment was motored by such a small engine.

As the season progressed towards the coming fruit harvest so did the urgency for new equipment and additionally the forgotten malfunctioning old ones began to arrive for repairing.

They all vary in design according to the price, but a basic one consists of a trailer with an inverted umbrella about six metres diameter which is opened around the circumference of a tree. Underneath the umbrella there is a mechanism which clamps around the trunk and shakes the living daylights out of the whole tree causing the plums to fall into the open umbrella for collection.

On a more sophisticated unit they are transported from the umbrella via a conveyor belt which houses a fan to blow all the leaf debris away. Then via a second conveyor, the fruit fills the waiting boxes, for the journey to the ovens for drying.

Broken machines don't receive prior cleaning before they arrival at Laurent's workshop and therefore the mulch of fruit casualties adhered everywhere on the machines gives off a sweet and sickly smell, most attractive to wasps and hornets.

Wasp stings are not much more than an irritation but hornets can be deadly. Three stings can kill you. Folk unfortunate enough to have a hornets' nest a bit too close for comfort would normally call the fire fighters - the *Sapeurs-Pompiers,* who would don appropriate clothing and deal with it. Now because of the recent fatalities during the process they will not undertake to do it, and recommend instead that you contact a specialist company at great expense.

Laurent though was a clever man with a mind on the future development of his business. I questioned him about the origins of his engineering career and he revealed that he has diplomas in welding and fabrication, and additionally not only is he a qualified machinist and centre-lathe turner but is also a qualified hydraulic engineer. He said that a farming community had little money and would never make him rich!

Instead his sights were on the increasing European second home owner and the recent new legislation concerning the security of children and swimming pools. He felt that the implementation of electronic alarm systems would soon give way permanently to the alternative of complete fencing with childproof gates, and fortunately I was involved in the design and manufacture of the first orders. This I hoped would secure a good future for me and his business.

Philippe had secured a friendship that seemed to be a reciprocal arrangement. He turned up at home out of the blue to drink my whisky and I received the next instalment in my on-going French lessons. As such evenings progressed, so did the subsequent glasses and my linguistic trepidations evaporated allowing us to become involved in some serious philosophical conversation.

But there was a limit to both my concentration and my depleting bottle and eventually I had to advise him that I was ready for bed. Only after I had fulfilled his final request for - 'one for the road', was I able to re-join Jenny who had been asleep in bed for an hour.

29

At seventeen years old, Sulin the female Siamese was slowing down and her arthritic joints were obviously causing her some discomfort. We had a close call recently, with the vet intervening, it seemed her kidneys were not what they should be and with the medication he gave her she was on borrowed time. She regularly walked around the house meowing, and appeared confused as to why she was where she found herself.

She has always loved heat, preferring to sit as close to any source of it as is possible – either sunshine or the wood-burning stove, but just far enough away to avoid catching fire. During the winter months her only movement was between her bed, and the kitchen to satisfy her primary functions – both ends.

Her memory also didn't seem to be what it was previously. As soon as we arrived within the kitchen area she would loudly demand feeding, forgetting that she had been fed quite recently. Keeping her body weight up was a constant struggle as well. She frequently ate a few mouthfuls and then retired back to bed; if she went further and gorged, it frequently ended up in the bed next to her. So we continued to love her and made her later years as comfortable as we could.

Minka the younger male was now six and we rarely saw him. He had been born within a litter just before the breeder went on holiday and only saw a human twice daily at feeding times, subsequently had never learned to interact with people. Even as a kitten any movement caused him to dart away and hide behind a chair. He was a total loner who only came home for food. It was disappointing because he was an elegant Blue-point cat.

I suppose it was this history of our cats that prompted Jenny to give a home to another free offering, this time from a car-boot sale. I can see what the attraction was, kittens are adorable and she was convinced that the colour of the coat and the blue eyes spelled 'Siamese.' I was not convinced because people do not give away Siamese cats.

Jenny named this tiny little ball Mia, and she was installed within a large cage for her own security away from the inquisitive dogs, along with all the other necessary requirements; she was a little too young to have left the litter really, as we estimated her age at four weeks.

On the occasions when we supervised her freedom within the house, Sulin ignored her despite Mia's attempts at inter-cat bonding. Minka sniffed the cage and notched up yet another reason to stay away. In consequence the only mother figure available to her was Spanner, with Arran close behind as maiden aunt.

When it was play time it was Spanner she turned to, and our early worries of the damage he could inadvertently inflict were unfounded. Still a puppy himself they became inseparable and played for hours. His continuing trait is to use his nose and poke when he wants attention and Mia found this a great game. She would launch into the air and wrap herself around his head fiercely biting as hard as her needle-like teeth would allow. When either of them became a bit too boisterous a quick yelp soon put things into perspective and a mutual respect for each other developed which lasts to this day.

Eventually as she tired, we would become aware of a lull and fearing some awful injury we'd search for her and there she would be – tucked up and nearly invisible within Arran's copious fur, fast asleep.

Our protection of her soon diminished and the cage went back into the barn along with the cat tray – we have never to this day had any little accidents from her. She became an excellent mouser within the garden and later the fields – always leaving the carcasses outside the house for our approval. Spanner also has become quite good at catching mice, although he still prefers to rely on Mia and usurp her catch before rolling on it!

As we left the garden for a dog walk and before we entered the fields opposite, Mia – who regularly came on such excursions - would leap out from her chosen cover and launch herself upon Spanner's back catching him by surprise. This ambush technique has developed into regular fun and games and has taught him to react with the agility of a cat. As yet she doesn't bark, but when yawning Spanner often makes a noise which is very similar to a meow?

Jenny of-course has regimented ideas for their diets but Mia prefers moths, spiders, and beetles and if she's lucky the occasional lizard. Spanner has his own ideas too; wood, leaves, one of Jenny's best shoes, and any paper that we forget to move out of reach, but we think for his main source of protein he still prefers the contents of the un-emptied cat tray. UGH!

Earlier in the year, Jenny had erected her new polytunnel; a commercial metal-framed construction six metres long and four and a half metres wide and high enough to walk through with ease. We hoped it would extend the season for growing our own vegetables and salads.

Jenny's endless time under the plastic proved very successful; she had grown three varieties of tomato plants with stalks as thick as your thumb, and now they were up to the roof with copious fruit slowly turning bright red. Cucumbers we couldn't eat or give away quick enough and the Melons were as big as small footballs. The first crop of our three varieties of Lettuce had been eaten and the second crop was on the way.

There were sweet peppers still to ripen and the aubergines were soon to be cropped as they were already a good size. Green chillies hung drying from the kitchen ceiling.

Outside, two frames of runner beans were just ready for picking and we had Brussels sprouts growing ready for the frosts that would make them at their best, and of course French beans and Peas.

The three courgettes plants that François had given us definitely did not need the accompanying three we bought to go with them. Despite our attempts to introduce this bounty of fresh produce into our diet we always found one more courgette that had turned into a marrow under the copious leaves. All in all, it seemed that it had become a very worthwhile project, even though we might have to buy a new freezer.

Spanner barked and I was alerted to François's presence in his orchard and so climbed up the bank and through the hedge to further *l'entente cordiale*. A chat with François was always a pleasure and I nearly always learned something.

He had a scythe and was cutting down and collecting what looked to me like weeds. Registering my enquiring look he explained, "*C'est pour les poulet.*"

Ah the chickens and he added the gesture with his finger-tips touching and a pecking motion towards his mouth. We had been tearing up the same plants from the garden for years and placing them disparagingly on the compost heap!

Our conversation turned towards the Acacia trees just inside our garden and I remarked upon the sweet smell from the abundance of blossoms and how quickly it disappears until next year. We discussed the overriding hum from the thousands of bees taking advantage of the brief supply of nectar and prompted by this he related how Renée makes omelettes using the blossoms and again the gesture towards the mouth indicated his pleasure from the taste.

"*Ah, vous avez une nouvelle camionnette; l'ancien camionnette de Jacques?*" He recognised my latest acquisition sitting on the drive; the old and battered Renault van. He doesn't miss a thing and his recognition of Jacques's old van was correct.

I had mentioned to Jacques some months ago that a van like his, old and inexpensive would suit me very well for work.

"You can have this one," he said, "When my new one arrives in a month or two."

Expecting a generous price I asked, "Yes, but how much?"

"Nothing – what is an old van like this worth – nothing."...and with a wave into the far distance he dismissed the idea that money would change hands.

Great, I just had to wait until his new van arrived, it seemed too good to be true and after another few months had elapsed I discovered that it probably was.

His new van arrived but, his son-in-law Didier had borrowed my van while his own car was being repaired which was a disappointment. I enquired again over the next few months which rather seemed to oblige me to eventually take it, and now it had been slipped into the conversation that legally, he would have to provide it with a certificate of testing before change of ownership, so I now presumed that some money was going to have to change hands.

Eventually when I did take possession I couldn't help but feel the disappointment. For a lesser price I could have bought a van with a heater and fan that worked, a comfortable seat, a working fuel gauge and paint-work that showed less rusting. Other than that is suited me fine, it ran well, always started and constantly amazed me at its capacity behind the seats. C'est la vie.

30

Creative pictorial art in any form takes a special gift. To be able to conceive an idea then transfer it to a chosen medium is beyond most people and yet those same people rarely see it for what it portrays, only to rapidly assess it for like or dislike. It is the sheer pleasure of creating something from an idea; to see eventually in reality what the artist has seen in their mind.

From the first saw cut in a piece of wood, a master carpenter can see the beautifully inlaid writing table with cabriole legs, and likewise a sculptor chipping away at a block of fresh hewn stone can visualise the highly polished bust hidden inside, but while the finished work is the overall aim, it must be the pleasure of the journey which appeals or they would never start.

It is this creativity which is the buzz and Jenny has that buzz, like most of us she has her preferences but she is creative. She can see the potential in gnarly old vines lying uprooted and discarded because they are too old and unproductive, and in that instant that she sees them she has cleaned, varnished and joined three together to create an unusual candelabra.

She can visualise the old worm eaten oak beam that she is creating from four pieces of plasterboard that are fit for the dump, and as she applies her special mixture of plaster, she will grain and texture it before it dries, making a pure white copy of her visualised oaken beam, ready for colouring.

As a young woman she worked as a freehand painter for Royal Doulton. Now many years later her creative instincts have blended with her love of glass. She had conceived an idea, nothing that she wanted to share yet, but it was there in her mind being evaluated.

She is always reluctant to share with me the development of her creativity and so carrying the idea with her she browsed local art shops in search of likely materials until she eventually found what she was looking.

In my absence during the day the dining room table became her studio and taking a framed picture bought from a charity shop, she discard the unwanted print, degreased and cleaned the glass and began to apply her design directly onto the glass. Her image was created using a fine self-adhesive lead strip and then she hand painted it with vibrant colours. The result was a stunning stain glass abstract in the 'art nouveau' style which she proudly hung upon the dining room wall for my approval and then described how she had achieved it.

A second design soon followed and as this new skill developed, the clock and resident pictures on our dining room walls began to disappear and be replaced. The dining room had become her gallery and much to her delight some of our friends wanted to buy them. So she sold them and continued to experiment with many new ideas and designs. She created cartoon animals and many abstract patterns, but her best pictures were the floral displays, of Sunflowers and Arum Lilies, Irises and Roses, all produced in various sizes and her own unique style.

She was greatly encouraged by the response to her work and started to develop the possibility of a permanent outlet in addition to many other ideas for her art. One afternoon, she spent over an hour rummaging amongst our copious store of unopened boxes, until she triumphantly produced a set of latex chess moulds and our kitchen was turned into a moulding workshop. She just hoped that the moulds hadn't deteriorated while in storage for so many years.

The moulds were patterned from medieval chess pieces that were found in 1831, on the isle of Lewis in the Outer Hebrides and Jenny's first pieces were transported straight into the bin as she felt that the plaster she had used wasn't quite right.

My involvement was now being openly encouraged and together with a very patient art shop proprietor, we searched his catalogues trying to find a suitable moulding plaster without going to the expense of resin figurines. Fortunately one of his catalogues had English text and so we were able to place an order. Although significantly cheaper than resin would have been, it was a high quality German porcelain moulding plaster, and the twenty five kilo sack still cost a pretty penny!

Jenny was delighted with the results; firm solid figurines with a strong resistance to breakage, and which dried to a smooth finish showing all the fine detail ready for painting and varnish. Of course I knew it wouldn't stop here, once she had got the bit between her teeth she wanted to research different styles and designs of chess moulds that eventually took her range up to four and in the time that she waited for her new moulds to arrive in the post, she increased her stock of leaded pictures on our walls.

When there was no more space for pictures she started to investigate other artwork possibilities using card and glue, ribbons and dried leaves; then very soon a small range of very different greeting cards began filling boxes. She was unstoppable as different ideas began to appear and as her reputation grew she received a great opportunity.

A local farmer and his wife had extensive acres of plum orchards and the annual fruit was mostly converted into prunes. But in addition they were producing their own home preserves; delicious prune aperitifs in a variety of flavours, prunes preserved in eau de vie plus a selection of jams and much more were all selling well in their farm shop which was a converted milking parlour, and now the farm shop had become a regular spot for visiting tourists.

They had always been keen to support local art, so in their shop they had devoted the space within each of the six cow byres, free of charge, to any willing artist who wanted to make a display, and the advantage for them was that it would attract more clients to their shop.

The introduction to the farmer and his wife was made through some friends who bought one of Jenny's pictures, and so it was that she had her first mini exhibition. She was thrilled to have sold one picture in consideration that it was quite late in the season, but she was thrilled with the reason why she had to later collect back all her work.

Lynn's husband Jacques was involved at the mayor's office concerning the twinning of our village with Algolsheim in Alsace, and he was also a friend of our mayor Mr Gouget. He arrived on our drive and after our greetings he said…

"Would Jenny like to hold an exhibition in the town?"

"I'm sure she would," I replied and explained that as she wasn't here at present, I would tell her later and get back to him. WOW! her very own exhibition.

He went on to explain that the tiny old chapel next to the Mayors' offices had been converted for use as a function room, and that it had hanging rails for use as a gallery. I asked how much it would cost.

"Nothing…" he said, "…she can have it free for a week, just say when you'd like it to be."

Jenny was delighted when I told her and as Christmas was approaching the obvious choice was the first week in December when people start to think of presents for family and friends.

I spent hours finding the right translations to produce the flyers which the local shop owners kindly allowed us to place in their windows, and on Jacques' suggestion and with his help linguistically we sent out a number of invitations to local prominent people, to come and enjoy an apératif at the opening ceremony.

We formed a great idea of how we could show our gratitude to the Mayor with a gift, and at the same time attract a little free publicity. Knowing that our village had a coat of arms we researched the design and Jenny produced her version of it as one of her leaded glass pictures. As a close friend of the Mayor, we enlisted Jacques' assistance to ensure that Monsieur Gouget accepted the invitation to attend her opening and drinks party. Jacques' instructions were that if necessary he could divulge that there might be a presentation and that the press would be in attendance.

At the height of attendance and just after the journalist had arrived I called for silence and Jenny presented her gift. On reflection we think he had some idea but he was totally unprepared for what he received. As he opened the wrapping his eyes opened wide with the surprise as he asked.

"Where on earth did you find the design?"

We satisfied his curiosity by admitting that we had photographed it from the side of the village football ground changing rooms. He promised it would hang in pride of place in the council chambers.

The event was an enormous success and Jenny received acclaim for her work from all who had visited including the local newspaper who did a splendid write-up with a photo of the presentation.

Over the next few months as the stocks and range of her artwork increased even more, we started to consider the possibilities of a more permanent outlet which led us into the minefield of French bureaucracy for starting a small business, and not wishing to take the plunge directly into a shop, we thought it would be a great idea to have a stall at the village markets.

Frequently visiting one very busy Sunday market we had often chatted to a friendly English trader and so we decided to elicit his help to advise us on the route to take. Little did we know at that time that this route would prove to be one of the most stressful experiences of Jenny's life, one that would reduce her to tears and make us question whether we still wanted a market stall.

'*Le stage*' is obligatory if you want to start a business in France. It is a five-day course which is essential to complete before you can register and receive the all-important *Siret* number. You can't start a business in France without a registration number. Our initial enquiries took us to the nearest '*Chambre de Commerce*' at Villeneuve sûr Lot and they were they were very helpful in directing us instead to the '*Chambre de Métier*' across to the other side of the city. They in turn were also most helpful and directed us to the '*Sous Préfecture*' right in the centre of town.

Off we went to the Under Prefecture whose offices we had driven past an hour earlier, only to find that we were 10 minutes late for their four o'clock closing and hence we returned the following day making sure we took with us the profuse documentation they required.

After the initial struggle with the three receptionists, a very frosty lady interviewed us. The ice eventually broke over a problem with one of her questions; Collins pocket dictionary couldn't solve it, the three receptionists couldn't, but a passing colleague did, and we all had a good laugh. After nearly an hour we eventually left with the completed '*attestation d' intente*' and returned to the '*Chambre de Commerce*.'

We met once more with a very nice lady who again assisted us with her near perfect English and furthered our understanding of bureaucracy in France. She now explained we needed to return to the '*Chambre de Métier*,' and make an appointment to register our intention to join the five-day training course, which when completed would allow us to apply for the permit to trade. Quite simple really!

We arrived at the duly appointed hour, expecting to produce all relevant documents, sign some papers, and leave shortly afterwards with a date when Jenny would attend the next course in January.

We left nearly three hours later, after sitting in stifling heat through an introductory lecture alongside thirty other students, to explain the contents of the future course and what we could all expect to gain from it. I concentrated really hard listening to the lecture but it was a hot day and the upstairs room was airless despite the open windows, eventually after just over thirty minutes the intensity of trying to absorb spoken French overcame me and I intermittently dropped off!

As we left the building in the bright afternoon sun we stopped at a cafe for a much needed drink to re-adjust mentally after the exhausting concentration, it had drained us both, and we were disappointed to learn that the nearest course was held at Agen, a busy metropolis and the department administrative centre.

Her application and fee had been accepted and she left home early on the appointed day for the hour-long journey to Agen. Entering the busy rush hour traffic she did three circuits after missing the turn before successfully placing herself in the right lane. Eventually she found the course class room and sat down to await the arrival of the other students and the lowering of her stress level.

During the introductory conversations with the other students she was greatly relieved to find that there were three other English students who fortunately understood and spoke better French than she did. They soon had a car share organised for the journey which meant that Jenny only had to drive locally each day, but their unfailing support during the course was what got her through it. The caring encouragement they gave when she dissolved into tears, embarrassed by her lack of understanding in front of the tutor and class kept her going.

Although speaking little English, her tutor understood very well the problem within the system for foreign students and conceded that many aspects of the course were irrelevant to Jenny's business. But she made it through unscathed, made some good new friends and registered as a market trader. Now all we needed was some sort of market stall to trade from.

I had become a trusted key holder for the workshop and with Laurent's approval I hooked up our old and tired trailer and took it to work. I soon cannibalised it saving only the wiring loom and the sprung axle, and slowly each evening our old trailer grew into our market stall. From a plain-looking box on wheels it opened out into a marvellous display stand with a smart canvas roof made from our old frame tent.

It could be assembled in minutes giving a stepped display top and plenty of hanging space for her pictures and cards. It had ample storage space inside for the canopy and poles plus loads of extra space for the boxes of Jenny's diverse art; we could keep it loaded then just hook up and go.

The first time we tried it was a major disappointment. We arrived at Villeréal and parked the car to seek out the '*Placeuse*'. She is the person who says who goes where and she would show us our allotted space for the morning market and return later for the fee. Soon we had everything assembled as on-looking traders marvelled at the transformation unfolding beside them. We congratulated ourselves and were thankful for the previous day's rehearsal at home.

Unpacking the stock from within the trailer our hearts sank. The suspension on the old camping trailer had been totally inadequate to stop the bouncing along the road and every precaution for safe packaging had been a gross underestimation.

The chess sets took the brunt of it and hardly a complete set was worthy of display. Boxed and individually wrapped in tissue paper they had knocked against each other inside the boxes chipping the paint and were now un-saleable. We could no longer use the trailer for Jenny's stock and serious research was needed for proper packaging materials.

As the summer season progressed so did our experience. We gave up the busy market in Villeréal on a Saturday because we were always placed in some obscure corner and rarely sold. Instead we tried the medieval town of Issigeac on a Sunday. Market days for us started around six in the morning. Quickly dressed we would load the car with all Jenny's boxes, hook up and go.

Although we became familiar regulars we still had to go through the same procedure with the '*Placeuse*'; a stressful time as until we have our allocation we can be anywhere along the long narrow main street or any of its side streets. Like children on a school outing we hopeful summer traders all dutifully followed her in the ritual parade through the streets stopping as each of us was re-questioned about our products when a space became apparent.

We were still being eyed suspiciously by some regular traders, and newcomers similar to us saw us as a threat to their preferred pitches, but after a few weeks and as we approached the spot that has become a favourite of ours Madame Placeuse searched for us within the group.

"*Madame Cooper, C'est bon la*?"

Relieved at the allocation of our usual spot we replied, "*Oui merci*," and as Jenny guarded it like a coveted space in a busy car park I dashed off for the car and the repetition of our weekly agenda. The narrow streets were now almost impassable; stallholders with their goods who have arrived before us were sprawled across the road and it was a relief when at last I navigated the car away through the mayhem to find the nearest parking space.

On my return the priority was to level the trailer and prop the wheels, then together we assembled the tubes and poles and fittted the canvas canopy before I could assemble and stabilise the additional trestles and table top which had now become necessary for the ever-growing display.

As eight o'clock approached everyone was busy setting out their wares. It was a process perfected over many years and we quickly fell into the same ritual while chatting briefly with our neighbours of the week. Involvement for me in the setting up of the display was not allowed by Jenny so I seized the opportunity to go in search of breakfast and enjoy the market atmosphere.

The Boulangerie was usually my first stop, to buy the breakfast baguette and one of their excellent nut loaves, before they all disappeared. A stallholder I often chat with threw me a cheery *bonjour* and I stoppped to swap our weekly news, but I was anxious to tear myself away when the delicious aroma coming from the next stall I was heading for reached me.

It was a scrupulously clean stall run by two guys who looked very much to me like they were a couple. Huge pans filled with today's dishes were giving off a delicious aroma as they gently simmered away; there was bœuf bourguignon and curries, casseroled pork and spicy chicken, spit roasting hams and game birds, belly pork and big fat Toulouse sausages gently browning on a griddle surrounded by caramelised onions.

I have to arrive early because it's a very popular stall and my preference - the sausages, soon sold out and reluctantly I would have to revert to the thickly sliced roasted ham. One Sunday I missed both but on returning through the market I bought two spit roasted quails instead; nice breakfast!

As I passed the café a rich aroma of coffee wafted into the street along with the sound of busy conversation, and through the open door I could see that the tables were all taken by breakfasting traders who were way ahead of us.

It was still early so I chatted with Paul who sold cheese. Unlike some who trade the markets he has a solid reputation for excellent cheeses, and says he regularly sells Stilton to the French.

One unfortunate day we were placed next to a disreputable vendor of cheeses whose sales tactics left a lot to be desired. The cheese in question was without doubt excellent but I doubt it was worth the extortionate price he was charging for it.

His patter was to offer a sliver to passing tourists who of-course found it most palatable, then in contrast he offered samples of inferior cheeses. Of course they said they preferred the first sample and readily agreed to buy, as he cut and wrapped a huge slice and placed it upon the counter and waited while the tourist fumbled for the money, a huge inflation of what you would expect. Unfamiliar with a strange currency they were often totally unaware of the price they were paying. Each week the same stall but a different salesman selling the cheese.

We watched them take six hundred Euros during one morning, so given a chance we would casually give tourists a warning when possible. I know because I fell into his trap shortly after we came to live here.

I discussed this problem with my cheese pal Paul. He told me that respected regular traders had unsuccessfully tried to put a stop to it as it was destroying the essence of

French markets but that the *Placeuse* was powerless to stop it and the culprits knew it.

It was mid-morning and the sun had now risen high. The weekly parade of shoppers had reached maximum with summer visitors and passing became almost impossible as tourists stopped at each stall to view the goods on sale. It's interesting to watch how people behave and interact with each other when unaware that they are being observed.

As midday approached, the streets slowly begin to empty as people headed home for lunch and the traders, we included started to dismantle and pack away. Our placement was fortunately close to where the market ends but for many, exit was strictly by convoy through the narrow streets and at some ungiven signal all the vans and cars lined up in order to repack and leave. Miss your turn to bring your vehicle in at your peril because you will then have to wait until all others have left or carry it back to the car piled high on the trailer, wherever it may be parked.

French people go to market to buy fresh produce at a cheaper price and have a good chat, it's a social event and they do plenty of the latter, so Jenny biased her products towards the tourists who come to this beautiful medieval town. Unfortunately people do not come to market expecting to spend a reasonable amount of money on art so sales were slow and she was glad she had her stocks of greeting cards and smaller pictures which went well.

We stayed throughout the summer season and some weeks were quite encouraging, others very discouraging but we met some lovely people amongst the French traders who encouraged and helped us. It was a pleasurable social event, a wonderful experience and a great learning curve for the future. But for us a future that we felt didn't include market trading as an outlet for Jen's art.

31

It had been many years since I had spent eight hours a day on my feet in any workshop. During the first weeks I sorely missed the benefit of the English 10 o'clock tea-break, and I was glad of the French two hour lunch break. It gave me time to have a good lunch, and afterwards I developed the habit of putting my feet up and resting my complaining back during a quick siesta. As the outdoor warmth increased I took my siesta naked in the full sunshine, often falling into a deep sleep. My tan was coming along nicely – one day the back, the next the front.

Jenny had strict instructions when to wake me so that I had time for a refreshing dip in the pool to bring me fully awake. My reliance upon Jenny's timing didn't always work as she herself would be absorbed in some occupation and forget, then it was a quick in-and-out and a frantic dash back to work.

One afternoon I walked sheepishly back into the workshop at five minutes past two and, receiving a disapproving look from Laurent as he tapped his watch, I felt really guilty. Although he was my employer, there was also a strong friendship and I felt like I had let him down.

He knew that in England I had owned my own similar business and he knew I had a kindred understanding of the problems he faced because we had discussed it. Although it was difficult with the language, sometimes he would speak about his future ideas and ask my opinion, and I became increasingly involved when he dealt with English clients and site visits.

He came with his family to the Saturday market at Villeréal, to support Jenny's first market and showed great enthusiasm for her venture, and with this same enthusiasm he invited us to join with him and exhibit at the renowned craft fair, in the medieval streets of Tombebœuf during the warm summer days of August.

The *Salle de fête,* a beautifully renovated stone built village hall, had a large arched entrance that was now fully glazed. Laurent was just outside with his display of wrought-iron work and pool fencing, and a new range of inexpensive steel patio furniture which we had developed between us. We had an equally good spot just inside the windows where Jenny set up a magnificent display of all her work.

When all the other exhibitors had finalised their displays, we were disappointed to realise that there were very few actual craft stalls, and that it wasn't much more than a village WI affair.

This craft fair has a reputation for attracting visitors from miles around, but this year it seemed that the only visitors were the village inhabitants which was a little disheartening, but we did meet some nice folk, especially an elderly wood turner. He had numerous items on display and was also giving practical demonstrations on his lathe, which gave us an idea.

Jenny had recently bought an antique oak dining room dresser in one of our local *brocantes.* It had a lower section with two doors below two drawers, and an upper section that also had two doors but with superb stained glass windows mounted in the frames, and much of the woodwork was beautifully carved. Between the upper and lower sections was a small gallery plate shelf with turned balusters five centimetres high and eight of them were missing.

The whole piece was in a poor condition with many areas needing minor repairs and it had been reduced in price more than once during the six months it had been in the shop. Jenny had bided her time over the months and now felt it was the right time to offer a substantial reduction and luckily got it.

When we went back to the craft fair for the second day, we took with us one of the balusters and sought out the old wood turner to ask him if he could make us eight new ones to replace those missing.

His face lit up with a warm smile as he affectionately revolved our sample in his fingers, feeling its age and quality. We explained that there was no hurry, and exchanged our details so he could contact us on completion. He strolled over to us about an hour later proudly displaying the one new piece and our sample and gave it to us at no charge. A little embarrassed, I explained that we wanted eight, but not today, again saying that he could take his time and make them at home on his more sophisticated lathe.

Jenny took his call two weeks afterwards and because we were unable to fully understand his directions, we set off armed with his address and a map. His village was only fifteen minutes from us and we soon arrived, searching for someone to ask the final directions to his house. The only person we found hadn't a clue, so we set off again along the only road not yet investigated.

We soon found a sign which directed us towards his house; it took us up hill and down dale, round bends through farms, to yet another sign for his house. Travelling along a woodland track we began to feel a little lost when suddenly the woods parted and there stood a smartly painted house encircled by an assortment of large wooden sheds that were defying gravity.

As we got out of the car the front door opened and we saw him register our familiar faces. We shook hands and exchanged greetings before he led us on a tour of his workshops and as our tour progressed he explained each machine and its function before proudly displaying items that he had made to emphasise each point.

We continued to follow him, climbing over ankle-deep wood shavings and various offcuts in this Aladdin's cave while he showed us tables and spiralled legs for chairs, wooden mushrooms, bookcases and lecterns, and an assortment of other items all equally well made.

Finally he delved into in an old shoe box and retrieved our beautifully turned and polished balusters. When I asked him the price he reluctantly charged us one Euro each, and when I asked him his age he shyly admitted he was eighty four!

We followed his directions and left by a different route passing through yet another farm which he proudly told us was his son's business, a market garden. As the woodland bordering the road opened to fields, we passed a deer farm and saw a stag with huge antlers leading the grazing herd across the enclosure, and then in contrast as the enclosure passed behind us, Jenny noticed a quick movement to our right as a wild deer frantically darted from the roadside. I quickly braked as it narrowly missed the oncoming vehicle to disappear into the orchard on our left and escaped unharmed.

Soon back on the main road, we found ourselves back home in half the time, but we had seen a part of France not before ventured into, and met a wonderful character who we hope we will see again.

32

The season for '*la chasse*' starts mid-September. It is the season when every able-bodied gun owner takes to the countryside in search of a meal he doesn't have to pay for. Habitually French hunters feel they have '*carte-blanche*' to roam anywhere with their dogs and will often shoot at anything that moves.

Modern laws have regulated hunting to suit a modern society and where wild deer and boar are concerned, the balance between control of these free-ranging animals and extinction is strictly controlled by the deterrent fines. Inbred traditions change slowly and little respect is shown towards garden boundaries if it means a shortcut to the woodland beyond.

We respect these traditions, they are part of the France we love; but we expect a reciprocal respect towards the sign at the top of our drive which says – '*Propriété privée - défense d'entrée.*' It hadn't stopped one intrepid hunter whose vehicle we came home to find parked and blocking the lower part of the drive; and it hadn't stopped the two dogs who tried to savage some of our chickens while the owner strolled casually through the garden. When brought to his attention that it was in fact our garden the usual reply goes something like…

"Well this is France – what do you expect?"

One Sunday towards the end of Jenny's market career, we had arrived home just after lunch, tired and hungry and incensed to find three hunters making their way towards our boundary and their exit to the road via our drive.

Fired by Jenny's "You get over there and tell them," routine I stomped off to deliver a well-rehearsed bollocking.

"*Excusez-moi mais…Ah Philippe, c'est vous !*" As I suddenly realised it was indeed my friend Philippe. He introduced me to his eldest son Frederic, a tall man in his early twenties with a ragged beard and hair that was ripe for dreadlocks, and then Frederic's girl-friend Annabelle who although short and rounded, had skin like silk and I imagined she would be very cuddly.

Philippe had taken lunch with his aged mother who lives behind the hill that borders our valley, and had then decided that an afternoon walk accompanied by the shotgun and family would be good for his digestion; as I suspected, would be my whiskey.

Lunch for us was to be a quick re-heat and then we could crash in front of a good movie before we probably dozed off. Now events had taken a different turn I could feel Jenny's displeasure and so tried to lighten things a little. Passing through the kitchen door, my attention was drawn to the pheasant we had suspended from one of our beams in a muslin bag.

"Philippe, did you shoot anything?" I enquired.

"Non." He replied, and so I launched into teasing him.

"Well look," I said, and pointing to the pheasant, "I haven't been hunting yet I have a plump pheasant to eat."

"Oh that's disgusting," he remarked, "... what are you doing…"

"It's hanging…" I said, "... to tenderise the meat then…"

"NO - NO, you can't eat a pheasant when it's rotten."

I was a little stunned by his adamant opinion but ventured forward in the hope that I might learn something. "*D'accord* – OK - so tell me how would you prepare and cook it."

"You do this, and you do that and then…" He forcefully retorted.

"Philippe…" I asked, "...are you free tomorrow evening?"

"*Err – Oui.*"

"Good, then you can come to our house and you cook the pheasant and then we can all eat it together, yes?"

He thought about it for a second and immediately mellowed saying, "Why not…but Jenny…"

"Yes Philippe."

"…You have to pluck and clean the bird and buy me a *chou.*"

"A what?"

"A *chou*, it's a round green leafy vegetable – like a football."

"I think he means a cabbage, let me get a book."…and I left them discussing shoes and went for a confirming picture. Although quite why he wanted a cabbage to cook a pheasant neither of us could fathom out but we're always ready to learn something new.

Now the fate of the pheasant had been decided we all settled in the lounge and the afternoon soon blended into the early evening. All three later accepted Jenny's offer of a ride home, especially Philippe who by that time I suspected would have found any walk difficult. I promised myself to phone him later the next day as I could visualise the uncooked bird patiently waiting for the Chef!

The pheasant itself had an interesting history. Keith and Margaret were in France at their barn for a couple of weeks and Keith phoned to ask if we liked pheasant. "Yes." I replied and expecting to be invited over for one of Margaret's gourmet dinners, I was surprised to be offered the bird for our own kitchen.

We later learned that the pheasant had appeared one morning on their patio table and Keith was under the impression that having landed there, the hunter was reluctant to retrieve it from their patio; a scenario which I very much doubted. If it had fallen through their window and landed on the kitchen table the hunter would have walked in with a quick and friendly 'Bonjour', retrieved the bird and left with it without a second word.

Despite the fact that hunters think they own the countryside which they may well do, there does exists a code of protocol amongst all but a rogue, and if someone has had a 'good morning' upon your land he will often show his appreciation – like leaving a pheasant upon your patio table – *voila.*

So Jenny cleaned and dressed the pheasant and bought a cabbage and Philippe arrived buzzing with enthusiasm and a carrier bag of goodies; we were pleased that Frederic and his girlfriend could come as well because we had enjoyed their company the previous day.

Like two students at a master-class we watched Philippe with keen interest as he rolled up his sleeves, and giving a nod of approval to the dressed bird he produced a home-made stuffing which he skilfully placed inside the bird, and while sealing the flap he explained its intricate recipe.

In the base and around the sides of a large oven pot he placed a layer of cabbage leaves and carefully lowered the pheasant inside, then enclosing the parcel with a top layer of leaves, a good shake of seasoning and a few tablespoons of water, he sealed the pot with the lid. This he said would suffice for the hour and a half cooking time in the oven and added…

"Now, can I have a whiskey please while we wait?"

As the rich if not strange aroma began to drift from the kitchen, Frederic tinkered with my banjo and Jenny introduced him to some of my blue-grass music.

Philippe and I became involved in his ongoing English lessons. What seems to us to be quite a simple multi-meaning English word always causes him problems which he requests to be clarified. It is at this point that the conversation really takes an in-depth turn as I search for an explanation using my limited French vocabulary and eventually give up.

Philippe confirmed that the pheasant was now cooked and while Jenny put the accompanying vegetables in serving dishes he broke open the cooked bird onto a platter. The meat was superbly tender and succulent with a slight flavour of the cabbage and the stuffing he had made suited it perfectly; as did the bottle of Cahors.

Fortunately Philippe's intake the previous afternoon had taken the edge of his appetite for my whiskey and we bade them all farewell at a reasonable hour and went to bed with the memory of another very pleasant evening.

33

The ten-year-old gas boiler mounted on our kitchen wall was showing all the signs of terminal illness. It had been ill before and had received a new thermal couple twice. The third time it wouldn't respond to treatment and had refused to light when the open tap called for hot water.

Last winter during the Christmas holiday when my son Greg was here with his girlfriend, we had a warning of its impending death and became used to the two huge saucepans constantly heating water on the top of the dining room wood-burning stove.

I was sure that the gas valve service kit and another thermal couple would do the trick, and when this failed I called in a pal who was convinced his experience with like water heaters would soon have the thing fired into life. After a frustrating hour of dissection and re-assembly it still refused to rally, and then after one last attempt it fired.

It didn't last for long and in my acceptance of the situation I administered a kindly blow of euthanasia with a large hammer.

Collecting together all our meagre savings we spent the next day within the isles of France's equivalent to B&Q, and came away with a car load of materials. It would seem that the planned make-over for the kitchen and bathroom which included the hot and cold water system had just taken a major leap forward out of necessity.

Within a week all the plumbing was renewed and within the loft, inside its very own double insulated enclosure was a cylinder containing two hundred litres of hot water, waiting to dispense to a modern shower cubicle and a new sink in the kitchen.

It wasn't really quite the disaster it seemed because as always, when something we needed for the future appeared at a bargain price, we had bought it. We had the sink and taps for the kitchen, and along with the shower cubicle we had a new bowl and taps for the bathroom, but the best bargains were the bathroom and kitchen units.

Months previously I had visited an English couple who wanted some work done. During the conversation they realised my diverse capabilities and announced their regret at having just placed an order for a new kitchen elsewhere. I couldn't see anything wrong with the old one, but their opinion was that they just didn't like it, so it was going to the dump.

My Mother always said, "Don't ask – don't get."

When we later went to collect it the client had directed his builders to take care with its removal and had safely stored it out of the weather. It was solidly made in real wood and the journey home tested the springs of both the car and the trailer which were both fully laden.

We did have to pay for the bathroom units however but the price was nothing because it came from the 'casualty corner' of the showroom and the minor repair necessary made it worthwhile.

Part of the initial problem with the boiler had been caused by the extreme hardness of our water. We were constantly removing the lime scale from the filters of the tap outlets and assumed that the old piping would be the same, so it seemed prudent to fit the double cartridge water filters under the sink where the water main entered the house. This was probably the most expensive single part of the whole make-over, and one that later proved to have a hidden expense that cost us far more.

Up and down between the barn and the house collecting and returning different tools while working on the kitchen, I spied François in his orchard and climbing the embankment into his land where our garden ends, I could see his ready smile as he waited to greet me.

"Bonjour Bob." His pronunciation of my name with a French accent sounds strange every time I hear it, and as I returned his greeting the smile creased my face as I replied.

"Bonjour François, ça va?"

"Ah oui, ça va bien merci." He replied.

I was always interested in what he was doing and he never tired of my questions, always offering a ready explanation. He had just finished pruning his vines and the cuttings were laying everywhere. He said that he would be bundling them together to tie into parcels for storage somewhere that I couldn't quite catch. Nothing was wasted because he said he used them to light his fire.

We conversed about the weather, and I remarked about the smell emanating from the beef farm behind us. François was well tuned to what was happening in farming around us, and he explained that it was time for them to move the dung heap from the farm to the fields that bordered us all, in readiness for the annual muck spreading. I looked forward to that!

It took a while for him to locate the words that I knew and could understand, but eventually it registered with me that he was offering me some pumpkins that he had grown and he added that his wife Renée made delicious soup with it. I had no doubt in this as everything Renée made was delicious, well almost.

Later in the evening when we arrived to collect the pumpkins, we were invited in as usual and were greeted to a wonderful aroma of garlic and cooking. As we greeted Renée and François's sister we could see the reason why because on the kitchen table there were two huge bowls of freshly made sausages that the two ladies had made that afternoon.

Pinching and lifting the skin on the back of his hand while saying *"Porc, Porc"*, I assumed that he was trying to tell me that the skins were made from pigs' gut, but with the exception of garlic and parsley, we were unable to decipher what the contents were.

We were invited to sit and he produced a carton of nibbles with an unlabelled bottle which he said was Pinot de Charente. It was a rich aperitif full of the flavour of fruit and he then added that it was given to him for a present. We discussed Renée's health and Jenny was saddened to learn that one of her toes was blackening, one more symptom of her declining health through diabetes.

As we were leaving François took us through to collect the pumpkins from their utility room and store where Jenny and I were amazed to see how much produce they had stored there. In addition to many Kilner jars full of fruit and vegetables from François' garden, Renée had obviously just made a fresh batch of pâté, and Jenny drew my attention to the strings of saucisson that were hanging from the beams to dry.

As usual our departure was delayed, this time because we received an explanation from François about the contents of each container and how best to eat it. Eventually we made our way into their kitchen towards the exit and I realised why Renée hadn't joined us in the storeroom because she had foil wrapped two freshly made sausages which she then pressed into Jenny's hand for our supper. She must have read my mind!

Back home and hungry after all the talk of food, we restocked the fires and silenced the whingeing Siamese with yet more food before we then turned our attention to supper.

François was emphatic; we should only cook the sausages really slowly under a medium grill to prevent them from exploding, and following his recommendation we decided to accompany them with some French beans and mashed potatoes.

We laid the table and because one sausage each would be a little smaller than our usual meal, we decided to eat an entrée of *pâté de campagne* and some crusty *bannette* loaf while they cooked. I was always eager to try most different foods but I commented to Jenny. "I hope I'm going to like this?"

Taking my knife and fork in hand, I tentatively made a cut as my mouth salivated profusely. Jenny was ahead of me, "Oh they're delicious!" She managed between mouthfuls.

Lifting the fork to my mouth I placed the first morsel inside and began to chew and that's as far as I got. My eyes registered the contents at the same time as my mouth and I realised at last what François had been trying to tell me; the contents were pigs' skin, roughly chopped and boiled and then flavoured with the parsley and garlic. As if in a dream all of François' descriptions from an hour previous came flooding back and at last I understood his explanation and watched while Jenny devoured both sausages.

The shops at the beginning of December are full of the build-up to Christmas and here in France there still remains a magic of Christmas that is not yet totally lost to commercialisation. It is however a time where little cost is spared in gastronomic celebration, a time for families to come together around the table, when sons and daughters return home from distant universities to celebrate with rarely seen relatives, and children excitedly await the arrival of *Pierre Noël.*

Any shop remotely concerned with the sale of anything edible has something special on offer, but the first prize must go to the *Boucher, Charcuter et Traiteur* – the butchers who produce their own variety of cooked meats, pâtés and prepared dishes. My local butcher Julien has a display that is difficult to pass without admiration. His village shop is by no means cheap in comparison to the nearest supermarket but his meats and charcuterie are always excellent, and in the weeks preceding Christmas his additional marble-topped tables overflow with goodies.

Whole poached salmon *en croute* stuffed with scallops, pâtés of *foie gras* and a sea food mousse encased in a pastry so fine it melts in the mouth; it takes a strong will to come away without a bill that would half fill the car with fuel.

The *Boulanger* comes a very close second with his displays of Christmas *patisserie* that has become an art form. Mini tartlets and pastries filled with an assortment of fruits, cakes and *gâteaux* with toppings and fillings of amazing flavours.

I visually enjoy the display of fresh fruit and vegetables in supermarkets and while not a great lover of fruits, the vegetables can inspire many different dishes. At Christmas the aisles in our nearest big supermarket shrink as they accommodate the influx of seasonal fruit and vegetables from far-away places, many of which I have never seen before.

The feel of Christmas was also evident within the workshop where my employment fortunately continued. After harvest time the pressure reduced as less machinery arrived for repair and Laurent turned his attention towards developing products for the increasing number of holiday-home owners.

Most of the English clients spoke enough French to phone and make an appointment for a site visit but still they were visibly relieved when it became apparent that they were not going to have to conduct a technical conversation in French. I knew how Laurent's mind worked; keep it simple and at the same time give the customer what they wanted at a price that fitted well. It was after one such meeting that had gone well that he showed his appreciation unexpectedly.

I sat in the car on my own contemplating the meeting while he had stopped to visit a small village store. Returning to the car he handed me a bottle of very good malt whiskey.

"This is for you," he said, "*Bon Noël*."

In France, Christmas day is a time for recuperation and relaxation, celebrations are during Christmas Eve and we felt honoured to have been invited to share it with Laurent and his family.

There seems to be some strange history within Laurent's family of eleven brothers and sisters that protocol demands - don't ask, so we were not surprised to find that the family we joined were all from his wife Corrine's side. Her father Clovis and her mother with her second husband all seemed to get along fine, two brothers and a younger sister with their respective partners and an entourage of children of varying ages down to a highly excited three-year-old.

I knew most of them by sight and some of them like Clovis, well enough to have a good joke with. Jenny had met Clovis before when we attended a summer drinks party and he seemed to have taken a shine to her despite being in his seventies. A handsome solid man who always wore an immaculate cap which when removed displayed a meagre rim of shining silver hair surrounding skin the colour of freshly laundered white sheets.

Ninety minutes passed quickly while we enjoyed the delicious nibbles and drinks, engrossed in the family camaraderie before we were all summoned to the table. I could see Jenny was a little anxious about her language skills because it was the men at one end and the women at the other, with the children somewhere between the two. I knew she would somehow cope when I noticed her dispensing the fish soup amongst the girls at her end.

We lads were already on the second bowlful, and when at last the bowl is finished – *Chabrol*, the custom of adding a little red wine to the dregs and drinking it from the dish. Checking on how Jenny was coping at her end I didn't notice Clovis overfilling my bowl and waiting for me to say, *C'est tout, merci* – that's enough. He thought it a great joke watching me struggle to finish it all saying, "Well you didn't say stop!"

Peeling huge prawns from the immense platter in front of us didn't come easy when my head was beginning to feel a little muzzy, but this next course was well worth the effort and the supply seemed endless. Corrine's brother handed me a huge loaf with a knife, which I used and passed on to Michele her other brother across the table from me, then following the paralysing liquid to cleanse the pallet the *foie gras* arrived.

The guinea fowl was excellent and perfectly complimented by the flageolet green beans, though what was added to produce the mouth-watering flavour I couldn't guess. Cheese was a simple affair; one large brie and a hunk of blue served with green salad and a titillating dressing of balsamic vinegar.

As midnight was drawing near, two steaming fruit tarts were placed upon heat mats and a pile of plates was being passed from one to the other down the table in an ever-decreasing stack. Corrine's brother-in-law finished his dessert in record time, then left the table and disappeared; nobody except me seemed to think anything of it!

Suddenly someone was frantically ringing the doorbell. At three years old Laurent's nephew was probably the only believer in *Pierre Noël* and as the continuous ring on the doorbell was brought to his attention he timidly opened the door. His eyes opened wide as he turned to the assembled family announcing, "*C'est Pierre Noël!*"

Father Christmas had indeed arrived and this wide-eyed boy sat absolutely spellbound upon a little stool watching and hoping as Father Christmas reached into his sack again and again, and frequently became a recipient. As the children played unaffected by the late hour we assisted in clearing the tables and ferrying what remained of the dishes back into the kitchen.

We danced, we laughed and we watched as Laurent drilled a hole in the centre of the lounge wall to mount his new electronic dart board. Eventually at two thirty on a frosty Christmas morning, we bid our grateful thanks and left the family to it.

We suspect that they were still at it when dawn broke on our Christmas morning and our thoughts turned to our Christmas lunch, but we were both in no hurry for a midday meal and agreed that mid-afternoon would suit us nicely. We now knew why French people spent Christmas day recuperating and relaxing and happily spent a lazy day on our own thankful that we weren't entertaining.

We awoke on boxing morning feeling quite refreshed if not totally recovered after an early night, and so took advantage of the brisk sunny day to blow away the cobwebs working in the garden. It is not a national holiday in France although many businesses have adopted the idea to carry the break through to the New Year. We had no special plans to celebrate the turn of the year and neither did Philippe, so we invited him to join us for the evening and together we shared its arrival.

34

I promised myself to make a concerted effort during the New Year to finish the pool and terracing, after all it had sat there unfinished though usable for well over three years.

The problem had been that it was usable; and even before the water temperature reached my preferred minimum I couldn't resist a quick dip, safe in the knowledge that the early season sunshine would soon take away those shivers. Failing that – I could have always popped back indoors for a hot shower.

I had been known to swim with the frogs - to take the first naked plunge of the season while the last residue of winter algae was still reluctant to relinquish its residency on the bottom and all that I could see was a sludgy-green carpet harbouring I knew-not-what! Of course it would have made the annual 'clean up' of the water a much easier task if I had fitted the winter cover, but that's a little hard when we didn't have a terrace to fit it to. I was asked to promise "no more new projects", until some of the others have been finished, game set and match – I lost.

A few days later Jenny answered a knock on the door.

"Jenny, I've got a problem," explained a very worried looking Lynne. "My wood burning stove has smoke billowing out of all the joints and around the door, and it won't draw properly. Now it's gone out."

"Your chimney probably needs sweeping, have you had it done lately?" Jenny asked, realising that the answer was written all over Lynn's face.

"You had better come in, I'm having coffee… will you join me?"

We hadn't seen much of our neighbour Lynn since she left her French husband Jacques and renting a small Gite had ventured out to start a new life on her own. Of course sadly we had seen it coming during our first years here in south west France when she often confided to us as kindred English, that she felt Jacques manipulated her life. But I guess we thought, or hoped that she would never do it, fearing that she lacked the skills for a solitary existence.

Once inside the house in the warm, Lynne continued. "I need some of those rods and a brush, have you got some?"

Jenny saw the worried look begin to wane as she replied. "Yes, have you ever used them?"

"No," she replied as the look of doom was starting to return.

Taking a deep breath Jenny ventured "Will it help if I bring them over after lunch and see what I can do."

Visibly relieved she answered. "Oh Jenny, is there anything you can't do?

Arriving as promised, Jenny the chimney sweep in her green boiler suit quickly attended to the problem, and by safely negotiating the damper valve with her brushes she soon had soot audibly falling into the fire grate. With no children to rush excitedly outside to shout when the brush was out at the top, it was left to Lynne who performed the task admirably.

Following a good clean up of the spoils she laid a new fire which once alight burned so well that Lynne remarked, "Oh it's never burned that well, and its giving off heat now, thank you Jenny."

Watching the proceedings with keen interest was neighbour Muriel from the adjoining house and owner of Lynne's temporary home. Muriel had realised that her own chimney had never been swept since its installation two years previously, and not wanting to miss a golden opportunity had ask whether Jenny would do a second one? Jenny of course obliged returning home three hours later and happy to have been of service.

A month later, I was sitting for lunch at a table in a harbour-front restaurant in *Boulogne-Sur-Mer.* Through the window I could see the weak February sun reflecting from the masts of numerous yachts, but it was cold outside and dark clouds were looming. The quiet roads of Lot-et-Garonne that I'd left early evening yesterday were far behind me after my overnight drive, and as I waited for my channel crossing I shuddered as to what I could expect on the roads when I left Dover enroute for my home town, two hours further north.

I had started my journey later than planned and by mid-evening hunger had forced me to stop outside a dimly lit bar and restaurant; it was a good opportunity to phone Jenny back at home and report on my progress. This would be only the third time I'd returned during six years, but even so Jenny hates it when I go and I worry about her. God knows what inadvisable projects she will attempt on her own in my absence or what minor injury she will inflict upon herself this time.

On my return last time I found her face bruised and covered in scratches, which she brushed off as some minor incident with a bramble bush. Later when she was wincing from rib pain I questioned her further and discovered the whole truth. She had clambered up over the top of head high boxes stored in the garage to hoist out a bicycle.

Raising it above her head she had proceeded to climb back out – with the bicycle. She then slipped back down within the boxes catching her ribs on a corner of one, and the bicycle had crashed down on top of her. She wonders why I worry!

Reassured as to each other's welfare by my call, we said goodbye on the promise of further up-dates along my route. The road where I had parked and the few adjacent houses were in total darkness except for a faint yellow light bathing the immediate pathway outside the bar door. A beer would be refreshing and I just hoped that they would be serving food as well.

The door opened with a clang from an aged bell mounted above my head and five inquisitive faces turned towards me. One man sat alone at a table to my right nursing a half empty glass of beer, and three others sat to my left on bar-stools conversing with my host - an ample woman who reminded me of my favourite aunt; she gave a welcoming smile to greet my "*Bonsoir*".

I ordered a beer and was relieved when she asked me if I wanted to eat, it saved me fumbling for the words but I was intrigued why she kept looking at something behind me while she poured and eventually my curiosity got the better of me and I turned.

My lone drinker at the table was now beaming a smile and said, "Good evening."

"And good evening to you," I replied now sporting my own grin, "I certainly didn't expect English company tonight."

He gestured me to sit at his table so I made my thanks for the beer and joined him. Auntie confirmed we would like to eat together and placing an unlabelled bottle of red wine and a carafe of iced water on the table, she laid the cutlery while explaining today's menu.

Pied du porc vinaigrette, I must confess I had never tried Pig's trotters but after a delicious soup my appetite was aroused. It looked and smelled good as I broke open the skin and a rich fatty jelly oozed across the plate, so mostly I selected the meatier parts which melted in the mouth.

As we ate, we swapped backgrounds and reaffirmed all the reasons we both came to be living in France. I learned how his wife had thankfully left him and gone back home and I heard how this 'Saint Francis of Assisi' character was somewhat of a magnet to wildlife. He told me tales that I couldn't doubt of birds who flew into his house and sat on the arm of his chair; of deer in his garden that were not frightened by his presence.

He described his house two doors away, adding that his kitchen was rarely used; and who could blame him the food here was excellent value and after the roasted *cote du porc* (it seems it was pork night) with green beans and baby potatoes, I hardly had room for a dessert and feared for my drowsiness during the drive before me. I was already losing concentration but that I think was from a one-way conversation that it was time to terminate.

The three lorry drivers had finished their dinner an hour ago, showered upstairs then retired to their cabs to sleep until four in the morning when, according to my resident diner they once again took to the road, *comme d'habitude.*

I thanked him and auntie for their company and rang the doorbell once more as I relished the awakening cold air outside. Back in the comfort of the driving seat I settled without my jacket and fired the engine. It felt dishonest to rob the village of its darkened mystery as I flooded my route once more with headlights.

This was a new route to me which gently meandered through a forest, a detour that avoided some unpleasant bends on my usual journey north, a route I expected to rejoin somewhere during the early hours of the morning. At one in the morning and back on familiar roads my eyes said 'enough', and I parked under the bare trees of a village square, crawled into the back seat and buried myself under a duvet. I could have chosen somewhere better than underneath the hourly chimes of the village church clock.

I awoke to complaints from my bladder two hours later and reluctantly gave up the warmth of the duvet to brave the bracing night air. The silence made me feel like I was trespassing and I was glad I'd closed the car door with a quiet 'click'. The stroll to find suitable discretion in the middle of the night was probably unnecessary, in France men pee anywhere. But it brought my stiffened joints and eyes back to working condition for another push towards the English Channel.

A misty dawn showed little promise when I awoke from a second short sleep in a layby and called home knowing that Jenny would be awake. On her own, she would have shuttered the house and gone to bed early, and consequently risen at some ungodly hour for her obligatory pot of tea.

The ringing tone in my ear from the home telephone brought her voice to me for my overnight report. She was reassured that I had eaten a good meal as I relayed my adventures, and also that I had slept twice now. With so many miles now between us we said a sad goodbye and I promised to call as soon as I reached my son Greg's home later in the day.

The Boulogne restaurant was empty so I paid and left in favour of a stroll round the harbour to kill the time before sailing mid-afternoon. The stiff sea breeze soon chilled me so I left the car a little closer to embarkation and sought good hot French coffee while I still had the chance.

Within the bowels of the vessel I parked and headed aloft alongside excited children and stressed-out parents, found the first available seat and opened a book. Cross-channel ferries are like buses and planes; there's always too much hubbub to sleep or read and there is always the necessity to re-read at some later date when I can properly digest the words. It passed the time during a smooth and uneventful crossing, as did the visual analysis of my fellow passengers.

Climbing away from the docks at Dover I glanced in the rear view mirror to see the immensity of the port growing smaller behind me as I passed the familiar signs reminding me to 'drive on the left'. At the first roundabout another sign pointed towards Deal and I realised that my Aunt lived ten minutes away. A pang of guilt came and went and I promised myself I'd make an effort to visit on the way back.

Kent was awful and I began to wish I hadn't decided to take a cross-country route and look up an old pal. It had snowed and the verges of the narrow roads were awash in a grubby slush that clung to the hedgerows in frozen festoons. Landing had put me at the front of rush-hour traffic and I could feel the all too familiar pressure from behind as dusk began its descent. I was low on fuel and the two hours it eventually took me to find his address would have seen me safely in Greg's home via the motorways.

They were glad of my surprise, we hadn't seen each other since their now adult boys were on their first bicycles; we caught up on many years apart and I left with all the usual promises to keep in touch. It was a much more enjoyable way to negotiate the rush hour.

The only sadness was that I revealed to them my reason for the trip back; the funeral of my eldest daughter Sally.

35

Sally was born on the twenty second of December 1974 at two thirty in the afternoon after a difficult labour. I shared the utter joy of her birth with her mother – my first wife Dulcie, and together we cried in the delivery suite. When we named her we added a middle name and she became our Sally Joy.

She was adored by parents and grandparents alike. My mother's longing for her own daughter was never fulfilled and she doted on Sally. I have always loved new babies and will happily attend to their needs at both ends and shared all that a new baby demands. She slept and fed well, quickly increasing her weight; I marvelled at her sleeping form in my arms after I fed her.

She was six months old when we knew something was radically wrong. It took months of tests and consultations with the staff at the Hospital for sick children at Great Ormond Street before Dulcie mentioned the white spots on her skin to a fellow nurse who said they could be important. They were, and formed a vital clue to her diagnosis.

Tuberous Sclerosis they concluded; a genetic disorder that causes calcifying lesions within the body and its organs; some people have the modifying gene – some don't and live a normal life. Sally did and it was manifesting in traumatic fits.

The drugs controlled the fits but Sally was severely handicapped. She retained every need of a new born baby; except she could cope with food of a minced consistency when fed to her, and she could hold a drinking bottle with her one usable hand.

We loved and cared for her for seven years, but following genetic counselling and the birth of two subsequent healthy children we had to admit we could no longer cope and had to seek residential full-time care for her.

She lived close-by within a specially designed unit with excellent staff who cared for her every need and we believe that in her own way she was happy until her illness eventually released her aged thirty one.

We laid her to rest in Welwyn cemetery and celebrated her life along with the staff of her home, and our family and many friends.

Her laughter was better than the birds in the morning,
Her smile turned the edge of the wind,
Her memory disarms death and charms the surly grave.
Early she went to bed; too early we saw her light put out;
Yet we could not grieve more than a little while,
For she lives in the earth around us and laughs from the sky.
Anon

It is always a strange feeling when I leave the places where I've spent most of my life. My aged Father was coping well for his age, my brother had his life and my two adult children continued with their lives without me and I yearned to be at back home in France with Jenny.

The M25 had been kinder than usual and nearly forgotten from mid-channel. The sea breeze was strong up on deck and as it took my cigarette butt from view before it landed in the wash behind, I scurried back inside the warmth of the ship.

Back on French soil I hurried out of the port and straight into the adjacent service station at E.Leclerc. The fuel would last me nearly all the way home and I relaxed to some daylight driving for a change; at least for the first few hours.

My Father had packed me a luncheon box - bless him, which I saved for as long as possible to keep me going through the later night drive. I stopped and relished the flask of his home-made soup and sandwiches as I looked skyward to the weak late afternoon sunshine and watched it obliterated by threatening clouds. The day's earlier snow flurry lay unmelted upon the unkempt tarmac of the pull-in.

I crossed the wide river Loire as the last threads of daylight disappeared and leaving Blois behind me, I turned into the tree-lined avenue that would enfold me for the next hours, apprehensive about what might lie before me through the onset of falling snowflakes.

The wide road through the forest was long and straight like a tunnel for many miles ahead and across the wide grass verges the trees formed a barrier of darkness that my headlights side-wash failed to penetrate. It felt eerie; I was glad to be passing through despite the wall of white I was driving into and my concentration barely allowed a second thought for what might lay ahead.

After an hour the falling snow stopped. Everything in sight had received a dusting, and it was getting deeper the further I went. The only tyre tracks in the snow were the ones in my rear view mirror and I felt very isolated. Yet I had to absorb the rare beauty of this monochrome scene around me, like a curtain that had been drawn back to reveal the inner secrets of the forest in darkness, now brought alive after the snowfall in contrasting white. Inside the warmth of the car with the hum of the engine I couldn't experience the silence outside, but I could feel it.

At ten o'clock I reached St-Aignan, and relaxing my concentration upon the clear roads within the town I sought a café for fortification of mind and body. My feet crunched upon the frozen pavements and humid warmth enveloped me as I entered through the glass door frosted by condensation. I drank two large steaming cups of coffee to reawaken my senses, and following my questions to the owner about what lay ahead of me, I followed them with a large whiskey.

He reported that most of central France had suffered a freak snowstorm and that temperatures through the night were being forecast at well below freezing.

Strangely it never occurred to me to find a bed for the night; my only concern was to get back home as quickly and as safely as possible. Reluctantly I left my new found pals to ponder why the crazy Englishman wanted to drive through the night when he could have stayed drinking for at least another hour.

Beyond the confines of the town the roads once again seriously deteriorated. The snow had fallen to a depth of four or five inches and a few tyre tracks had crushed it to a now frozen slush. St-Aignan lies in the Cher valley and the road leaving it climbs through a steady continuation of bends that require prudence in good weather. I kept my speed low to make sure the car stayed on the road. I just couldn't begin to imagine the problems if I lost control and ended up in a ditch in the middle of the night, with the difficulty of arranging recovery at first light miles from anywhere and against this I worried about losing traction on the slippery surfaces and every slight incline had my reactions on full alert.

Concentration was extreme but eventually the road levelled and the bends were behind me, and although the conditions didn't improve I relaxed and made good progress in second gear, rarely achieving third. I tried to keep going during the night for as long as possible, fearing the increased possibility of an accident in daylight hours; French drivers are known for their lack of prudence in bad conditions.

Just before midnight I pulled off the road and hauled myself into the rear seats, again I was pleased that I'd had the foresight to bring a duvet. I thought I would never sleep as all I could visualise behind my closed eyes was a vast white tunnel disappearing into the distance. Ninety minutes later I melted the snow at the base of the wall where I'd parked and cursed my full bladder for my all too short respite.

The sharp night air brought me further awake so I pushed on until four o'clock when I had to stop once more. A faint dawn greeted me as my dream faded, a dream of a snow plough clearing the road before me.

Daylight brought into full perspective the extent of the snow coverage and I searched each passing hamlet for coffee and croissants, desperate for breakfast of some sort; Dad's fortification in the lay-by was now just a pleasant memory.

To my surprise, although the covering of snow was now much thinner it did stay with me until I passed Perigueux, then at last I managed to relax a little and make good speed driving on clear roads and with an hour to go before I arrived back home my thoughts turned from the elusive French breakfast to a full English fry up, and my hunger became intense.

My dog Spanner went ballistic when he realised who had arrived, and even Arron who barely musters a flick of the tail now he's aging came up and rubbed all around my legs to greet me, and Jenny, she was just relieved that I'd arrived safely home.

I too was just glad to be home again and desperately sought an overdue shower and a change of clothes. I towelled off in the warm dampness and then opening the bathroom door I could smell the aroma wafting from the kitchen and immediately began to salivate; brunch cooking and fresh coffee. Such bliss waits!

36

I'd decided, or rather Jenny had decided for me that it was about time we got moving on the construction of the pool terrace. Five pallets of concrete blocks and a large pile of sand were sitting on the drive, and the weather was now beginning to improve with little chance of frost.

I had no experience of driving a mini-digger but I hired one anyway. David had offered to drive it for me and dig the footings for the walls which would enclose the pool and therefore ensure that the terrace would conform to new regulations for pool safety.

The old tiny pump house became a chemical store and I incorporated a much larger room into the build which gave us the opportunity to realise a vast improvement idea in pool filtration, by dispensing with the in-pool system in favour of a sand filter. It worked brilliantly and saved me hours of cleaning.

Jenny had also thought that the weed infested rear courtyard outside our bedroom patio doors was a disgrace, and she had decided to create an area that we could use. Revamping a multitude of old pallets, she laid a ground membrane then levelled the pallets to create this amazing decked terrace with bordering gardens and ornaments, and installed a garden table with four chairs.

We tied a ribbon across the entrance from the garden, prepared diner for four people and invited David and Rhoda for an opening ceremony. Rhoda cut the ribbon after a short speech interspersed with hoots of laughter, then after unveiling a plaque we served diner and drank too much. Very nice evening!

Later that summer, after a busy day in the mid-July sunshine we had dined earlier than usual and retired just as dusk arrived. Jenny had snuggled down and was nearly asleep, and my eyes were drooping over my book when suddenly we heard this roaring wind and both shot up in bed to look through the window into the failing light. The patio table suddenly took off and along with the umbrella it smashed into the wall outside.

We were out of bed and fully awake again in an instant and looking across the rear garden we could see the trees bending against the force of wind. As the rain started to hammer on the roof tiles above our heads we rushed into the lounge to view the storm through the front windows and were seriously worried.

The garden was absolutely covered in leaves and the heavy rain had turned to hail stones the size of glass marbles. The plastic sun loungers were crushed underneath a huge branch that had been ripped from the acacia tree and the plastic table was laying upside-down nearby. Only two of the four chairs were visible and one of those was broken.

Suddenly… as quickly as the wind had arrived - it stopped, and as the rain reduced to a drizzle we could see the devastation everywhere. The whole episode lasted no more than fifteen minutes and there was nothing to be done tonight in the failing light, so we went back to bed for a restless night's sleep.

In the morning mist it looked like a war zone with debris everywhere. One of the barn doors had been ripped off and flattened another of the chairs and we found the other in the pool underneath a densely-leaved oak branch. The drive was impassable and François' oak woodland had been devastated; four mature oak trees lost all the top branches leaving the trunks with ragged stumps on top, and two others fell midway across our drive, while another small acacia blocked the drive entrance.

I walked up past François' vineyard at the rear to inspect the top of the drive and found it hard to take in the condition of his precious vines. Huge round bales of hay that had been awaiting collection by the roadside had been sent spinning down the hill to cascade through his vineyard, and the wind and hailstones had stripped his vines of leaves and the developing fruit. I was opening up the drive with the chainsaw when he saw it for the first time and he stood there stunned and very near to tears.

"Never, ever…" did he eventually managed to say, "…have I seen such devastation here by a storm."

Days later, the office of the *Marie* officially declared it a tornado. It had cut a path half of a kilometre wide starting from somewhere south of us, and burned itself out a little further north.

Some friends came to help us and together we cleared the garden of debris and made the trees safe, before I drove to another friend to offer the same help. On the way back I saw François struggling to replace the edging tiles on his low barn roof.

"I'll get on the roof…" I said, "…and you pass me the tiles from the ladder."

I know he would have done it himself because that's the way he was, but nevertheless he looked so relieved to have had my help.

I'd cleared a space in the undergrowth at the edge of Francois' woodland and cut and stacked all the fallen branches from after I'd cleared the drive, just like he would have done. When he saw it he was most impressed and then, looking into the woodland he could see the remaining fallen trees and the enormity of work still to be done there, and he said…

"Look at my woodland, thirty years some of those trees have been growing, my father planted some of them!"

I could see his sadness and I said, "Tell me when you're going to do it and I'll be there to help."

"Merci." He quietly spoke, and then with a determination, "Take it, take it all, I've got more wood than I know what to do with and haven't the time or energy for all this as well as my other woodland."

I couldn't thank him enough and when Jenny and I, with my son Greg's help, eventually cleared, cut and stacked it all in one metre lengths at the edge of the woodland, I realised the magnitude of his gift to us. To buy the same amount of logs from a supplier would have cost us a few hundred Euros.

Our vegetable garden had also been stripped and the Pumpkin vines were now just leaf-less green arteries across the lawn. The ends of the plastic covered greenhouse and the contents inside looked like a car had driven through. The field of ripening maize below us was eventually ploughed back into the soil, but amazingly our vegetables rallied and we had a splendid crop of everything.

Because our house is cut into a hillside, most of the wind passed over it taking just one tile from the chimney top. Jacques' farm was not so lucky and it bore the full force of wind which ripped the roof from his cow sheds.

It seemed that this was the season for mini disasters because the next one was waiting just around the corner.

At 5-30am on a warm August morning Jenny got out of bed to answer a call of nature and suddenly felt her feet sloshing in water. She says that her first reaction was that I might have had an accident; well, that would have had to be a big accident wouldn't it?

However, quickly roused I shot out of bed and discovered that the aforementioned under-sink water filter system had failed miserably and mains-pressure water was quickly flooding throughout the house. I stopped the water flow and we stood stunned for a few seconds assessing the implications.

Fortunately the water hadn't made it into the lounge but having flooded from the kitchen into the dining room it had passed into the hall and entered the bedrooms. Our room was the least affected while in the other two the carpets were under water.

We moved the furniture to one side and dragged them sopping wet onto the back lawn to drain. The better quality rugs we laid out to dry in the warm sunshine while we mopped all the water up, and we discarded the thin fitted ones from the bedrooms, they were after all only cheap flooring on top of the concrete until we could afford something better.

The warm summer breeze passing through the open doors and windows soon dried the floors, and outside on the lawn the carpets didn't take much longer, so everything was back to working order quite quickly. The first figure the insurance assessor gave us revealed his utter lack of understanding, so I showed him the numerous photographs and doubled it. He agreed without too much argument and when the cheque arrived, it paid for the floor tiling in the hallway and all three bedrooms.

We had been reading a local newspaper that was published in English, and as well as French news it often published interesting articles with a local theme, and I thought… I could do that. So I wrote 'Nuts about Cancon' - an article about our village and its claim to fame as the Hazelnut capital of France; it was published in the Dordogne News the following October and before they paid me for it they went into liquidation; not the best start to a writing career!

However I was inspired and a few weeks later I received a complimentary magazine from an editor who had just published my work, an article which started a relationship with H&E Naturist magazine that still exists today. Now all I needed was an area where I could write in peace and quiet.

I decided that I needed an office, so with a lot of help from my Dad I started the first phase of work in the barn and created my office and one other room which was destined to be a library. My new office was spacious and modern with a window that overlooked the pool and garden and it also doubled as my music room where I could play my banjo in solitude which greatly pleased Jenny.

'What shall we do with the fish' introduced H&E Naturist readers to our life here in France, and paved the way for me to become the magazine's correspondent in France. My monthly column of news and reviews about the naturist scene in France led me to meet some interesting people in unusual places, like the afternoon when I met Kees and Sanne.

I was on my way to visit a naturist holiday centre, and turning into a tree-lined drive I approached a pair of wrought iron gates and imagined that they were the entrance to a fine Chateaux. But the sign where I left the road was quite specific and this was Domaine Laborde, and eventually the drive opened into a vast car park with directions to reception where I met Kees, the Dutch owner.

He greeted me warmly and over coffee in the bar he told me the history of this immaculate place. After selling his successful engineering company, he'd purchased this fifty acre site and the derelict farm that stood upon it, with a dream to create a rural holiday centre for naturists. Now twenty two years later, Kees and his wife Yvonne had secured an international reputation for their holiday centre.

Concluding our interview I asked if I could spend some time enjoying the naked freedom of the grounds and perhaps take a swim, and I was also hoping that I might see an opportunity to interview some naturist holiday makers.

"Of course..." He replied, "...although there are not many campers here because it's a little early in the season, but yes take as long as you want."

The derelict farm buildings had become a fine family home, a restaurant and a shop, and a clubhouse with a comfortable bar. It was like entering a fairy tale village, nothing was out of place and the roads, paths and buildings all looked like they had just been cleaned and swept.

I took my towel and the meandering road that led down the gentle slope towards the expansive fresh water lake. It was a beautiful place with wide lawns bordering the lake which was encircled by trees and the water was like glass reflecting the sunshine that filtered through the trees.

I noticed a shoal of fish near the slipway and bent down to take pictures when I became aware of someone behind me, a girl in a purple dress wearing a straw hat.

"Bonjour"...I said and added "Hello," because many Dutch people speak excellent English.

"Hello..." she replied, "...are you taking pictures of the fish?"

I confirmed that I was and explained to her why I was visiting.

"Do you want me to model for you?" she asked.

"If you are offering..." I said, "...yes please." and I couldn't believe my luck at being granted such an opportunity as she dropped the straw hat, lifted the dress over her head and entered the water's edge naked.

We chatted while she posed for my pictures and she told me how the natural water left her skin feeling so much better than chlorinated pool water, so when she decided to swim, I decided I had to join her and share the experience. We swam across the lake to the other side and back again, and both agreed than while the top two feet of water depth was quite warm, underneath the spring-fed lake was quite icy.

Back on the grass and towelled dry I had to agree with her, my skin did feel lovely and I bid her goodbye and left as she laid drying on her towel in the sunshine.

37

The old butcher's shop in the village had been empty for as long as we had lived there. Uncollected mail and circulars were piled inside the glass door and the only sign of usage was an estate agent's poster hanging in the window. It was a scruffy little place inside and out but it still excited Jenny.

She had been saying for a long time how it would make a nice little gallery for her, and I was surprised to learn that she'd done something about it. Now here I was making a bespoke wooden serving counter for her gallery while she cleaned and decorated the little shop.

'Galerie Jenny' opened a few weeks before Christmas and the sudden awakening of the old shop with its bright seasonal window display attracted a lot of attention. Mr. Gouget our mayor was delighted to see a new and exciting enterprise opening in the village, and it was ideally positioned a few doors away from the busiest boulangerie.

Sales were good and dismissed any doubts that Jenny may have had, but it was the enthusiasm for her art which gave her the most encouragement. A parisienne man spent ages enthusiastically viewing her work before he said,

"I could never find contemporary art like this in Paris, everything there is all too classical."

But unfortunately Galerie Jenny in Cancon had to close after a few months because the building was being sold. The owner was sad to give this news to Jenny because she had hoped her son would buy the building and stay living in the flat above, giving Jenny security of tenure; he had declined.

Our thoughts turned to a neighbouring medieval village, in the hope that we might open the gallery there. Historic Monflanquin was built upon a hill and has narrow streets of magnificent stone houses and many restaurants and bars encircle the Bastide square. It has a thriving community and attracts a flood of summer tourists. I spoke to an estate agent we knew there.

"Yes…" he said, "…the shop just next door is to let."

Inside I was excited at the prospect because it was perfect for Jenny's requirements, and calmly I asked if I could view it.

"Of course…" he said, "…I'll just get the keys."

Inside was in good decorative order with exposed stone walls and there was double the space to exhibit. To one rear corner there was a small lobby with a toilet while the other corner housed a small kitchen and the space between the two would be ideal for a working studio where visitors to the gallery would be able to watch Jenny creating her art. I arrived home barely able to contain the news and spoke to Jenny who had just returned home from her Cancon shop.

"I think you had better put your coat back on." I said.

"Why?" she reluctantly enquired. I took a deep breath…

"Because…" I said, "…I'm taking you to Monflanquin to see your new gallery!"

Her coat was on in a flash as I received a barrage of questions about it, most of which I declined to answer so as to heighten her first impression. She loved it and although the rental was more expensive the increased footfall would justify the extra, and Max the estate agent – the same agent who sold Jenny our house many years ago, was delighted to welcome us into the community.

Packing up all the boxes of art and materials and then transporting it all to the new gallery took us days, and then I had to modify the counter to suit its new environment. The shop had previously been a tea room and the lighting was just not adequate and I had to renew it all to suit the studio and gallery needs, as well as satisfying Jenny's every request for new shelves, work surfaces and picture hook placement, all on a very tight budget.

During the next weeks I rarely saw Jenny between early morning and mid-evening. She was determined to organise all her work studio and to create a breath-taking display in the gallery before the approaching summer season.

Now though it wasn't just her glass pictures; her many new ideas had slowly increased her variety of goods in the gallery and she now had the addition of acrylic paintings and pictures made from dried flowers and leaves. Then there were her painted glass bottles for oils or vinaigrette, trinket boxes and candle burners, oven gloves and designer handbags in every colour and style for all ages. Finally her stunning chess sets of many character themes and colours which were all displayed floating on hidden stands. She made everything, it was obligatory under her new business status as an artist.

During the time she spent as a market trader she had been inundated with the official costs involved in having a small business and so we went to the offices of taxation in the hope that we might be able to negotiate a reduction. In France you pay the equivalent of National insurance contributions for a business in advance, it's costly and the gallery wasn't even earning what they were asking for.

We explained the predicament to a very nice tax inspector who listened patiently, asking a few questions for clarification before he gave us his verdict. He said that because Jenny was an artist who made everything, and not a commercial enterprise that buys and sells, he would de-register her so that she could then trade as an artist. This meant no more costs until she had earned above a certain amount, which she never would do and we were able to claim back what she had paid. Brilliant!

Jenny came away with a new spring in her step, and I was very relieved that I would no longer be trying to find the money that the gallery as yet didn't have, and although we could ill afford it we decided to celebrate and investigate the culinary delight of the Restaurant du Lac.

The Restaurant du Lac is off the beaten track just outside of the village of Cancon within the stunning grounds of the municipal holiday resort, where it sits opposite an expansive lake with woodland on the far side. The building is raised up from ground level and disguised to look like a huge log cabin with a wide terrace across the whole length at the front with stairs at both ends.

The restaurant enjoys a reputation for excellent food at very reasonable prices in a comfortable ambience, and has become a Friday night hotspot for the locals because of the live music bands. Of course we knew none of this when we arrived early on a Friday evening after our meeting with the tax man and tried to book a table. We were very lucky because there was only one small table for two on the terrace remaining, so we booked it and went for a walk around the lake.

By the time we returned it was dusk and the outside terrace was bathed in coloured lights and beginning to fill with diners. We found our table and an attentive waitress gave us the à la carte menu and then drew our attention to the blackboard which showed our much preferred choices for the night's specials; there was a choice of three entrées, three plats, and three desserts at an incredible price of €10.50 per person, no wonder the tables were fully booked!

Our starter was a safe choice of goats' cheese salad; a bed of mixed green leaves topped with grilled slices of goats' cheese on toasted French bread and drizzled with honey, and for two hungry and happy lake-side walkers, very tasty!

The main course was veal in a white wine and mushroom sauce, served with seasonal vegetables and fries. It was just as delicious as the starter and then after a short break, somewhat enforced by the multitude of other diners, we chose our dessert. For Jenny a *tarte au fruits,* but for me is has to be the *tarte au chocolat.*

We saw many faces that we recognised as we sat contently full, and couldn't understand why we had never heard of this excellent venue that was only five minutes from home. We listened as the band tuned their instruments, and then later the whole interior started to rock as they burst into action with a fine mixture of rock music. We also learned how beneficial it could be to have a table inside. While the terrace dining area had a preferable ambience, it later became chilly in the early season air, and inside diners had a ringside view of the bands and this particular band had a great image. They were all dressed in school uniforms and they played instruments that looked like toys – a tiny drum kit and what looked like toy guitars. At first glance they were an amusing sight but it worked very well and we enjoyed some great music and a fine evening out. It was a restaurant we were confident we would visit many more times in the future.

It was late September and the flood of summer tourists visiting Jenny's new gallery had dwindled to a mere trickle – if any at all. Footsteps in the doorway broke the spell from her latest paperback as her interest grew towards a potential sale.

From where she sat behind her serving counter she could only see two moving heads; one was uncovered and neatly bobbed, the other was clad in a blue denim pork-pie hat with a frayed and turned up rim; both people had hair the colour of soot.

Eventually they registered her presence and smiling warmly they attempted a synchronised bow which didn't quite come off. Jenny said bonjour and offered a nod of the head; somehow it seemed good manners to offer some sort of bow in return.

"Bahjor." he said about halfway through the second bow and then on the way back up – meeting his wife on the way down, several times before they continued with their tour of the gallery.

Under the brim of his hat, the large horn-rimmed glasses perched on his nose made his eyes look bulbous, like they had been transplanted from an alien. His blue denim waistcoat with a long-sleeved blue check shirt underneath nicely matched his mid-calf blue cotton jeans, and the sandals and orange socks really set off the whole outfit.

His wife wore tight black leggings with a beautiful floral top and on her tiny feet were a pair of new-looking sandals that would have fitted a five-year-old. Jenny's eyes were back on the pages but she wasn't reading - she was listening.

"Hoor... ahhh!"... They exclaimed before a muffled brief conversation in Japanese; it seemed they approved. They moved around the walls pointing and oohing and ahing and eventually settled between a choice of two, a picture of a sunflower on one wall and one other in a tiny frame opposite of a dragonfly. They caught Jenny's uplifted eyes and the whole discordant bowing procedure began again.

His happy face dissolved into seriousness and as he timidly approached and Jenny could see that he was searching for words he didn't have. He hadn't expected to find an English speaking person in a French gallery and was visibly relieved when she asked,

"Would you like to speak English?"

"Arrr yaw ingleesh…" he ventured, and pointing an arm around all the walls he added,"…velly gord, velly gord." and he went into double-time bowing to catch his wife up who had started two bows before him.

Tentatively he reached to touch the dragonfly and was immediately chided like an errant child by his wife. Although the words were unrecognisable, the meaning was clear, so Jenny reached up and unhooked the picture from the wall and when the bowing stopped she handed it to him so he could feel it. He bowed and they huddled together over the frame for a closer inspection and a further discussion.

From the body language it wasn't hard to work it out; Jenny had heard the same conversations many times in words that she knew.

"What is…?" he asked gently tapping the glass as his wife's questioning look swivelled between Jenny and her husband.

"It's glass," didn't quite seem to register and so walking to the shop window Jenny tapped the pane and repeated the word. "Glass."

"Ahh… glarss." And the bowing was replaced by numerous nods of the head between them as the word registered.

His next request took a little more explanation as he felt the leaded outline of the dragonfly and its painted colours like a blind man reading braille.

"What is..?" he asked…

"That is lead and special paint." Jenny said but it drew a blank expression from both of them as expected and so beckoning them towards her work station she showed them an off-cut and her pots of paint to explain the procedure the best that she could, and for this she received three more bows. The timing between them was by now getting better and she obviously had firm ideas where she wanted to hang the dragonfly back home in Japan.

"Myee wive, she like velly mush pictar..." but he was cut short from either lack of words or the instructions he was receiving from her. From his expression Jenny deduced his retort must have been something like, "But I don't know how to ask." And hers was probably, "Well try!"

Resigned to saying something he swallowed and took a deep breath.

"Pictar is gord to go…?" and lost for words he pointed with it towards the doors. Jenny kept his questioning gaze as they all inched towards the outside and he held it to the outer wall,

"Ah" Jenny said, "Outside."

"Yes, outside." He repeated brimming with confidence having been reminded of a forgotten word, "Myee wive, she like it to go outside."

Explaining how it would deteriorate when exposed to the elements took all Jenny's efforts but eventually they grasped it and their disappointment was evident.

To rekindle their interest she described how dragonflies will hunt in our garden at home and received a warm,

"Yes, we have in Japan."

For that little gem Jenny was obviously back in favour as the bowing started again. To lessen the blow she demonstrated how it could be hung in front of any window internally and showed them how splendid it looked with the light behind it, but all to no avail because she had her heart set on hanging it outside and that was that. They prepared to leave and by alternating between two backward steps and two bows they eventually found themselves outside the gallery and with one last bow in perfect unison they turned and disappeared.

In amazement Jenny watched for some thirty seconds the empty space where they had stood, half expecting them to reappear for an encore bow but they didn't

38

Autumn had become quite a wet affair, so wet in fact that the ripened sunflowers in the field below us were too wet to be harvested and it was feared that this late in the season they would never dry sufficiently to cut; the drooping seed heads looked depressing in the damp air.

Jenny had braved the damp air to attack the long overdue job of cleaning out the chicken house; she wanted to dump the spoil onto the vegetable patch so it would rot down over winter. As she emptied the wheelbarrow and turned around, a sudden movement on the sunflowers caught her eye and a massive flock of small birds lifted skywards in an amazing murmuration.

She dropped the barrow and watched in awe as she carefully made her way to the office window, where she made me jump out of my skin banging on the glass. I thought the woman had finally gone mad during the few seconds it took me to realise what the hell she was on about, whereupon I joined her outside to watch the spectacle.

Finally the little birds settled among the high branches within François' woodland where we could hear them noisily chirping, and then a few at a time they descended back to the sunflowers to feed on the bounty of un-harvested seeds. Again and again they repeated the process as some hidden alarm spooked them, and on two or three occasions throughout the day they flew so close to the house that there were the inevitable casualties. One of these poor dead birds was a Brambling, such a beautiful little bird and one we hadn't even realised was in our locality.

I knew that many small birds flocked together in colder months, but I had never seen so many small birds flocking together before my very eyes, and I've not seen a spectacle like it since, there were so many that it darkened the sky.

In addition to the flocks in the sky, our birds on the ground had grown considerably. Lynne once again had found it necessary to dispose of chickens that were too small for her commercial buyers, so Jenny of course accepted another six. She gave them all names and they grew into nice hens and became good layers, but Snowflake seemed to grow just a little bit more.

She was twice the size of the other hens and even the cats gave her a wide berth. She was eating enormous amounts of chicken feed and gradually she started to be a bit aggressive towards our cockerel. Jenny came back into the kitchen one day and announced…

"Snowflake has just had a go at me; she attacked me like a cockerel would."

"That's weird…" I replied, "…she's a hen.

"Well I thought she was too, but maybe she's a cockerel after all."

So we kept a watchful eye on her behaviour and sure enough although she didn't have a cockerel's comb or wattle, she was definitely behaving like one. Then her aggression towards Jenny became a regular thing so we decided that because she was getting dangerous as well as upsetting the other birds, she would have to go; we just hadn't decided when.

I'd gone into the enclosure to top up the seed-feeders one day and had to dodge her attack, and then from the corner of my eye I saw her coming in for a second attempt. I swung round quickly and gave her a sharp kick, lifting her off the ground into the air where she bounced off the fencing and scuttled away to the other end. I nearly broke my foot; it was like kicking a large sports medicine ball.

She had now sealed her fate and was destined for the pot, so we separated and captured her and put her in a cage on water only rations to await execution. Unfortunately we had to go out the following day and it was too late when we returned to do the dirty deed, then pluck and clean the carcass, so I decided on the humane thing to do and I shot her with my air rifle. It seemed that our approach to Christmas was being fraught with animals dying.

Minka the younger of our two Siamese cats had never been what you might call a homely cat, always preferring to return home for food then zoom back out of the door and away somewhere. But despite this truancy he was often visible around the house apart from the time when he disappeared for three days, and then came rushing back indoors desperate for food; we assumed he had managed to get himself locked inside a farm building close by.

This time he'd been missing for nine days, and Jenny was getting worried. She toured the adjacent beef farm during the quiet of the evening when all the staff had returned home, calling his name and listening to all the closed doors without success.

He was a loner and I told Jenny months previously that there would be a day in the future when he wouldn't come back, and now everything told us that the day had arrived.

Weeks later François took me aside and told me that he had found Minka's body inside an old shallow well at the bottom of the valley; he had probably slipped in and couldn't climb out. I wish we had been there when he needed us.

There are rare occasions when Jenny's artwork cannot be measured by sales, when just a small comment can be a priceless reward.

The village of *Saint Colomb de Lauzun* annually hosts a weekend Christmas market of thirty five different artisan exhibitors. It is an excellent venue within a stylish modern built village hall which is always decorated for the occasion and it attracts many visitors from far and wide.

The quality of artwork is high and the committee who organise it take great care not to duplicate the exhibits for sale; an invitation to display is prestigious. Each artisan has something unique to offer and there exists a mutual respect for each other's art as stories are swapped, re-kindling friendships from previous years.

Jenny's display was awesome, yet as Saturday afternoon proceeded into early evening a gloom began to descend upon her; it was a miserable day outside, dull and overcast with the threat of snow as the temperature hovered at zero. Visitor attendance was good and many had shown great delight at the visual extravaganza as they filed from stand to stand amongst the hubbub, but very few were buying.

Taking advantage of a brief lull in visitors Jenny had spoken to other exhibitors and discovered that many other artists were experiencing similar meagre takings, and together they had formed the opinion that the world financial crisis was to blame and people were just being prudent.

Returning to her exhibition, she found a smartly dressed French lady bending at the waist to admire a picture of a group of pansies.

"Bonjour Madame," surprised the lady from her thoughts and she stood pensive, composing a question.

"Are you Jenny?" She asked, in French.

With her interest aroused Jenny replied, *"Oui, C'est Moi,"* and then watched as the lady's eyes returned to the picture and an affectionate smile arrived.

"I have a picture like that, but not three pansies it is a bunch of eight blue pansies, and all my friends admire it when they come to my house in Duras. My son gave it to me as a present last year, could it be one of yours?"

Unsure where this conversation was going Jenny said, *"C'est possible."*

Explaining a little further the lady said, "My son lives in Bordeaux and he was on his way to a rugby match when he passed through Cancon on the *route Nationale.* He spotted this little gallery and paused for a brief look through the car window before continuing his journey."

"Yes," said Jenny, "I used to have a gallery in Cancon but I had to move when the building was sold, but I remember your son, he came in after the match on his way home."

Thrilled that her recognition of the artwork had been confirmed she beamed a smile and added, "Ah, so it is yours, and the oil bottle as well – not the same as these you have here but similar. My son has the ability to buy me presents that are so unique and different, and I'm so thrilled that I have actually met you. The painted oil bottle has pride of place in my kitchen, I use it every day – I think it's beautiful."

"*Merci Madame,* I am very happy for you." Said Jenny as she watched her move off and imagined how she would relate the experience to her son at some later date.

Then there was Jack who stood in front of the stall gazing at the empty space with tears welling up in his eyes, and at nine years old he was making a brave attempt to keep them hidden. His voice gave away his absolute disappointment when he asked, "Have you sold it?"

Jenny mustered every bit of sympathy in her expression when she said, "Yes, I'm sorry, someone has just taken it."

What Jack didn't know was that following his unsuccessful pleading for the medieval chess set and board for a Christmas present, his mother had sneaked back and paid for it, asking Jenny to wrap it discreetly in readiness for its secret collection by his father.

On Christmas morning Jenny asked me, "I wonder if Jack is having a nice surprise right now?" Then we talked about how Father Christmas was alive and still working!

During the following year's *Marché Noël* Jenny spotted the same family when they arrived. Jack was taller and it looked as if Jack and his younger brother were soon to expect a brand new brother, or sister.

At ten the memory is very short and it took a few seconds for him to realise when Jenny asked, "Hello Jack, did you have a nice surprise last Christmas?"

"Oh yea," he eventually replied as it dawned on him who he was speaking to, and a broad grin spread across his face as he turned towards his family. Mum and Dad later described an account of Jack's Christmas surprise for Jenny who was please to know that it had been her craft-work that had given this lad so much pleasure.

Christmas was over and I found myself feeling restless during the idle days before the New Year. There was still a considerable amount of fallen branches within François's woodland that needed to be cut and stacked, and in winter it was much more accessible. I looked out of the window and the mid-morning low sunlight filtering through the leafless branches was enticing me into activity.

It felt good to be doing something after the days of over-indulgent festivities; the air was clear and fresh, with the musty smell of woodland very evident. The exhaust smoke from the chain-saw drifted slowly away, reluctant to rise within the cold damp air.

Turning off the motor, I began to lift and stack near to the woodland boundary and soon had a satisfying pile. Then turning back again towards my cutting area, I saw all the trimmings laying everywhere and sighed as I recalled how long it had taken Jenny and I to dispose of it all the last time. We had dragged all the trimmings out of the woodland and across our drive, traversing the two flanking ditches to feed the roaring bonfire we had lit in the open field opposite. So I was quite glad when François later presented a much better solution.

Considering his age, François's ability at land and woodland management amazes me. For a few hours at a time each day, he nibbles away at some task in preference to vegetating during his retirement. Nature will always take back what is rightfully hers and his woodland was slowly becoming impenetrable to all but the brave in search of precious winter fuel.

During a previous discussion with him about the woodland he had told me how he used to clear the undergrowth and leave just the new saplings, and gesturing towards the thicket he added…

"Poof – look at it now…I'm not as young as I used to be!"

This conversation must have stuck in his mind, because as I looked around for a suitable site to pile up all my cuttings, I noticed that further into the trees many such piles had already been made; it was evident now that François had taken the initiative and was clearing his woodland once more.

Later when I returned with the trailer attached to the tractor mower to retrieve my wood stack, he appeared through the clearing carrying his razor sharp ancient tools across his shoulder.

We shook hands, "*Bonjour François, Ca-va?*"

"*Oui merci*," and placing his tools against a tree he scribed an arc with his free hand towards his worked area, "*Eh voila!*"

"That's marvellous." I told him, "You must have worked very hard?"

"Oh poof, it's just a little each day until it's done." He grinned in appreciation of my praise and in answer to my question recalled that it was in excess of ten years since he last did it.

"Will you be here after lunch?" I asked and following his confirmation he gladly accepted my promise to help. It is a small price to pay for the winter's fuel that has cost us nothing but a few hours labouring in the peace and tranquillity of his woodland.

By mid-afternoon we had three bonfires in different areas crackling away as we crunched back and forth across the carpet of twigs and fallen leaves collected the cuttings and feeding them with pitch-forks onto the infernos.

Resting for a few minutes we discussed the progress and overall effect of our joint woodland management, and somehow the conversation turned to his memories of farming before he owned a tractor. I knew from previous conversations that his tractor was fifty years old, which gave me a clue to the years he was recalling now, and I also knew that until he bought his tractor he farmed the land with oxen.

Pointing to the field in the valley below which his nephew had recently ploughed with a modern tractor and four swivelling plough blades, I questioned him about ploughing and suggested that his plough-lines were probably straighter than those of the land in front of us.

"*Bien sûr*"... of course! He stated with his eyes wide open, almost indignant that I might suggest otherwise. He went on to explain how in those days they didn't have a plough with four blades but one single blade, and it didn't turn for the return furrow so they had to drive the oxen back up the field for the subsequent row.

But today he was going back even further to a time in his youth when he worked alongside his father. He said that in the summer they would rise in the middle of the night to harness and prepare the oxen for haymaking. He said they had to be in the fields as dawn broke so as to capitalise on the cool early morning temperature before the heat became too much for the oxen to work, and also because the animals would need to ruminate. He smiled and explained how his mother would arrive in the field and together they would share the French equivalent of a Ploughman's lunch, then she'd leave them and go back to prepare the evening meal while they would find some shade under the cart and take a siesta; probably assisted by some good home-made red wine!

As our bonfires became little more than piles of smouldering ash he shouldered his tools and bid me farewell, thanking me for my help.

"*C'est mon plaisir pour tous les bois de chauffage vous avez donnez-moi.*" My pleasure for all the wood you have given me.

Back home later, I heaved the wood basket full of split logs into the house for the evening's warmth and I smiled to myself at what I had seen in the front garden; an old relic that we had retrieved from the redundant junk in our barn and lovingly repainted. Standing in the front garden and supporting two hanging baskets full of winter pansies stood Francois' old plough.

39

The phone rang, it was Muriel.

"I have an English couple staying in my Gite; they have been looking at properties for sale in the area and have now decided to buy the old cottage where Jim and you did the conversion. They say that they would like to meet you because you were builder who did the work, so if you would like to come over and meet them, they're here until Friday."

"Would tomorrow after lunch be a good time for them?" I asked, and the reply was yes, that suited them fine.

I met Sonya first and I liked her immediately, her easy conversation and attractive looks made it easy to be attentive to her and I felt quite guilty when Brian arrived onto the patio some ten minutes later. I was surprised to see that he was obviously quite a lot older than his wife, but we chatted easily together as I answered his questions about the history of the house and my involvement with the previous owner; evidently he had only heard one side of the story from Muriel.

He wanted to know what the house looked like originally, and showed a keen interest in how we had achieved its new layout, but his greater interest was my ideas and planning for the adjacent barn and he listened intently as I explained, and then he revealed the reasons why he was so interested.

"I wanted to meet you…" he said, "…because we really like what you have achieved with the house, and we want you to come and work for us and finish the project by converting the barn into the holiday Gite that you originally planned,"

Wow!

I was flattered that my designs and workmanship had made such an impression and extremely pleased with the income potential. We met on site to discuss working plans in more detail and Brian admitted that although he was not a tradesman he wanted to work alongside me, and we developed a good working relationship filled with friendly camaraderie.

It was eerie to be back inside the barn where nothing had changed in over two years since I left and I was amazed to see a box of Jim's old tools still there, although not really surprised because he put little value on material things, that's the way Jim was.

The work for Brian and Sonya was a challenging experience and one that I found most fulfilling. To be now completing the project that I had conceived and designed so long ago put to rest all those demons that still haunted me in the back of my mind, and when the Gite was eventually finished and ready for paying guests, I took pride in our achievement.

While we had been working on the barn conversion Brian had become interested in a farm building across the lane and opposite his house and barn. It was a large open fronted stone building that had housed farm machinery. It had needed a new roof but the walls were sound, and attached to the rear was another section which had probably been living quarters for a farm worker, but the roof of this part had completely collapsed and it was now derelict.

It had once been for sale at a ridiculously inflated price, but then the price had been greatly reduced and despite not yet having a planning certificate for habitation it would still have been an attractive proposition for anyone wanting a renovation project.

Brian and Sonya didn't want that to happen so they decided to buy the building and a generous amount of land around it, firstly because it would secure the immediate area against building development, and secondly because a good proportion of the land was flat, and that would enable them to install a swimming pool which would complement their holiday Gite.

They installed their swimming pool and I constructed a wooden decking to surround it, and then I built a timber framed lean-to roof over a sizable poolside terrace. We rebuilt the derelict farm worker's accommodation at the back of the garage and incorporated a toilet and a small kitchen. Guests in the Gite could now have a poolside barbecue or just make a hot drink.

Brian was not the sort of person to throw compliments around, but I know he also was proud of what we had all achieved. I had been in their employ for the best part of two years.

Damis de Neef was a trombone player with the Monflanquin village band – *Les Vert à Pied*, and everyone called him Dick, it seemed easier. He became a great pal of ours and his dry sense of humour was always entertaining; his outlook on life was, "It's there to be enjoyed - with as little work as possible."

Through him we came to know many band members and they all seemed to share the same philosophy of life. Dick summed it up very well.

"We're all very lucky really, we go away to interesting places where we all enjoy playing our music and entertaining folks and the proceeds from it fund a very nice social life for us all."

They were certainly an interesting group from mixed backgrounds, and the magazine Brass Band World paid me very well for the article about them that they published alongside my pictures, and now an opportunity had presented itself for a sequel.

During the thirteenth century the hilltop village of

Montréal near Carcassonne was at the centre of the bloodbath of the Cathar heresy, and then during the fourteenth century it was raised to the ground by the Black Prince; I just hoped that there would be no bloodshed during the tournament that I had been invited to as band photographer.

The village was hosting its annual festival - *Bandas en Malepère*, and although one brass band would be taking away the winning trophy the competition was not expected to be fierce, it was a social time where friendships would be renewed, a time to party for the nearly two hundred musicians that were expected to attend.

At their base in Monflanquin, the first band members of *'Les Verts à Pieds'* were boarding the coach early on the Saturday morning to travel south for the festival. The banter was in full flow as more members joined the coach en-route thirty minutes later. Before they were seated the driver hurtled off once more, skilfully negotiating the narrow winding streets towards Agen and the motorway. A final musician boarded at the slip road where the bus barely stopped before it joined the motorway and settled to a generous speed.

Spirits were high for the twenty five musicians, and at ten o'clock in the morning the party had begun and the cry went up for *Ricard* - an aniseed apératif taken with water; no one was driving for the next two days. A cushion provided a makeshift card table for five at the back, while the centre seats hosted a mini jam session when a guitar and my harmonica were produced and voices clustered around a wad of song sheets someone had brought.

Near lunch time, the coach was free of the motorway and climbed along the narrow roads towards the approaching village of Montréal with its backdrop of the Pyrenees. All the musicians - men and women of all ages excitedly spilled from the parked coach as luggage doors were flung wide open. Instruments lay everywhere between the coach and a wall as the owners struggled on the pavement to change into the band's uniform of white dungarees with green gingham shirts and red bandanas.

Eventually they were all ready to play music and excitedly grouped together upon a grassy verge for yet more of my photographs. Climbing the low hill towards the village centre they knew exactly where they were going; this was the eighth festival and they had been there many times before. They usually went just to enjoy themselves, play music and entertain, but this year they had decided that they would compete as well.

Base drummer Jean-Michel raised his hand in signal as they neared the village centre and just before they turned the last corner the band started to play and made its entrance into the welcome marquee which was reserved for the eight bands. *Les Vert à Pieds* had arrived – they were the first.

The heat from the sun was radiating through the canvas roof, it was approaching twenty five degrees outside but a breeze was circulating through the open sides. The bar which was staffed by many volunteers was now busy as the festival committee members welcomed back old friends.

Then conversation became impossible as '*In Vino Veritas Banda*' official band of the 'Wines of Bergerac' arrived in the same fashion, and as they too lay down their instruments and made towards the bar there was much back slapping and hugs as they circulated to meet old friends.

Movement within the marquee had become a calculated affair now that all the musicians had made their entry, and lunch was being served in relays. But for *Les Vert à Pieds* it had to be quick because their coach was waiting to take them to their first appointment – the old people's home where they make an annual visit and play for the old folks, despite that most of the residents hardly register that they are there.

For the band it's a way to say thank you to the village for their hospitality. The nurses had opened bottles of a local sparkling white wine - *Blanquette Méthode Ancestrale*; just to fortify the band for their effort. Outside as they left, a few mobile residents waved a cheery goodbye through the fence as the band boarded the coach for the return to *Centre Ville* and the start of the afternoon playing throughout the village.

By early evening the town was beginning to swell with revellers. There was parking provisions for four thousand vehicles and fifteen thousand people were expected over the two day festival. The smell of cooking was everywhere and an array of food vendors was set within the beautiful gardens where tables and chairs could seat four hundred diners.

The choice was mouth-watering; paella or cassoulet – a regional speciality, sirloins and duck breasts, mussels and chips, grilled veal, and of course escargots. Three courses would have cost a fiver with numerous other choices for those with lesser appetites. Whichever way you turned and looked there was a beer tent and the bar staff were run off their feet trying to keep up.

I followed the band back to the welcome marquee for dinner; it was going to be a long evening. First an apératif to line the stomach, then cold meats, paté and vegetable salad, followed by cassoulet and dessert - and plenty of bread, with red wine to wash it down. I didn't realise how hungry I was.

There were stages erected in three locations around the centre of the village where the bands could perform, and in front of the beer tents had also become a firm favourite, but the streets were packed with revellers and moving from stage to stage as they circulated around the village had now become very difficult. There was brass band music everywhere with just sufficient distance between each band. As dusk began to fall the atmosphere was like a fairground and the youth were out in full force. There was not a Gendarme anywhere but security forces were discreetly keeping a watchful eye.

Midnight came and went and the crowds were thinning little; the music had changed much to everyone's delight and gone now were the regimented gay tunes. Players spilled from one band to another and any organisation had disappeared. 'When the Saints go marching in' developed into a forum of ad-lib jazz which went on for nearly twenty minutes and the crowds love it. This is what *Les Vert à Pieds* came for and they were expert at taking the audience with them.

With them also went the wheelie-bin covered in band stickers. It nearly caused one young man to blow his top when he wouldn't accept that it was not a dustbin but a container for the stocks of the band's comic book and accompanying CD which were for sale.

At 3-00 am the streets were almost bare, save for discarded plastic drinking vessels. Within the student dormitories at the local agricultural college, weary bandsmen and photographers were falling into bed for a brief night's sleep.

The coaches returned to collect us at 08-30, but the day didn't look good as we descended from the coach back in the village centre. It had rained during the night and the clouds that were rolling in over the distant Pyrenees looked threatening. Suddenly large plops of rain started to fall and we scurried back onto the coach as a full scale storm hammered on the roof. Sunday's proceedings looked like they might need to be cancelled, but the rules for a festival to make an insurance claim are strict, so the band waited and watched the sky.

During a generous breakfast in the *Salle de Fete* the

storm passed and the roads started to steam as a hot sun came breaking through the clouds. The band was going to play after all but today – as always at a two day festival – it was to be a different costume, and the locals couldn't believe their eyes when twenty five grown men and women with musical instruments, made their way into the village dressed as schoolgirls!

They were an immediate hit and the afternoon got off to a good start as music filled the air once more and yesterday's crowds started to re-appear. It was a long afternoon, the storm had delayed the timetable and the speeches and presentations were much later than normal.

At 6-00pm the master of ceremony called for attention to the main stage and a very slow hour passed giving thanks to all the committee, their helpers and volunteers; all interspersed with joint fanfares from the bands in appreciation.

Eventually a winner was declared - Charanga Las Peñas, a Spanish band who well deserved the trophy of 'Le Festival de Banda Champion en Malepère', and the winners gave a final display which after a few minutes developed into a mass of musicians all playing together in celebration for them.

Mid-evening the massed crowds had mostly returned home save those few who will never go until all the music stops. The bands, including our ragged looking schoolgirls had decided that enough was enough, but now they had all been invited to reassemble back in the *Salle de Fete* for a final apératif and nibbles.

Les Verts à Pied had gone to Montréal because they love to play music, and back in the village hall that's exactly what they continued to do. When eventually their coach driver started insisting and darkness was descending, they said their final goodbyes and walked back to the coach, and those they left behind were still playing!

'*Les Verts à Pieds*' went to party, and party they did – but as they boarded the coach for the journey home their added pleasure was that the second prize - the 'Phacochère D'Argent', was coming home with them.

I arrived back home at Prieu somewhere after 3 o'clock in the morning, and was very glad to slide quietly into a soft bed after trying to sleep curled up on a coach seat. During what was left of the morning when I got out of bed, I downloaded rather a lot of pictures I'd taken and related my adventures for Jenny and I had to admit that it had been a great weekend.

Jenny was busy in the kitchen getting lunch, and I was outside on a sun lounger absorbing the sunshine as usual and quietly thinking about things in general when she woke me from my thoughts.

"Penny for them?" she said.

"Oh… I was just thinking," I replied, still rather absorbed in my discovery.

"Thinking about what?" She questioned, and I suddenly felt very contented as I answered her.

"Well you know how we have often talked about how we are building our dream and if in fact we are actually ever going to get there."

She looked just a little alarmed but I could see that I now had her full attention.

"Yes…" she said, "…go on."

"Well I've just realised something… we are actually living it!"

Robert Cooper left school at fifteen and began a long career in engineering where he achieved management level and eventually opened his own company. Disillusioned with engineering he later closed the company and became a home improvements salesman.

He moved to France with his wife in 2001 where he augmented his income by writing articles for English magazines. Later he secured his own monthly column in H&E Naturist magazine; a leading world-wide publication for English-speaking naturists.

His published articles paved the way to turn his diaries into his first book.

Lightning Source UK Ltd.
Milton Keynes UK
UKOW03f1517250314

228763UK00002B/11/P

9 781784 075040